OBJECTIVES, METHODS, AND EVALUATION FOR SECONDARY TEACHING

second edition

OBJECTIVES, METHODS, AND EVALUATION FOR SECONDARY TEACHING

MICHAEL A. LORBER
WALTER D. PIERCE

Illinois State University

Prentice-Hall, Inc., Englewood Cliffs, New Jersey 07632

Library of Congress Cataloging in Publication Data

LORBER, MICHAEL A., (date)
   Objectives, methods, and evaluation for secondary teaching.

   Rev. ed. of: Objectives and methods for secondary teaching/Walter D. Pierce.
   Includes index.
   1. High school teaching. I. Pierce, Walter D.   II. Title.
LB1737.A3L65 1982   373.11'02   82-3763
ISBN 0-13-629014-0   AACR2

Table 1, p. 44 is from *Taxonomy of Educational Objectives: The Classification of Educational Goals: Handbook I: Cognitive Domain* edited by B.S. Bloom et al. © 1956 by Longman, Inc. Reprinted by permission of Longman Inc., New York.

Table 2, p. 50 is from *Taxonomy of Educational Objectives: The Classification of Educational Goals: Handbook II: Affective Domain* by D.R. Krathwohl et al. © 1964 by Longman Inc. Reprinted by permission of Longman Inc., New York.

Table 3, p. 57 is from *A Taxonomy of the Psychomotor Domain: A Guide for Developing Behavioral Objectives* by A. J. Harrow. © 1972 by Longman Inc. Reprinted by permission of Longman Inc., New York.

PRENTICE-HALL CURRICULUM AND TEACHING SERIES
Ronald T. Hyman, Editor

This title is the second edition of a book formerly titled
Objectives and Methods for Secondary Teaching

Editorial Production/Supervision: Barbara Kelly
Cover Design: Wanda Lubelska
Manufacturing Buyer: Edmund W. Leone

Printed in the United States of America

10 9 8 7 6 5 4 3 2 1

ISBN 0-13-629014-0

Prentice-Hall International, Inc., *London*
Prentice-Hall of Australia Pty. Limited, *Sydney*
Prentice-Hall of Canada, Ltd., *Toronto*
Prentice-Hall of India Private Limited, *New Delhi*
Prentice-Hall of Japan, Inc., *Tokyo*
Prentice-Hall of Southeast Asia Pte. Ltd., *Singapore*
Whitehall Books Limited, *Wellington, New Zealand*

To our wives, Ellen and Pam,
whose patience is infinite

CONTENTS

THREE

WRITING PRECISE INSTRUCTIONAL OBJECTIVES, 25

FOUR

CLASSIFYING AND USING PRECISE INSTRUCTIONAL OBJECTIVES 39

FIVE

PREASSESSMENT
The Great Time Saver, 68

SIX

SELECTING INSTRUCTIONAL PROCEDURES, 79

NINE

PUTTING THE PIECES TOGETHER—PLANNING A UNIT, 167

Objectives, 167
Planning Units, 168

What is a Unit Plan? Generating Appropriate Objectives,
Writing a Rationale, Sample Rationales, Specifying Content,
Collecting Mediated Instructional Aids, Selecting Instructional Experiences

Organizing the Parts of a Unit: An Abbreviated Model, 173
Deciding on Optional Activities, 175
Planning for Evaluation and Future Use, 175
Summary, 176

TEN

ORGANIZING FOR DAILY INSTRUCTION—LESSON PLANS, 178

Objectives, 178
Pros and Cons of Lesson Planning, 179
Lesson Plan Components, 180

Objectives, Content, Teaching-Learning Activities, Materials, Evaluation,
Time, Miscellaneous Components

Writing a Lesson Plan, 185
Summary, 187
Model Lesson Plans, 188

ELEVEN

INDIVIDUALIZING INSTRUCTION, 192

Objectives, 192
The Systems Approach to Individualizing, 193
The Effect of Self-Instructional Packages On the Curriculum, 195

The Purpose of Package Programs, The Teacher as Advisor,
Packages as Enrichment Activities, Remedial Use of Packages, Extended Absence,
Partial Package Programs, Modified Systems Programs

Building A Self-Instructional Package—Model Package, 199

Part 1: Objective for Model Package, Part 2: Self-Preassessment,
Part 3: Learning Activities, Part 4: Evaluation

Summary, 210

XI

TWELVE

DISCIPLINE, 211

Objectives, 211
Four Positions Concerning Disciplines, 212
Maslow's Hierarchy, 213

Physiological Needs, Safety Needs, Love Needs, Esteem Needs, Self-Actualization Needs

Guidelines for Precluding Discipline Problems, 221
Behavior Modification: Operant Conditioning, 225
Behavior Modification: Reality Therapy, 228
A Discipline Procedure Involving the School Disciplinarian 231

The Six Steps in a Model Discipline Procedure Involving the School Disciplinarian

Potentially Dangerous Problems, 234
Hyperactivity and Chemotherapy, 234
Summary, 236

THIRTEEN

THE MANAGEMENT OF CO-CURRICULAR ACTIVITIES, 237

Objectives, 237
Extra Pay, 238
Types of Sponsorship, 239

Clubs, Student Government, Pep Groups, Service Organizations, Classroom-Associated Organizations, Events, Trips, Dances

Sales and Money Management, 244
Elections and Appointments, 248
Contracts, 249
Working With Off-Campus Organizations, 250
Assemblies, 251
Disruption of Classes, 251
Objectives and Extra Curricular Activities, 252
The School Calendar, 253
Summary, 254

FOURTEEN

TRENDS AND ISSUES IN EDUCATION, 255

Objectives, 255
Competency Testing—Students, 256

PREFACE

This book is based on the idea that you can acquire certain skills and information which will help you become a humane and effective teacher. Since you will be teaching in an era that emphasizes technology and competency-based instruction, we have incorporated into both the content and the structure of the text principles which are central to the uses of technology in education and to the competency-based movement. We have, for example, suggested certain precise instructional objectives at the beginning of each chapter. We have also included a model to help you understand competency-based instruction, an example of a self-instructional package, an in-depth look at computer applications in education, and ways of evaluating and maintaining classroom control that are consistent with competency-based approaches.

While we believe there is much of value in the competency-based movement we do not believe the teaching-learning process is quite as precise or clear-cut as some proponents of the movement imply. Your success as a teacher will depend as much on your development of personal characteristics conducive to good teaching as on your mastery of specific teaching skills and procedures. You must, for example, be tolerant of individual differences and opinions, be fair with people, and be receptive to new ideas. These attributes, and others like them, are difficult to specify as precise instructional objectives or to evaluate as specific competencies. Nonetheless, they are as crucial to good teaching as any of the skills and procedures about to be presented.

Many people contributed time, effort and ideas to this book. We particularly want to thank Dr. Leo Eastman, who was a leader in the competency-based movement; Dr. Albert Upton, who patiently explained many things that should have been obvious; and the members of the Professional Sequence staff at Illinois State University, who contributed many of the key concepts.

M.A.L./W.D.P.

ONE
A LOGICAL MODEL
FOR INSTRUCTION

One of the most intriguing problems confronting the educator bent upon improvement is determining where to start. One could focus first on the processes within the classroom and the transactions between pupil and teacher, or one could begin by considering the rationale behind any particular educational endeavor. However, after careful consideraton of various starting points, it becomes apparent that the components of any logical instructional process are intertwined and inseparable. Hence, it is recommended that one conceptualize a complete process initially and subsequently examine its parts in relation to the whole.

The procedure used most often in this regard is that of focusing initial and continued attention on the activities involved in teaching-learning situations. Concern about instructional activities not only dominates most texts dealing with education, but it frequently dominates everyday discussions among teachers as well. It is not uncommon, for example, for students to hear one teacher ask another, "What are you doing in class today?" The question seems perfectly appropriate to students because, when they get home and their parents inquire about school, their parents are likely to approach the matter in exactly the same way, for example, "What did you do in school today?"

A more appropriate question, however, would be, "What will your students be able to do after instruction that they were unable to do prior to instruction?" But this question is not usually addressed. Many students and teachers seem to accept the idea that activities such as talking about the economy or going on a field trip are of prime importance in and of themselves. The fact that they are vehicles by which skills and information are acquired is usually overlooked. This is not to say that instructional activities are unimportant; a major portion of this book is devoted to helping you improve such activities. What is even more important, however, is understanding how to select particular activities and how the activities can be made into an effective instructional program. This understanding can be facilitated by analyzing models for instruction because such analyses will help you understand what the parts of the teaching-learning process are and how they fit together. This chapter will help you with that analysis.

Objectives

When you complete this chapter, you will be able to:

1. Label, in writing and without error, each stage of a blank schematic of the Logical Instructional Model.
2. Explain orally the function of each stage of the Logical Instructional Model and its relationship to each of the other stages.
3. Observe a fifty-minute lesson and specify, in writing, which stages of the Logical Instructional Model were manifested and which specific activities support those assessments.

FOUR-STAGE MODELS OF INSTRUCTION

In recent years a number of educators have developed models of instruction that consist of four basic elements: (1) preparation of precise instructional objectives, (2) preassessment of students to determine their abilities relative to the objectives, (3) instructional activities to ensure achievement of the objectives, and (4) evaluation to determine whether students are able to achieve the objectives.

In 1970 Popham and Baker, in *Systematic Instruction*,[1] and Kibler, Barker, and Miles, in *Behavioral Objectives and Instruction*,[2] depicted these four stages in schematic diagrams. Popham and Baker used the diagram in Figure 1 to show the model and its self-correcting features.

The diagram by Kibler, Barker, and Miles is very similar. Using the title "General Model of Instruction" and somewhat different labels, they

[1]James Popham and Eva Baker, *Systematic Instruction* (Englewood Cliffs, N.J. Prentice-Hall, 1970), pp. 13 and 18.

[2]Robert J. Kibler, Larry L. Barker, and David T. Miles, *Behavioral Objectives and Instruction* (Boston: Allyn & Bacon, 1970), p.13.

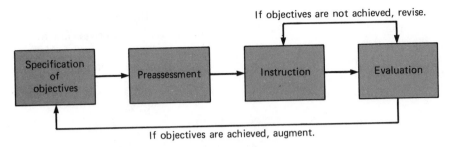

FIGURE 1 A Goal-Referenced Instructional Model with Courses of Action Dictated by Evaluation of Results

included a *feedback loop* to examine the first three stages when such an examination was indicated by the results of the evaluation. The General Model of Instruction is illustrated in Figure 2.

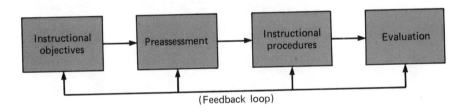

FIGURE 2 A General Model of Instruction

As basic and revealing as they are, both schematics leave a number of questions unanswered. Both, for example, imply that instruction must follow preassessment. This ignores those instances in which preassessment indicates that students already possess the competencies sought. In the model diagrammed in Figure 1, it is assumed that if the objectives are not achieved the fault lies in the instruction. Although this point is taken up in accompanying materials, the model itself could be interpreted as not considering those instances in which students enter the class without the beginning competencies necessary for success. The model presented in Figure 2 carries a number of implications in the feedback loop, but if students are unable to achieve the objectives, no specific course of action is implied other than a general reassessment of each and every stage of the model. A more precise and detailed model might be even more helpful.

A LOGICAL INSTRUCTIONAL MODEL (LIM)

The Logical Instructional Model, which appears in Figure 3, builds upon the excellent work already done by Popham and Baker and Kibler, Barker, and Miles. It is an attempt to diagram a model of the instructional process that is more complete and more self-explanatory than preceding models. The remainder of this chapter is devoted to providing an overview of this model, and the following chapters are devoted largely to building the understandings and skills necessary to making the model a viable and sound basis for instruction.

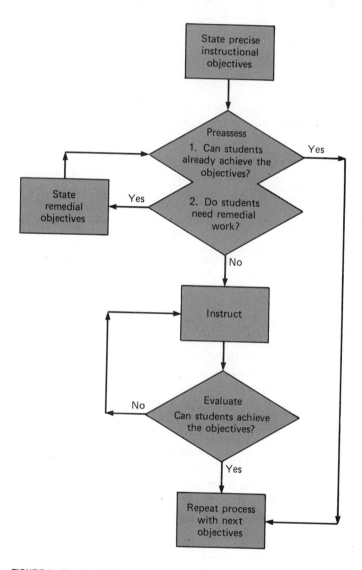

FIGURE 3   The Logical Instructional Model

State Precise Instructional Objectives

Although it may sound like a contradiction in terms, the place to begin planning an instructional procedure is with the instructional results. The first and most important point to be considered is *what students should be able to do after instruction.* Making this decision is the single most complex and difficult step in planning for instruction.

In every community there are political, sociological, psychological, practical, and subject-matter considerations that must be taken into account when curricula are being built and objectives decided upon. What individual teachers must do is sort out the various factors, organize them according to importance, and use them to assist in the selection or writing of precise instructional objectives that will satisfy students, parents, administrators, boards of education, and themselves. This is no simple task, especially considering that most teachers have had little, if any, formal training in the writing of precise instructional objectives.

School systems throughout the country are going about the task of acquiring precise instructional objectives in a variety of ways. Some, for example, are purchasing compilations of objectives and asking their teachers to choose and alter objectives rather than write them originally. Other school systems are asking teachers to write objectives for their own classes, while still others are organizing teachers according to subject matter or grade levels and asking them to write objectives on a collective basis.

The following are specific, but typical, kinds of questions teachers must ask themselves as they begin to focus on their objectives.

1. Have ideas for objectives been considered from sources such as students and parents?
2. Will the necessary human, physical, and financial resources be available?
3. Are the objectives relevant and reflective of social and cultural realities?
4. Are the objectives compatible with the overall goals of the community and school?
5. Do the objectives lead to a series of increasingly more important objectives?
6. Will the objectives assist in satisfying student needs?

In addition to being able to justify the inclusion of each objective, the teacher must phrase each so that it conveys the exact instructional intent. At the very least, each objective should specify exactly what each student is to be able to do at the end of the instruction and how well he or she must do it. In addition, most objectives will need some clarification of the exact conditions under which the specific competency will be demonstrated.

Obviously the stating of precise instructional objectives is a thought-provoking and time-consuming task, but since every other part of the instructional process depends directly on the objectives, they are all important. If the objectives are poor, the rest of the instructional process is likely to be poor also, but if the objectives are well stated, include an observable behavior, and are measurable, then the instructional process is more likely to be equally strong.

Preassess

Once the precise instructional objectives have been explained to the students, the teacher's next step should be to preassess students' abilities. Since the teacher is seeking to compare the abilities students possess prior to instruction with those they will need to demonstrate the specified competencies, the preassessment often consists of an equivalent form of the final evaluation instrument. Conducted properly, preassessments can yield valuable information, but primarily they provide data related to two specific questions.

The first question is: "Do students already possess the specified competencies?" If it is revealed that students already posssess the skills and /or information necessary to demonstrate the stated competencies, it would be pointless to proceed with the planned instruction because it is not needed and would only bore the students. Once the determination is made that students can, in fact, perform as required, they may move on to new objectives.

The second question is: "Do students need remedial work?" If it is revealed that students lack the basic skills and/or information needed to begin working toward achievement of the stated objectives, the teacher has no logical alternative but to state remedial objectives that will provide students with the background necessary for further progress and to go through the instructional model with these alternate objectives as the starting point. Students are then more likely to profit from instruction relating to the original objectives.

It is unfortunate when students need remediation because less time is then available for work toward the original objectives. In most cases, however, students will have the background necessary for further instruction and the teacher may need to provide only a brief review of background material. It is obviously crucial to determine, as accurately as possible, if students do need remediation.

The facts that preassessing reveals about students may indicate that a teacher must go back and provide instruction other than that for which he or she is specifically responsible or that the teacher must skip over instruction that has been carefully and painstakingly planned. This may explain why many teachers simply do not preassess their students, which, in turn, may account for a good deal of the frustration and boredom of which many students complain.

Instruct

By and large, teachers are paid to help students learn. The skill with which this is done depends largely on the abilities of the teacher, but there are innumerable procedures for improving instruction. Some procedures concern themselves with specific kinds of instructional activities and ways of making them more interesting and therefore more effective. Other procedures focus on basic principles of learning. In this text, specific activities and principles are both explored, and it is at the risk of redundancy (but with the hope that if they are reviewed they may be seen in a new perspective) that a few basic principles are included here. Other collections of such principles can be found in a wide variety of sources from Kibler, Barker, and Miles[3] to the Wisconsin State Department of Public Instruction.[4]

1. *Students differ in ability and rate of learning just as they differ in more observable characteristics such as height, weight, and appearance.* Not only must teachers be aware of such differences, but they must make each student aware of his or her own learning characteristics.

Teachers need to help individual students overcome their weaknesses and increase their self-esteem by emphasizing their strengths. Because the weaknesses are so obvious and easy to pinpoint, many times teachers forget about the need to emphasize strengths and are thus less successful than they might be. Students will not respond as fully if they feel their weaknesses will continually be exposed. Provisions for fast learners to remain interested and occupied with enrichment material and for slow learners to obtain the help they need to continue learning are necessary, although sometimes difficult to achieve in every classroom.

2. *Principles of retention and practice govern learning.* There are certain psychological principles that, when applied properly, can assist students in the acquisition and use of information.

    a. Retention of information is increased if the information has meaning to the student.

    b. When teaching principles and abstractions for later application, the teacher can increase students' retention by using examples and illustrations.

    c. After an initial teacher presentation, the acts of the students are more important than are the acts of the teacher. The most obvious way for students to acquire a particular skill is to practice it and receive corrective feedback concerning their efforts.

    d. A number of short practice sessions distributed over a longer period of time will generally result in better retention of the information or skill than will a few long practice sessions grouped closely together.

[3]Kibler, Barker, and Miles, *Behavioral Objectives*, pp. 7–9.

[4]See "Learning Principles, Wisconsin State Department of Public Instruction" in Leonard Clark, ed., *Strategies and Tactics in Secondary School Teaching* (Toronto: Macmillan, 1968), pp. 100–107.

3. *Prior to beginning instruction teachers should determine which skills students must acquire to achieve the objectives.* Assuming that students have the prerequisite skills, the links between the skills to be acquired and those already acquired need to be clearly established to assure students that their abilities are steadily being increased, expanded, and strengthened. If students perceive the instruction as leading to goals they consider valid and important, they will participate actively in the activities and facilitate their own learning.

4. *Lack of student desire to learn (motivation) ensures instructional failure.* It is generally accepted that *intrinsic* motivation (a desire to learn that comes from within the student) is far superior to *extrinsic* motivation (a desire to learn that is generated by external pressure—either positive or negative). When a student arrives at a class without a built-in desire to learn, however, it becomes the responsibility of the teacher to foster such a desire in the student. The following are some points teachers should keep in mind concerning motivation.

a. If students perceive the learning as fulfilling a need, they will be more likely to be interested in engaging in that learning.

b. If students are permitted to help select objectives and activities, they tend to be more committed to the achievement of the objectives and the success of the activities.

c. If students can see visible progress toward a goal (positive feedback), motivation can be initiated and maintained.

d. The influence of peers and their attitudes toward learning can have tremendous influence on the success of the instruction. Trying to motivate a single student without considering the attitudes of his or her friends may be futile.

e. Competition can be an effective source of motivation if each student sees a chance to win, but either winning or losing too frequently reduces the effectiveness of competition.

f. When teachers use many extrinsic rewards to build motivation, they must be alert to the problem of students working for the rewards rather than to achieve the instructional objectives. The ends can become muddled.

5. *The proper organization of information into a knowledge structure will facilitate learning.* Most people have had at least one or two teachers who knew a great deal about their subject matter but who were not effective teachers. It is likely that many of these teachers' problems stemmed from their inability to organize their information into a pattern that made sense to their students. The arrangement of information into a hierarchical form, such as from general concepts to specific facts, makes the information more digestible for students and speeds learning.

6. *Students will achieve competencies more quickly if models of the desired skills or products are supplied early in the instructional process.* Models can help

students understand the individual components of a whole and the whole itself by pinpointing specific strengths and weaknesses and by facilitating the explanation of how the parts interact to make up the whole. Care must be taken, however, to see that students do not follow models slavishly and thereby stifle their own creativity.

Evaluate

The major purpose of instruction is to help students acquire the knowledge and skills they need to achieve the specified competencies. It makes sense, then, to follow instruction with evaluation. There are, however, a number of more specific reasons to evaluate the progress of students. One reason to evaluate, for example, is to help teachers determine the effectiveness of particular instructional activities. If students are unable to demonstrate achievement of specified objectives after engaging in what the teacher thought would be a helpful instructional activity, that activity obviously did not meet the teacher's expectations. The students' performance will provide the kind of data the teacher will need to justify modifying or eliminating that particular activity.

Evaluations are also used as part of the basis for the making of long-range plans by students and parents. The results of teacher-made tests and a wide variety of standardized tests are usually taken into consideration whenever students begin thinking about going to college or getting a job, and these forms of evaluation frequently have great influence on the final decision.

The single most important reason to engage in the evaluation of students' progress is, of course, to determine whether each student can demonstrate certain competencies. To make this determination, teachers have traditionally relied heavily on paper-and-pencil tests such as objective and essay tests. With the increased interest in precise instructional objectives, however, teachers are finding that there are other means of evaluating students' accomplishments that reflect instructional intents better. Today instead of having students demonstrate competence solely by passing tests, more and more teachers are writing objectives that call on students to demonstrate alternate skills more akin to those needed in life outside of the school setting.

If, at the evaluation stage, students cannot achieve the specified objectives, there should be little need for the teacher to reassess each stage of the entire instructional procedure, since the Logical Instructional Model provides specific checks as each stage is encountered. If students cannot achieve the objectives at this point, the problem most likely resides in the instruction stage. It could be that the instructional procedures were inadequate or that insufficient time was expended, but in any event the problem should be solvable with additional, and perhaps alternate kinds of, instruction. It would not be appropriate at this point to blame the objective or the preassessment for the students' inability to demonstrate the specified competency.

With practice, the steps described in the Logical Instructional Model will result in student achievement of specified objectives and may be repeated with successive sets of objectives.

EXTENT OF USE OF THE LOGICAL INSTRUCTIONAL MODEL

This discussion of the Logical Instructional Model and the place of precise instructional objectives within that model should not lead you to presume that the model or precise instructional objectives are meant to be all inclusive. Teachers are employed to help students learn, and there are many learning experiences that help students learn but that do not lend themselves to implementation via the LIM or to definition in precise terms. It would be foolish to advocate the elimination of all such activities and to rely solely upon the LIM. Instead, it is suggested that you view the LIM and the use of precise instructional objectives as a means of establishing the framework of an instructional program. The objectives that are stated and discussed with students are those that are most basic and most essential to a particular course of study. Other objectives will certainly be achieved by students along the way, but many crucial ones will have been specified in very precise terms.

The same line of reasoning pertains to utilization of the LIM. The LIM is a workable and efficient approach to instruction, but it is not necessarily the best approach to use in every single instance of instruction. There will be many times when common sense dictates some instructional approach other than the LIM, and in such instances deviation from the model is quite appropriate. By and large, you will find that everyday instruction will proceed more smoothly if the steps in the LIM are followed, but some circumstances may require different steps and, provided they are effective in helping students learn, they can, and should, augment the systematic process inherent in the model.

SUMMARY

This chapter has presented three instructional models, all based on the same general principles. The last, the Logical Instructional Model, is more detailed than its predecessors and is examined most fully.

The first step of the Logical Instructional Model is to state precise instructional objectives. The purpose of these objectives is to specify, in terms that are both observable and measurable, those minimal things students will be able to do after instruction.

The second step of the LIM is to preassess students' abilities with respect to the abilities required for achievement of the objectives. Two specific questions are answered via the preassessment and two specific courses of action are delineated. The first question is whether or not students can already achieve the objectives. If students already possess the needed skills and/or information and have no need of further instruction, they can simply move on to the next objectives. The second question is whether or not remediation is needed. If students have not acquired the beginning competencies required for successful progress, the teacher must write remedial objectives and provide the necessary background.

The next step in the LIM is the providing of needed instruction. The purpose of the instruction is to enable students to achieve the stated objectives.

The last step in the LIM is to evaluate. At this step you determine whether students have achieved the specified objectives and you evaluate the effectiveness of your instructional activities. If students have mastered the necessary objectives, then you repeat the process with a new objective. If the objectives were not achieved, then you must reassess your instructional activities and provide additional instruction to help students acquire the necessary skills and information. It is important to keep in mind that your success depends, to a large extent, on the success of your students. Help your students learn and you further your own success.

This chapter has presented a model of an instructional procedure. The remaining chapters will explore some of the reasons that prompted its development and will expand upon each stage of the model.

TWO
OBJECTIVES, AIMS, PURPOSES, GOALS
What Are We Really After?

One of the most important steps in a viable teaching-learning process is the specification of instructional objectives. For some time educators have been concerned with the formulation of instructional objectives, but consensus still has not been reached as to either their form or their content. One need only look at the objectives written in different secondary schools to confirm the lack of consensus concerning goals. The wide range of courses, services, and activities housed in public schools is testimony that disagreement about the specific objectives of the public schools is widespread. There is, however, a growing movement toward fewer elective and more required courses in an effort to raise academic standards.

This chapter will trace the development of educational "goals" through the years and examine a number of the more important attempts by educators to establish goals. This background information is intended to help you understand how and why the objectives stated by many typical schools came into being. This understanding, in turn, sheds light on the process by which these objectives may be improved.

Objectives

When you complete this chapter, you will be able to:

1. Write the names of at least three committees that have structured aims for secondary schools.

2. Explain in your own words the central themes that the three cited committees utilized in their construction of aims.

3. Distinguish, and describe in a paper of no more than three pages, at least two similarities and two differences between each of three sets of aims for the American secondary school.

4. Design, organize, and write a set of at least four aims for the American secondary school, giving rationales for each aim included, and organize these rationales into a series of criteria for judging secondary school aims.

5. When presented with a set of secondary school aims, apply your own criteria to the given aims, judge them as worthy or unworthy, and provide a rationale for each judgment.

EDUCATIONAL GOALS

Early Educational Goals

During prehistoric times, it can be assumed that education consisted of the young imitating their elders. Even if man had wanted to attempt formal education, there would have been little need to specify the goal of this instruction because it was obvious: survival. The penalty for failure to learn one's "lessons" could be early death.

Formal education itself probably began when the division of labor made it possible for some individuals to engage in activities other than hunting, fishing, and gathering. It is likely that, with the rise of a priest class and the training of future priests, formal education experienced its genesis.

During the Egyptian period, the priest class managed whatever formal education existed (mostly the training of more priests and scribes), and the general population had little benefit from the goals of that education. For the vast majority of youngsters during ancient Egyptian times, education involved an informal apprenticeship. Parents could apprentice a son with the "educational goal" in mind that the son would become a skilled workman. If this goal were not achieved, the parents would likely stop sending their sons to that particular master. Girls were taught homemaking skills in their homes but were not included in the "formal" education afforded the boys.

The parallel between popular interest in educational goals and popular participation in education can be illustrated in the case of the Hebrews. The Hebrews had a religious commitment to education in that each boy was to be taught the *Torah* (the five books of Moses). All Hebrew men were expected to help see that the goal was achieved and the rabbis (teachers) were elevated to the highest social position in recognition of their efforts in this study.

Greek and Roman education represented a different approach. If one could not afford a tutor for one's child, there was little chance for formal education in either ancient Greece or ancient Rome. Education among the aristocracy was of high caliber, but there was little interest in goals for education because education itself became the goal. No formal education for practical skills was necessary in aristocratic education because all manual work was done by the lower classes. In this environment, the study of music, mathematics, and rhetoric flourished, but there was no worry as to whether what was being learned was of immediate and practical value; this was simply not a point of concern.

During the Middle Ages the dichotomy between education for the aristocracy and education for the masses grew. Sons of wealthy families spent their time learning about grammar, rhetoric, and dialectic (the trivium) and arithmetic, geometry, astronomy, and music (the quadrivium). These subjects became the seven liberal arts, and their pursuit, by way of formal education, was limited to "gentlemen." As for the masses, a formal apprenticeship program emerged during the Middle Ages and attention to educational "goals" was manifested in the working of the law of supply and demand: the better a skilled craftsman was at achieving the goal of training other capable craftsmen, the more business he received.

The operation of early universities was also geared to the law of supply and demand with respect to goals. The compensation of teachers at these institutions depended upon the schools' ability to achieve goals deemed important by enough students to support the teachers financially. Precise goals became relevant during the nineteenth century when mass education began to take hold and, even more important, when people began to support education with public funds.

Today's Needs

When formal education involved a small percentage of the total population, there was little problem with its concern for matters that had little or no practical value. If scholars wanted to debate the number of fairies that could dance on the head of a pin, it was acceptable; the work of the world would still get done. Today's world is rather different. Since the founding of the first public secondary school in Boston in 1821, the United States has had publicly supported secondary schools, and virtually all of our current teenage population attends these schools. In this context, the broadening of mental horizons by the study of academic subjects is not sufficient. Taxpayers are demanding that high school graduates acquire marketable skills so they will not become burdens on society. Schools have accepted not only their traditional roles, but also the roles once assumed by parents, craftsmen, and guilds. Furthermore, since the masses are now paying for this educational process, they want to know what they are getting for their money. They want educators to state their goals so that it can be seen whether those goals are being accomplished. The movement associated with this thrust is often referred to as *accountability*.

Looking at education in the past, it can be seen that one rather consistent, if nebulous, goal has been to pass down the cultural heritage. A look at mankind's attempts to avoid continually rediscovering the wheel leads one to conclude that people wanted their children to benefit from their experiences, to avoid making the same mistakes, and to have a better life overall than they themselves had. There is, however, a basic dilemma built into this goal or hope, and the problem is now one of our most serious.

If the fact is accepted that the intellectual abilities, physical skills, and value structures of preceding generations form the substance of what the younger generation is to be taught, the implication must also be accepted that each generation attempts to make its successor as nearly like itself as possible. Proponents of this view might diagram the function of formal education as in Figure 4.

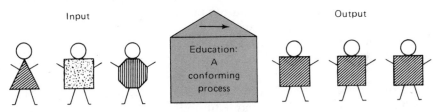

FIGURE 4

A shining example of the impact of this goal is the study of American history, which is mandated by all states in the Union. This particular course has traditionally been a curricular inclusion because many Americans have felt that youngsters should have a knowledge and appreciation of their country's past. If all students learned similar things, they might all end up with similar attitudes.

The problem with this view of the education process is that, as each succeeding generation learns of its past, it tends to reject much of what its predecessors held near and dear. Looking again at the requirement that all students study American history, it can be seen that, although the original goal was to make Americans more alike in their knowledge and appreciation of their past, things are not working out quite as expected. Today students learn that, while Washington championed freedom, he also kept slaves; that only some of the colonists supported the Revolution, while others were outright Tories and still others were relatively neutral; that many Americans treated the Indians and the Mexicans rather shabbily; and that industrialists were somewhat less than fair to their workers during the late 1800s and early 1900s. Each generation of graduating students is quite different as a result of formal education. Schools do change people, for better or for worse. A more accurate diagram of formal education might well look like that outlined in Figure 5.

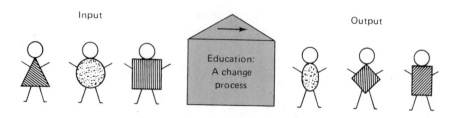

FIGURE 5

Two incompatible views of the function of education, one formal and one informal, are inherent in the foregoing. If the emphasis of education is to be on making people more alike, then goals for this end can be formulated and taxpayers can see if the goals are being accomplished. If the emphasis of education is to be on individuality, then goals for this end can be formulated and taxpayers can judge if these goals are being accomplished. Unfortunately, society has not taken a firm stand on what it wants its schools to do. In the United States, with a population of over 220 million, there are nearly as many different views of just what schools should be accomplishing. In an attempt to alienate no one, educators have tended to state goals nebulously. This, in turn, has opened the door to charges of doing the wrong thing and, conversely, of not doing anything at all. What attempts have been made to state educational goals? How did secondary education arrive at its present position? What is being done to remedy the situation? Let us see.

ATTEMPTS TO DEVELOP AIMS

The change in the purposes of secondary education over the past two hundred years has been enormous. Education has moved from the colonial period, in which a selected few fortunates attended the Latin Grammar School solely to gain entry into a colonial college, to today's mammoth network of comprehensive and specialized secondary schools that covers the nation. These schools are designed to serve the entire U.S. adolescent population, and they attempt to teach everything from how to drive a car and change a diaper to computer technology. They are accused of not doing enough (why else was Russia first in space and not the United States?) and of doing too much (as in sex education).

Have people tried to define the purposes of the American secondary school throughout its history? The answer is yes, but with varying degrees of skill and success. Some of the efforts are described in the discussion that follows.

The Committee of Ten

In 1893 the National Education Association attempted to formalize the purpose of the high school. A group of men prominent in higher education at the time gathered together and formalized a set of goals for secondary education. According to John S. Brubacher and Willis Rudy,[1]

> They wrestled with the basic problem of how to articulate the college with a dual-purpose high school, a high school which had to serve as preparation for college and also as preparation for life. Down to 1893, when the committee reported, the prestige of the college preparatory function had predominated, enabling the colleges to dictate the high school curriculum. After the report of the committee, however, the high school came to enjoy a more independent position.

Four of the specific recommendations are cited as examples of the Committee of Ten's efforts:

1. That all pupils should pursue a given subject in the same way and to the same extent as long as they study it at all.
2. That every subject studied should cultivate the pupil's powers of observation, memory, expression, and reasoning.
3. That the function of the high schools should be to prepare pupils for the duties of life as well as to prepare them for college.
4. That colleges and scientific schools should accept any one of the courses of study as preparation for admission.[2]

The Committee on College Entrance Requirements

In 1899 the Committee on College Entrance Requirements of the National Education Association reiterated a triple function of the secondary school:

1. Preparation for life.
2. Preparation of teachers for the common schools.
3. Preparation for college.[3]

That they additionally attempted to paint a more congenial educational picture by stating that programs should be flexible, have a variety of electives, and take into account the students' abilities, points up the NEA's growing concern for, and influence over, the conditions of learning.

[1]John S. Brubacher and Willis Rudy, *Higher Education in Transition* (New York and Evanston, Ill.: Harper & Row, 1958), pp. 241–242.

[2]*Report of the United States Commissioner of Education*, vol. 2, parts III and IV, 1892–1893, pp. 1474–75.

[3]*National Education Association Proceedings* (Washington D.C.: National Education Association, 1899), pp. 635–636.

The Commission
on the Reorganization
of Secondary Education

By 1913 the Commission on the Reorganization of Secondary Education, appointed by the NEA, recommended what was to become probably the most famous statement of the purposes of the high school. Labeled the "Seven Cardinal Principles of Secondary Education," these aims were memorized by countless numbers of prospective teachers as part of their pre-service training. In an informal study[4] conducted and replicated six times, with separate groups of thirty to forty prospective teachers who attempted to construct their own set of aims for the high school, at least six of the original seven principles were *still* on those groups' final lists of worthwhile aims for today's youngsters. A summarized version of the seven cardinal principles follows:[5]

1. *Health.* Good health habits need to be taught and encouraged by the school. The community and school should cooperate in fulfilling the health needs of all youngsters and adults.

2. *Command of fundamental processes.* The secondary school should accept a responsibility for continuing to teach and polish the basic tools of learning, such as arithmetical computation, reading, and writing, that were begun in the elementary school.

3. *Worthy home membership.* Students' understanding of the inter-relationships of the family in order for the give and take to be a healthy, happy affair should be advocated by the school. Proper adjustment as a family member will lead to proper acceptance of responsibility as a family leader in later life.

4. *Vocation.* The secondary school should develop an attitude in students that will lead to an appreciation for all vocations. The basic skills of a variety of vocations should be made available to students who have the need and/or desire for them.

5. *Citizenship.* A basic commitment to proper citizenship on the part of students needs to be fostered and strengthened during the adolescent years. The secondary school needs to assume this responsibility not only in the social sciences, where one would ordinarily assume it would be handled, but in all subjects.

6. *Proper use of leisure time.* The student should be provided opportunities while in secondary school to expand the available possibilities for leisure time. (The commission felt that leisure time properly used would enrich the total personality.)

7. *Ethical character.* The secondary school should organize its activities and personal relationships to reflect good ethical character, both to serve as an exemplár and to involve the student in a series of activities that will provide opportunities to make ethically correct decisions.

[4]Walter D. Pierce, unpublished informal study of broad goal setting by college students, Illinois State University, 1972.

[5]U.S. Bureau of Education, *Cardinal Principles of Education,* Bulletin No. 35 (1918), 2 pp. 5–10.

The seven cardinal principles were an attempt by a group of educators to use the needs of society and the individual as a basis for describing what secondary schools should accomplish. Other attempts were subsequently made to identify the central goals of schooling, and a few of the most noteworthy are described in the paragraphs that follow. Depending upon the prevailing issues of the particular time and place, the statements made by these groups show slight changes in emphasis and style. They are therefore best looked at in terms of the social situation in which they were articulated.

The American Youth Commission

By 1937 the country was deep in the Depression and educators were looking at education in terms of how it could help students get and hold jobs. The principle of vocational preparation became predominant: "American youth need opportunity for economic independence. They need information on how to prepare for, find, and hold a satisfying job."[6]

The Educational Policies Commission

In 1938 the Educational Policies Commission set forth a series of goals arranged in four major divisions with subsections concerning "the educated man." The four main divisions included (1) self-realization, (2) human relationships, (3) economic efficiency, and (4) civic responsibility. A typical goal format under the civil responsibility subsection was: "The educated person respects the law."[7]

The National Association
of Secondary School Principals

After World War II a shift in priorities increased the emphasis on science. John S. Brubacher[8] credits Herbert Spencer with a large portion of the responsibility for this shift because of an essay of Spencer's that drew wide attention entitled "What Knowledge Is of Most Worth." Spencer's opinion was that, in spite of the commonly held position that those things taught in the liberal studies are the most worthwhile, the priority should actually be on the practical, and he felt the knowledge of most practical worth was science. It is certain that the wartime development of radar, sonar, rockets, and atomic bombs did nothing to undermine this popular opinion.

[6]H. R. Douglass, *Secondary Education for Youth in Modern America* (Washington, D.C.: American Council on Education, 1937), p. 137.

[7]Educational Policies Commission, *The Purpose of Education in American Democracy* (Washington, D.C.: National Educational Association, 1938), pp. 50, 72, 90, and 108.

[8]John S. Brubacher, *A History of the Problems of Education* (New York: McGraw-Hill, 1947), p. 16.

In 1947, the National Association of Secondary School Principals delineated the "Imperative Needs of Youth." These goals repeated in essence the seven cardinal principles and added statements on appreciating aesthetics, becoming an intelligent consumer, and understanding the methods and influence of science. The thrust of the list of goals changed from a "command of fundamental processes" to an emphasis on rationality, clear expression of thoughts, and reading and listening with understanding.[9]

The Educational Policies Commission

In 1961 the Educational Policies Commission again set forth a series of goals for secondary schools. These goals, once again, caused a reassessment and restructuring of secondary schools. Without completely abandoning the ideas embodied in the preceding statements of goals, the Educational Policies Commission emphasized the idea that the primary objective of education should be to improve the rational powers of students. The specific aims included in the older lists were reexamined in light of the goal of creating the rational person.[10]

THE EFFECT OF BROAD AIMS

Contemplating the energy and effort expended to produce the lists of aims just cited, two specific questions come to mind: "Of what value are these lists of broad aims?" and "What forces really influence the schools?"

It is immediately obvious that, for school goals to have effect, the goals must *reach the student,* which means that ultimately it is up to the individual teacher to implement the goals. Does the publishing of these lists affect the teacher in the classroom? Probably not as much as one would like. Teachers, by and large, tend to teach not only the *way* they themselves were taught, but also *what* they themselves were taught. The rewording of a broad aim by a new commission in Washington will not necessarily bring about a major change in a tenth-grade English class in Normal, Illinois.

What really influences a typical secondary school then? The most obvious answer is that, when someone in a *position of power* perceives a needed change, he or she then goes about making it happen. A few hypothetical examples follow:

1. The PTA president thinks sex education is needed and influences a community action group to push for the adoption of a course. Pressure is exerted through appropriate channels until a course is adopted by the board.

[9]National Association of Secondary School Principals, *The Imperative Needs of Youth of Secondary School Age,* Bulletin No. 31 (March 1947).

[10]*The Central Purpose of American Education* (Washington, D.C.: National Education Association, 1961).

2. In a new suburb the superintendent is able to get a bond issue passed for a new high school after several failures by promising the voters open classrooms and a modified schedule.
3. The Russians beat the United States in launching the first satellite. The schools are blamed for not teaching scientific know-how. Congress approves funds for improving the teaching of science, math, and foreign languages, and thousands of teachers are given additional training in these areas.
4. The black majority in a suburb of a large city picket and petition until courses in black studies are offered.
5. Microcomputers become inexpensive enough for thousands of people to buy them, and schools start buying them because administrators want to stay "up to date."

All these situations have produced changes that have influenced the lives of students—perhaps profoundly; yet none of them is based directly on an overview of the broad aims described in any of the official lists just surveyed.

How does a math teacher go about, in his or her regular teaching capacity, emphasizing good health? Surely there are incidental moments of reinforcement, and he or she can function as an exemplar, but the goal of good health would be viewed by most teachers as one for another subject area such as physical education or home economics. If it is the case then that each broad aim will be taken care of by specific subject-matter areas, what subject will emphasize ethical character? Where will the students who are not going to take home economics learn about worthy family membership?

The problem is obvious: if broad aims are to be implemented, they must be translated into programs at the local level with specificity and vigor. Consider the folowing "educational philosophy," which was prepared for an accreditation visit by the staff at Downey Senior High School in Downey, California.[11]

Communicate (read, write, listen, speak, view) with precision and discrimination.
Understand the methods and applications of science (observe, experiment, record, analyze, predict) and the implications of scientific facts concerning the world of man.
Develop mathematic skills for practical operations and subsequent training.
Have historical perspective to understand the rights and duties in a democratic society and to be able to assume these responsibilities.
Develop the foundation skills and information that enable individuals to pursue successfully a trade or a profession either immediately or after further training.
Know how to purchase goods and services intelligently, with a proper understanding of our economic system.

[11] *Accreditation Report from Downey Senior High School* (Downey, Calif.: Downey Unified School District, February 1969), Appendix 4-1.

Appreciate the significance of the family as the important unit of our society.
Develop and maintain good health.
Become aware of, and conform to, accepted moral values.
Appreciate the values of the arts, including literature, music, and fine arts.
Use leisure time in constructive and socially desirable activities.
Make a realistic evaluation of their interests, aptitudes, and achievements.

These aims are worthwhile. They are commendable and typical of broad goals used by thousands of high schools across the country. However, it is possible, and desirable, to effect a translation of such goals into precise objectives that will give specific directions for the accomplishment of those objectives. Why is this translation made so seldom? One can only surmise on the basis of an analysis of what is actually happening.

Education in America is built on a foundation of federal interest, state responsibility, and local control. When a prominent group such as the NEA or one of its subgroups voices a set of objectives for secondary schools, it is assumed by many local educators that these "experts" have researched the problem and speak from a position of knowledge. This knowledge, however, comes from the pooling of a variety of ideas, and the objectives thus generated are, of necessity, general guidelines suitable for use by almost all secondary schools in the United States. It has not been the intention of any of the national groups to prescribe instructional objectives for any particular school district because these groups are well aware of the wide variety of needs that exist. But because schools were not forced by law to have precise objectives or to monitor students' progress with vigor, they largely ignored these crucial responsibilities altogether. They acted as though freedom to act responsibly was freedom to not act at all.

As a consequence of neglecting to focus on precise educational *outcomes*, schools have tended to justify their existence by focusing on the *process* by which students are educated. This focus has often caused a misdirection in efforts to educate. Teachers, for example, are evaluated in terms of a series of political considerations, which include items such as "personal characteristics" and "maintenance of a neat classroom." Thus the emphasis is on the behavior of the teacher and how well he or she measures up to the conceptual model of the ideal teacher that the evaluator has in mind. Tragically, however, few evaluation forms include a section dealing with the *amount of learning* that is taking place as demonstrated by specific acts of the students. Very rarely does someone ask, "What are students achieving?" The most important aspect of teaching—increasing the knowledge and skills of students—is usually neglected. Just as it does not make much sense for a law firm to employ a lawyer who persists in losing cases, it does not make much sense for schools to employ teachers who consistently fail to help students learn. Educators must be able to tell the taxpayers what the schools are *really* after and demonstrate to them that they *can* achieve their goals. Taxpayers demand accountability.

Schools continually receive broadly stated goals from national and state organizations. To be workable in any given classroom, however, these goals need to be reworded into precisely stated objectives. Unfortunately, many schools try to make minor wording changes instead of the major changes actually needed and thus end up with nebulous goals that make competence assessment all but impossible. If school administrators evaluate teachers solely on the basis of process considerations, ignoring product considerations (i.e, student growth), public education may lose the support of the taxpayers. Taxpayers want to know what they are getting for their money, and schools must be prepared to tell them. Parents may soon be asking you, "How do you *know* that my Johnny is developing an ethical character?" and "What *specific* things can my Mary do now that you have taught her about worthy home membership?"

What are the implications? The changes coming about now in education will continue and accelerate. When teachers pass each other in the hall, the kind of question they ask each other will become, "What objectives are your students working on today?," rather than the current question, "What are you going to be doing with your kids today?" While the second question may be more sociable, it avoids the issue. Educators must define their purposes, goals, aims, objectives, and ends specifically and be able to tell the taxpayer what the students can accomplish as a result of schooling.

The teaching skills to be presented later in this book focus on those that are useful tools for enhancing learning. There is one tool, however, that is so basic and so useful that the following two chapters are devoted exclusively to its use. That tool is the *precise instructional objective*.

SUMMARY

The penchant for public education to fail to state any goals but very general ones grows out of the history of education, stretching back to prehistoric times when formal goals were unneeded. There seems to be a direct relationship between popular interest in educational goals and popular participation in education. Throughout biblical, Greek, Roman, medieval, and colonial times, when only a relatively few individuals received a formal education, the public was not concerned with the goals because they were not directly involved.

In the course of the development of mass education, overall goals underwent a significant change. Instead of focusing only on matters of the mind, as more and more people began going to school, schools also began to focus on more practical matters. In addition, as education came to be supported publicly, the need for formal statements of goals became more acute. Educators now must decide, for example, if education is attempting to make students more like or more unlike each other. The goals educators espouse have to reflect their decision and must satisfy the people paying the bills.

In the United States a number of attempts (from the Committee of Ten in 1893, through the development of the seven cardinal principles in 1913, to the Educational Policies Commission in 1961) have been made to formalize goals for secondary schools, but these broad goals were, necessarily, not specific enough to assist directly in the creation of proper educational experiences. The vacuum left by the failure of educators to specify their goals has been filled by people in positions of power who have perceived needs and wrought changes in particular schools. This trend has been obscured by educators who focus attention on the process of education rather than on its outcomes.

Education cannot continue to avoid its responsibility to state precise goals. Hard economic facts of life mandate that educators be able to specify educational objectives so that their accomplishment is observable. Precision in generating educational objectives has become imperative.

THREE
WRITING PRECISE
INSTRUCTIONAL
OBJECTIVES

Anyone who talks with educators today or who reads current educational journals cannot help but be aware of the increasing use of precise instructional objectives; they have become part of a continuing expansion of competency-based education programs and are crucial to increased efforts aimed at increasing accountability among educators. School systems throughout the country are providing (either by choice or by legislative fiat) in-service education for their teachers to prepare them to write and use precise instructional objectives. This in-service work is often followed by workshops during which teachers are expected to begin writing precise instructional objectives for their courses. Personnel directors in many districts are actively seeking teacher candidates who can demonstrate their ability to write and use precise instructional objectives, and more and more teacher preparation institutions are providing both undergraduate and graduate courses that include the study and use of precise instructional objectives.

With this increased interest, the wise prospective teacher will venture into a classroom (or a job interview) only after acquiring the basic skills of writing and implementing precise instructional objectives. This chapter is intended to help you develop the skills necessary to write and modify such objectives.

Objectives

When you complete this chapter, you will be able to:

1. When given ten instructional objectives, label in writing at least eight as (a) lacking an observable behavior, (b) lacking a minimum acceptable standard, (c) both a and b, or (d) acceptable.
2. Given two improperly stated instructional objectives, rewrite them so that each contains an observable terminal behavior, a condition, and a minimum acceptable standard and concerns the same topic as the original.
3. Given a topic within your teaching field, write three precise instructional objectives, each of which calls for a different kind of behavior and specifies a condition and a minimum acceptable standard.

GENERATING OBJECTIVES

Gathering the Content Base

Once written and distributed, precise instructional objectives are available for critical examination by a wide variety of people. Therefore, the wise teacher will make it a point to consider a number of factors when writing the objectives, among which are the needs and desires of the students, the teacher's own academic strengths, the expectations of the school and community, and the limitations imposed both by state requirements and by the nature of the subject itself.

A good way to begin the process of writing precise instructional objectives is to write down the particular skills and content you feel should logically be a part of the proposed course and would be of most help to students once they leave the class. Pay particular attention to including skill and information areas that will be of real help to students in their day-to-day affairs. For example, it makes little difference if a person can or cannot list the first ten presidents of the United States (except on a quiz show), but being able to describe the division of powers in the federal government may help a person to understand the antagonism that often exists between the legislative and executive branches and thus to explain the governmental problems that are so confusing and frustrating to one who lacks such knowledge.

After writing down your own ideas, you may obtain other ideas by scanning current texts in your subject area, reading through curriculum guides and resource units, and talking with other teachers, administrators, and parents. It is also helpful to pursue compilations of precise instructional objectives (see Appendix A). All these sources will help you develop objectives focusing on the subject matter at hand. It is your job to refine these ideas into objectives that have relevance to, and involve, today's technologically oriented world.

Having compiled what is likely to be a rather lengthy list, you are ready to begin converting the original list into a set of precise instructional objectives. You should not be alarmed if there is little student contribution at this point. The most valid student input will come after the initial work. The steps described here would take place prior to the first class and will provide you with a basic list of essential objectives to which student suggestions can be added.

THE BASIC PARTS OF PRECISE INSTRUCTIONAL OBJECTIVES

Observable Behavior

The first step in transforming the "raw material" into precise instructional objectives is to specify an *observable terminal behavior* for each objective. An observable terminal behavior describes, in terms of activities that a person can actually see and measure, exactly *what a student will be expected to do at the end of instruction.* Experience has shown that terms such as "define in writing," "underline," and "diagram" are more effective in describing expected behaviors than are terms such as "know," "learn," and "understand." The terms in the second group are not directly observable and can be interpreted in a number of ways. Consider the following examples:

1. You will know the difference between prose and poetry.
2. You will define, in writing, the terms *prose* and *poetry* and illustrate each definition with the name of an example.

Since the word "know" in the first objective represents a behavior that is not directly observable, the student cannot determine how you expect the knowledge to be demonstrated, and neither you nor the student can ascertain when, or if, the objective is finally achieved. If no observable behavior is stated, the objective is useless in terms of telling students exactly what is expected of them: it does not convey instructional intent.

The second objective contains an observable behavior: "define in writing." Since you and your students can now describe how achievement of the objective is to be demonstrated, it becomes easier to plan instruction that will help students acquire the necessary skills, easier for students to focus their efforts on achieving the specified skills, and easier for both you and your students to determine when, in fact, the objective *is* achieved.

It should be noted that words such as "know," "learn," "understand," "grasp," and "discern" do not necessarily have to be avoided when writing precise instructional objectives. If it is felt that such words are necessary to convey instructional intent, you may use them but should be sure to include an explanation of how the implied behavior is to be demonstrated. Consider, for example, the following objective.

You will demonstrate an understanding of prose and poetry by writing the definitions of these terms and illustrating each definition with the title of an appropriate example.

This objective contains an observable terminal behavior, but it is unnecessarily wordy. In many instances you will find that words such as "learn" and "understand" are superfluous and do not assist in clarifying the instructional intent. The fewer words used to convey the instructional intent clearly, the less chance there is for misinterpretation.

Some terms, such as "identify," "differentiate," and "solve," are less ambiguous than are such terms as "know" and "learn," yet they describe purely mental activities—activities that go on in the student's head—and are therefore not directly observable. To make these terms less ambiguous, you must again be sure to specify a means by which the activities can be observed: "identify in writing," "differentiate by recording on a checklist," or "record on paper the step-by-step procedure." By indicating to students what specific activity will be required to demonstrate the competence overtly, you not only sharpen the mental picture students have of what is expected of them, but you also tend to reduce anxiety. The expected behavior is now clear.

Sometimes it makes sense to have students demonstrate a competence orally. While this kind of competence demonstration has its place, there are disadvantages that must be kept in mind. If an objective requires a student to "state orally" certain specifics, the reliability of the competence demonstration is compromised if other students hear the recitation. It would be illogical, for example, to write an objective that stated, "The student will state orally three measures of central tendency," unless provisions were made for each student to demonstrate the competence privately. If the competence were demonstrated in a classroom setting, you would be unable to differentiate between those students who actually understood the material and those who were merely parroting what they heard others say.

Since it is likely that a large number of the objectives will be demonstrated in writing, it may be advantageous to state at the beginning of the list of objectives that all objectives will be demonstrated in writing unless specified otherwise. This procedure eliminates the need to include the words "in writing" in virtually every objective.

Conditions

Once the observable terminal behavior is decided upon, you are in a position to add any special limitations or freedoms that will exist when the behavior is demonstrated. Conditions frequently refer to time limits or to the use of aids or special equipment, but they can refer to whatever factors are considered important to the demonstration of the terminal behavior. A physical education teacher, for example, might consider it important to specify "using a regulation baseball" in an objective concerning the hitting of line drives to avoid any question as to whether a baseball or a softball is to be used. Again, the function of conditions is to clarify further the student's mental picture of the constraints or other conditions that will affect the demonstration of the specified competence. Consider the following objectives.

You will be able to:

1. Describe, in writing, at least two possible advantages associated with the use of precise instructional objectives.
2. Using only notes, describe, in a paper of no more than two pages, at least two possible advantages and two possible disadvantages associated with the use of precise instructional objectives.

The first objective contains an observable terminal behavior ("describe, in writing"), but students do not know if they will be expected to memorize the required information or if they can simply open a text and copy what they need. In the second objective doubts are removed. The condition that notes may be used is stated clearly, and there is little room for misunderstanding. Likewise, the specification of length ("in a paper of no more than two pages") gives students an even more complete description of constraints.

While statements of conditions are usually quite helpful and are sometimes absolutely necessary to avoid misunderstandings, some care must be taken in their use. Preconditions such as "after a lecture" or "after reading Chapter Ten" usually weaken an objective because they limit the sources from which a student may draw information in formulating responses. Certainly it would not be your intention to penalize a student for having acquired information or skills outside the class, and yet conditions such as those just mentioned imply such a penalty. If, on the other hand, the limitation is crucial to the objective for some specific reason, such preconditions must be included.

There are few instances in which the prerequisites for an objective need be included in the objective itself. Generally, a precise instructional objective should not concern itself with how a student acquires the knowledge or skill to demonstrate a particular competence. The manner in which a student prepares for eventual demonstration of a competence falls within the realm of teaching-learning activities. At this point in formulating objectives, your main concern is specifying the competence itself as clearly and concisely as possible.

Another point to remember is that it makes little sense to attempt to state all conditions for all objectives. For example, the condition "with no aids" will probably be common to many objectives. To include the words "with no aids" in each and every objective, however, would be both repetitive and distracting. A more logical solution would be to state the conditions common to most objectives at the beginning of the list of objectives and to discuss the general nature of these conditions with students prior to instruction.

As a general rule, you should state conditions whenever there is a possibility that doubts or misunderstandings may arise. If there are any doubts as to whether conditions are needed in a particular objective, be safe and include them. Keep in mind that if no conditions are specified in the objective, adding constraints at the time the competence is to be demonstrated may result in strong student resentment.

Minimum Acceptable Standard

The last element included in a complete precise instructional objective is a minimum acceptable standard of performance. You must decide how well each of the observable behaviors must be demonstrated for it to be deemed acceptable.

Given the kind of behavior called for in the objective, the minimum acceptable standard can be stated in quantitative terms, qualitative terms, or both. As the name suggests, quantitative terms specify amounts or numbers and qualitative terms specify particular points or aspects that are sought. The following are examples of objectives using quantitative and/or qualitative minimum acceptable standards.

You will be able to:

1. Given four sets of symptoms, diagnose, in writing, the correct disease in *at least three* of the cases.
2. Write *at least ten* precise instructional objectives, each of which contains *an observable terminal behavior, conditions,* and *a minimum acceptable standard.*
3. Explain, in writing, the proper use of the wood lathe including (a) *the procedure for mounting material* (b) *the proximity of the rest block to the material* (c) *the speed of the chuck* (d) *the proper use of tool bit,* and (e) *safety precautions.*

The first objective utilizes only a quantitative standard (at least three). The second example combines a quantitative standard (at least ten) with a qualitative standard (contains an observable terminal behavior, conditions, and a minimum acceptable standard). The third contains a qualitative standard that describes the minimum elements necessary in a student explantion (points a through e).

A common misconception concerning minimum acceptable standards is that the specification of allowable time or lengths of answers is, by itself, sufficient to clarify what is expected as a minimally acceptable performance.

Generally these are conditions, not minimum acceptable standards. Consider the following objectives.

You will be able to:

1. Describe, in a paper of no more than two pages, the results of World War II.
2. Type at least two letters in one class period.

In the first objective students could argue that they should receive credit for achieving the objective for writing simply, "The Allies won." This answer would meet the condition "in a paper of not more than two pages," but it confuses conditions with minimum standards because the teacher failed to include a minimum standard. According to the second objective the student could turn in two messy, error-filled pages at the end of the period and be upset if they were not accepted. In neither objective did the quantitative limitations convey the true minimum standards. The teacher did not state the complete instructional intention.

If, however, time or length is a consideration for achievement, then it can be a minimum standard. For instance, in the objective "You will be able to run the 100-yard dash in 13 seconds," thirteen seconds is certainly the minimum acceptable standard. Similarly, a teacher who is teaching how to summarize can include "in less than one page" as part of a minimum standard.

Qualitative standards present a more involved problem for those writing objectives, for they often imply subjective judgments, and it becomes difficult to describe the particular attributes or characteristics that must be included in the terminal behavior demonstration if that demonstration is to be declared acceptable. For example, the objectives stated in the instances given are improved as additional qualitative standards are added.

You will be able to:

1. Describe, in a paper of no more than two pages, the results of World War II in terms of at least two economic developments in France and Germany.
2. Within one class period, type a one-page personal letter and a one-page business letter, using the block style, with no typographical errors.

As rewritten, the objectives begin to communicate instructional intent more clearly and minimize the chances for misunderstandings. As more standards are added, the picture of the desired end product will become more and more clear in the mind of the student. To try to include every possible point, however, would make the objective so cumbersome that it would be virtually useless.

For instance, in attempting to establish qualitative standards for either of the two objectives given, the teacher will undoubtedly consider many factors such as logical organization, completeness, relevancy, neatness, spelling and punctuation errors, and other considerations that are either too common or too vague to specify. Common kinds of standards as well as common kinds of terminal behaviors and common kinds of conditions can be stated at the beginning of a list of objectives, thus eliminating the obligation of stating them for each objective.

Of course, the task of specifying standards for logical organization, completeness, relevancy, or other similarly nebulous factors is admittedly difficult; in fact, in some instances it may even be impossible. While it is desirable to communicate clearly to the student exactly what will be sought in the response or skill demonstration, at the same time it is necessary to keep the objective to a reasonable length. In the objective concerning the results of World War II, for example, the parameter "in terms of at least two economic developments in France and Germany" gives students a clearer picture of how they are to orient the answer. Adding the words "See the handout for further minimum standards" would allow the teacher to describe further minimum standards without loading down the objective with material that might detract from readability and interest.

The fact that all possible qualitative standards are not included in each objective should not be taken as an abdication of your right or professional obligation to make judgments concerning overall quality, and this point should be made clear to students. You should simply acknowledge the fact that many instructional objectives deal with complex concepts or human behaviors and that the objectives are therefore attempts to convey, as far as possible, the true instructional intent by specifying as many pertinent parameters as makes good sense. If you want students to refer to particular ideas, points, or aspects when demonstrating a competence, you should identify those points in the objective, but terms such as "main ideas," "most important points," and "major aspects" should be used with the understanding that you are willing to accept the student's opinion regarding these matters. If you are not precise in describing terminal behaviors or minimal acceptable standards, you should not hold the students accountable for the consequences of misinterpretation.

Objectives and Mainstreamed Students

Many schools are now following a policy of placing some handicapped students in "least restrictive environments." This policy, known as *mainstreaming*, means that some students who might have been placed previously in special education classes are now being placed in regular classes. This placement may pose special problems for you with respect to objectives.

The main reason for mainstreaming students is to enable them to work with nonhandicapped people and to perform as much like the non-handicapped people as possible. With this in mind, you will want to make as few changes in your objectives as possible, but you may find that some changes are necessary. If, for example, you have a visually impaired student in your class, that student might be allowed to demonstrate some objectives orally rather than in writing. Similarly, a spastic student might be given the opportunity to have papers typed rather than writing them in class.

While the adjustment of terminal behaviors might be time consuming, it is the possible adjustment of minimum acceptable standards that poses the real problem. Some of the mainstreamed students may have learning disabilities that make it difficult for them to meet the standards set for others in the class. If you find such students in your class, you should first check with your school administrators to find out if a policy has been established regarding the adjustment of standards for mainstreamed students. If no policy has been established, it is suggested that you work with special education teachers and/or guidance counselors to develop a set of objectives that are reasonable for the student and for the subject and grade level in which the student has been placed. It is *not* suggested that you abandon your own standards to accommodate the mainstreamed student(s). If mainstreamed students simply cannot meet reasonable standards for a particular subject at a particular grade level, consideration should be given to placing them in another class (perhaps a special education class) to give them a fair chance at success.

Review

In review, the first step in writing objectives is the decision as to what the teacher really wants students to do after instruction. You must consider not only the needs and desires of your students but also your own subject-matter strengths and weaknesses, the expectations of the school and community, and relevant state regulations. You should seek ideas for objectives from current texts, other teachers, administrators, parents, curriculum guides, resource units, and compilations of existing objectives.

After acquiring all this "raw material," it must be refined and converted into a series of precise instructional objectives by phrasing each idea so that it specifies a particular behavior to be demonstrated, describes the pertinent conditions that will exist at the time the behavior is demonstrated, and states clearly a minimum acceptable standard of performance. In short, you must convey to your students, as clearly as possible, exactly what they will be expected to do after instruction.

PRACTICE IN WORKING WITH OBJECTIVES

Practice Exercise 1: Characteristics of Objectives

Many of the following objectives are stated in unacceptable form. Use the following rating scale to pinpoint the weakness(es) in each objective, rewrite the objective in acceptable form, and check your responses with those furnished. An objective may be rated using more than one response.

(Note: It can be argued logically that, if an objective contains no observable behavior, then there is no way for it to contain a minimum standard. This is because, if it is impossible to observe *what* the student is going to be able to do, then it is impossible to determine *how well* he or she has to do it.)

RATING SCALE

1. Lacks an observable behavior
2. Lacks a minimum acceptable standard
3. Lacks conditions
4. Contains all three necessary elements

You will be able to:

1. Know the democratic principles upon which our country is founded.
2. Know the names of both U.S. senators from your home state.
3. Be an alert and an aware citizen.
4. Given a microcomputer and a diskette, correctly run a specified program.
5. Prescribe appropriate medication for a surgery patient.
6. Take an active role in society.
7. Demonstrate typing skill by retyping two letters in class, using block style, without errors.
8. Write a proper personal letter.
9. Understand the plight of the poor people in our country.
10. List orally the three branches of our federal government in class.
11. List orally the strengths and weaknesses of the United Nations.
12. Understand two steps in the committee process.
13. Appreciate the benefits of competency-based instruction.
14. Sincerely believe in just one reason to participate on a committee.
15. Demonstrate a comprehension of behavioral objectives by achieving a score of at least 80 percent on a forced choice test dealing with behavioral objectives.

RATING SCALE ANSWERS

1. 1, 2, 3
2. 1, 3 ("both" is a quantitative minimum standard)
3. 1, 2, 3
4. 4
5. 3
6. 1, 2, 3
7. 4
8. 2, 3 ("proper" does not prescribe a precise minimum standard)
9. 1, 2
10. 4
11. 2, 3 (how many strengths and weaknesses?)
12. 1, 3
13. 1, 2, 3
14. 1, 3
15. 4 (technically correct but somewhat ambiguous)

The following objectives are examples of rewrites based on the original and contain an observable behavior, minimum standard, and conditions. It is expected, of course, that rewrites may vary considerably from these models:

You will be able to:

1. Write, in class, all requirements for election and lengths of term for U.S. congressmen.
2. Write the names of both U.S. senators from your home state.
3. Select a current legislative issue, write a one-page letter to your U.S. senators expressing your views on that issue, and give at least two reasons for those views in the letter.
4. (No changes needed.)
5. Given a hypothetical description of a surgery situation, prescribe the medication necessary.
6. After reading the details in the local paper, write a letter to the editor of the local paper expressing your views on a current local problem containing at least two rationales for those views.
7. (No changes needed.)
8. Write a one-page personal letter containing at least a heading, salutation, body, and closing, without grammatical error.
9. State orally at least three factors inhibiting the elimination of poverty within our country.
10. (No changes needed.)
11. List, in writing, with no aids and within thirty minutes, at least two strengths and two weaknesses of the United Nations.
12. Describe, in writing, at least two steps in the committee process.
13. Describe, in writing, at least three benefits of competency-based instruction to students.
14. Describe orally to the class at least one reason to participate on a committee.
15. Recall and/or apply information concerning the structure of precise instructional objectives well enough to answer correctly at least 80 percent of a series of multiple-choice questions concerning such objectives.

Self-test: Rewriting Poorly Stated Objectives

Rewrite each of the following objectives so that they contain an observable behavior, minimum standard, and conditions.

1. You will develop good instructional objectives.
2. You will know why behavioral objectives are important.

Checking the Rewritten Objectives

1. Look at the rewritten objective. Ask yourself the question, "Does this objective tell me what the student is going to be able to do after the lesson that I can observe?" If it does, then the objective includes an *observable behavior*.

In objective 1, the word "develop" is imprecise. A person could develop objectives in his or her head but that would be unobservable. It would be better to say "develop and write," "state orally," or just "write."

In objective 2, the word "know" is not observable. Observable behavior could be "stated orally," "explain," "describe in writing," or "demonstrate understanding by taking a test."

2. Second, ask yourself if the rewritten objectives answer the question, "How well does the student have to demonstrate the observable behavior?" If your objective answers this question, then the objective has a *minimum standard*. In objective 1 "good" does not give us a minimum standard.

3. Third, ask yourself if the rewritten objective answers the question, "Under what circumstances will the student demonstrate the observable behavior?" If the objective answers this question, then it has the necessary condition or conditions.

Possible Rewrites

You will be able to:

1. Write, without aids and within ten minutes, two behavioral objectives each of which contains an observable terminal behavior, any necessary conditions, and a minimum acceptable standard.

2. State orally in class at least two reasons for the wide acceptance of behavioral objectives by educators.

Self-test: Characteristics of Objectives

Use the following rating scale to pinpoint the weakness(es), if any, in each of the following objectives:

RATING SCALE

1. Lacks an observable behavior
2. Lacks a minimum acceptable standard
3. Lacks conditions
4. The objective is acceptable

You will be able to:

1. Write a critical reaction to *Moby Dick.*
2. When asked by the teacher, state orally the names of two wartime presidents.
3. Recite the Pledge of Allegiance with no errors.
4. Demonstrate a knowledge of proper tool use by selecting a saw with which to cut plywood.
5. Understand quadratic equations well enough to solve, on paper, any three that are given, without the use of aids and within thirty minutes.
6. Demonstrate easy mathematical skills with at least 80 percent accuracy.
7. Understand fully the terms volt, ohm, and alternating current.

8. Demonstrate good physical condition, in part, by running the mile in less than six minutes.
9. Translate written French into written English.
10. Be proud to be an American 85 percent of the time.

Answers to Self-test on Characteristics of Objectives

1. 2, 3
2. 4
3. 3
4. 2, 3
5. 4
6. 1, 3
7. 1, 2, 3
8. 3
9. 2, 3
10. 1, 3

Summary

There is little doubt that the use of precise instructional objectives can be a useful tool in modern education. Since the number of school systems requiring teachers to learn to write and use precise instructional objectives is increasing, and since more and more recruiters are looking for teacher candidates who already possess these skills, prospective and practicing teachers need to become familiar with both the writing and use of such objectives.

The first step in writing precise instructional objectives is to determine exactly what it is students should be able to do after instruction. As a base for building objectives, you may turn to your own academic background, current texts, the needs and desires of your potential students, the expectations of the school and community, other teachers, administrators, resource units, curriculum guides, and compilations of existing instructional objectives.

The second step in the writing process is to rephrase each of the ideas so that it communicates instructional intent clearly, that is, so it specifies an observable terminal behavior, conditions under which that behavior will be demonstrated, and a minimum acceptable standard of performance.

Observable terminal behaviors such as writing, telling, and demonstrating need to be specified so that students, teachers, and any other interested parties can verify that certain knowledge or skills have, in fact, been mastered. Since actual thinking activities such as solving, identifying, and appreciating take place within the head, they cannot be used, directly, to verify that learning has taken place. For such verification the purely cognitive activities need to be reflected in observable behaviors. Obviously not all cognitive processes can be reflected in all their complexity but many can be and should be.

Conditions such as "with no aids," "within ten minutes," and "under test conditions" are stated to inform students of the particular circumstances under which they will be expected to demonstrate the terminal behavior. Since the statement of conditions enables students to practice the expected behavior appropriately, it is unfair to state conditions for the first time immediately before the behavior is to be demonstrated. Students should be as aware of the conditions that might affect their performance as they are of the expected behavior itself.

Minimum acceptable standards tell students how well they must do a particular thing for it to be acceptable. Standards can be quantitative ("at least 80 percent" or "in at least six cases") or qualitative ("emphasize the relationship between cost and quantity" or "in iambic pentameter, about spring"). In either case you must be sure to include the critical aspects you will use to evaluate the student's performance. Factors such as the length of a response are not usually useful as minimum acceptable standards since they imply that you intend to use sheer length (or weight) to evaluate the response rather than to read what has been written. The specification of standards is not easy, but it is a crucial step in clarifying and communicating instructional intent and will contribute, immeasurably, to your students' success and hence to your own success.

The following chapter will concern itself with a taxonomy that will enable you to classify objectives so as to determine which skills and abilities are being emphasized.

FOUR
CLASSIFYING AND USING PRECISE INSTRUCTIONAL OBJECTIVES

Instructional objectives that are stated precisely help improve the teaching-learning process by clarifying instructional intent, thereby enabling you and your students to work toward the same clear goals. It is possible, however, that the goals may focus on a very narrow range of skills and abilities and thus limit the development of your students and your own range of instructional activities. To avoid this development, many educators find it useful to classify their objectives on the basis of the kinds of skills and abilities expected of students.

One of the best known classification schemes was developed in 1956 and described in a book edited by Benjamin Bloom entitled *Taxonomy of Educational Objectives, Handbook I: Cognitive Domain.*[1] "Bloom's taxonomy" (as it is popularly known) is divided into three domains, and each domain is divided into levels. The cognitive domain, delineated in *Handbook I,* concerns the acquisition and manipulation of factual information. The affective domain, delineated in *Handbook II,*[2] concerns commitment toward values and attitudes. The psychomotor domain, delineated in a book entitled *A Taxonomy of the Psychomotor Domain,*[3] concerns the development of physical skills.

[1] Benjamin S. Bloom, ed., *Taxonomy of Educational Objectives, Handbook I: Cognitive Domain* (New York: David McKay, 1956).
[2] David R. Krathwohl, ed., *Taxonomy of Educational Objectives, Handbook II: Affective Domain* (New York: David McKay, 1964).
[3] Anita J. Harrow, *A Taxonomy of the Psychomotor Domain* (New York: David McKay, 1972).

This chapter will familiarize you with all three domains and the levels within them. It will also demonstrate how instructional objectives can be written to elicit a broad range of skills and abilities and give you some practice in classifying objectives. Both skills will help you to use objectives to their maximum advantage.

OBJECTIVES

When you complete this chapter, you will be able to:

1. List, in writing, each major level of the cognitive, affective, and psycho-motor domains. (Knowledge)
2. Describe, in writing, the distinguishing characteristics of each level of the cognitive domain. (Comprehension)
3. Within your teaching field, write one precise instructional objective at each major level of each appropriate domain. (Synthesis)
4. Rewrite at least three of the objectives written for objective 3 to accommodate a learning disabled student. (Synthesis)

THE TAXONOMY AND ITS USE

The taxonomy of educational objectives was developed to help educators classify objectives according to the skills and abilities they elicited from students. When working with any of the taxonomic domains or levels, it is important to keep in mind that you are working with a theoretical division of skills and abilities. It is extremely difficult to analyze the working of the human mind, and there are likely to be some objectives that do not seem to fit neatly into any specific level or even any specific domain. The possibility of haziness in classification does not seriously lessen the usefulness of the taxonomy because most objectives *will* fit into one or another domain and level. Further, if you classify your objectives according to the taxonomic divisions, you will be able to see if you have included a reasonable range of skills and abilities even if a few objectives are misclassified.

THE COGNITIVE DOMAIN

The cognitive domain is divided into six major levels, each of which is divided into sublevels. The exploration of the cognitive domain will be restricted primarily to the six major levels, but if you wish to explore any of the levels in greater depth, Bloom's handbook is recommended. The following discussion is intended to give you enough skill to make initial classifications of objectives for the purposes mentioned. Studying the material that follows and completing the exercises will enable you to examine and defend your objectives as to the variety of thinking skills they include:

Knowledge

The first, and lowest, level of the cognitive domain is knowledge. At this level students are expected simply to recall information to which they have been exposed or to recognize information presented. The main skill emphasized by objectives written at this level is simple recollection. Listed now are some examples of objectives written at the knowledge level.

You will be able, in writing and under test conditions, to:

1. List at least five parts and three formats characteristc of business letters.
2. List the unit of metric measure corresponding to (not equivalent to) pounds, ounces, quarts, gallons, inches, yards, and miles (e.g., miles/kilometers).
3. Define the terms "capitalism," "socialism," and "communism."

Comprehension

The second level of the cognitive domain is comprehension. It is the view of many educators that this level is the one most emphasized in today's schools. If this view is correct, our level of emphasis is disappointing because the comprehension level is low in the hierarchy of intellectual skills. This level indicates that the student can recall information and can also make some use of it.

Bloom includes three kinds of intellectual skills in the comprehension level. The first of these is translation, the ability to make a one-for-one conversion from one symbol form or language to another. The second skill is interpretation, which is the ability to generalize or paraphrase information. The third skill is extrapolation, which is the ability to make predictions based on the information presented. Examples of observable behaviors reflecting each of these skills are as follows.

You will be able, in writing and under test conditions, to:*

1. Describe what is meant by the tone of a letter and cite examples of two tones.
2. Translate the formula for converting degrees Fahrenheit to degrees Celsius, from sentence form to mathematical statement form.
3. Explain the idea of dialectical materialism (thesis, antithesis, synthesis) using the concepts of pure capitalism, socialism, and communism.

---

*NOTE: A visually-handicapped student might demonstrate these competencies orally rather than in writing.

Application

The third level of the cognitive domain is application. Application is essentially the act of applying some abstraction to a new or unique concrete example, without prompting. Bloom describes the distinction between the levels of comprehension and application as "A demonstration of 'Comprehension' shows that the student *can* use the abstraction when its use is specified. A demonstration of 'Application' shows that he *will* use it correctly, given an appropriate situation in which no mode of solution is specified."[4] It is useful to think of the student understanding a principle or rule at the comprehension level, and then using the principle or rule in a practical situation at the application level. Examples of objectives written at the application level are the following.

You will be able, under test conditions, to:

1. Given the unorganized components of a business letter, organize the components properly into any given business letter format and type the letter without error.
2. Given a series of temperatures in degrees Fahrenheit, convert, in writing, at least 80 percent of them to correct degrees Celsius.
3. Explain, in writing, how the idea of dialectical materialsim can be used to help understand some of the trauma being experienced by developing Third World countries.

Analysis

The fourth level of the cognitive domain is analysis. Many educators consider analysis the first of the higher-cognitive levels. At this level students should be able to break down an idea into its constituent elements or internal organizational principles and to perceive relationships among those elements or principles, within one "whole," or between several "wholes." Analysis, in its fundamental form, is seeing similarities and differences between things. Examples of skills included in the analysis level are shown in the objectives that follow.

You will be able, in writing and under test conditions, to:

1. Given a letter of complaint, modify it to eliminate unnecessary information and improve its tone.
2. Explain at least three advantages and three disadvantages associated with the utilization of the metric system in the United States.
3. Given a description of a business operation, explain the kind of economic system exemplified and support your analysis with specific facts and examples.

[4]Bloom, ed., *Taxonomy of Educational Objectives, Handbook I*, p. 120.

Synthesis

The fifth level of the cognitive domain is synthesis. Synthesis means the creation of something new from previously existing elements or principles. The levels of the cognitive domain are cumulative, and this cumulative aspect becomes evident when a student is asked to create, from the knowledge and skills previously acquired, something that is new and unique (at least to the student). Certainly students need to have mastered material in the area at the preceding levels before they can be successful at the synthesis level. Even then, developing something that is unique is not often an easy task. You must be careful not to mistake the simple accumulation of related parts for synthesis. For example, if you create a menu by simply selecting X servings from Y food groups it would be difficult to justify the menu as a product reflecting high-level thought. If, on the other hand, the menu had to appeal to, and meet the nutritional needs of, a particular kind of person, the complexity of the task increases significantly. Some objectives written at the synthesis level are shown now.

You will be able, under test conditions, to:

1. Write a letter to an appropriate public official, using one of the commonly accepted formats, explaining three reasons why you feel that the official should try to bring about a particular change.
2. Construct a crossword puzzle with at least six words down and six words across that focuses on the metric system.
3. Create a written checklist of at least ten points that could assess the efficiency with which goods and services are produced.

Evaluation

The last, and highest, level of the cognitive domain is evaluation. Evaluation means the formation of a judgment and the substantiation or justification of that judgment by reference to facts, examples, or specific criteria. Evaluation, then, means considerably more than simply saying that this is better than that. The judgment must be made on the basis of specific criteria. Examples of objectives written at the evaluation level are the following.

You will be able, in writing and under test conditions, to:

1. Given two business letters, explain, in less than two pages, which you believe is the more effective and support your decision by citing at least three specific facts and/or examples.
2. State your position with respect to learning the metric system and defend your position by citing at least three specific facts and/or examples.
3. Explain which economic system you believe has the greatest long-term growth potential and support your belief by citing at least three specific facts and/or examples.

Table 1 is included to help you review the characteristics differentiating the various levels of the cognitive domain.

TABLE 1 Behavioral Terms for Objectives in the Major Categories of the Cognitive Domain, *Handbook I*

TAXONOMIC CLASSIFICATION	EXAMPLES OF BEHAVIORAL TERMS FOR SPECIFIC LEARNING OUTCOMES
1.00 Knowledge	Defines terms, recalls facts, recognizes symbols, recites information, states theories, identifies criteria, lists events, selects procedures, matches names and dates, describes phenomena.
2.00 Comprehension 2.10 Translation	Translates phrases, illustrates meanings, restates meanings, illustrates abstractions, prepares representations.
2.20 Interpretation	Interprets theories, explains relationships, draws conclusions, makes qualifications, differentiates among views, demonstrates abstractions.
2.30 Extrapolation	Predicts consequences, infers meaning, determies implications, extends conclusions, predicts effects, estimates probabilities.
3.00 Application	Applies principles, generalizes conclusions, chooses methods, organizes situations, develops processes, uses abstractions.
4.00 Analysis	Distinguishes among facts and intents, recognizes particulars, identifies assumptions, distinguishes relevancies, identifies consistencies and inconsistencies in arguments, compares relationships, identifies patterns, detects organization, determines biases, deduces purposes.
5.00 Synthesis	Writes a unique composition, produces a unique design, proposes a plan, organizes a schematic, formulates hypotheses, combines relationships, develops theories, modifies abstractions.
6.00 Evaluation	Judges accuracy, assesses consistency, determines quality, rates efficiency, judges courses of action, determines precision, determines flaws and errors, and defends judgment.

THE AFFECTIVE DOMAIN

When Bloom and his co-workers published *Handbook I*[5] in 1956, most educators readily accepted the concept of a three-domain taxonomy and just as readily accepted the levels within the cognitive domain. Most educators

[5]Bloom, ed., *Taxonomy of Educational Objectives, Handbook I.*

agreed then, and still agree, that a primary responsibility is to help students acquire and manipulate factual information. When David Krathwohl edited *Handbook II*[6] in 1964 however, many educators were confronted with a dilemma.

Most educators agree that affects such as emotions, attitudes, and values exist and profoundly affect human endeavors. Further, most educators agree that a typical classroom, with its myriad human interactions, is an important force in shaping values and attitudes. The dilemma concerns the extent to which teachers should focus attention and instructional time on affective objectives.

Some feel that, since values and attitudes are going to be developed either deliberately or inadvertently, it is wiser to plan for this development than to allow it to occur by chance. Others feel the development of attitudes and values should be the responsibility of parents and/or churches. They also point out that to observe an affect you must first select an observable behavior that you believe reflects or indicates that affect and then accept the behavioral indicator as the affect. If a poor behavioral indicator is selected, assessment of the affect will be distorted. These educators point out further that, even if it were possible to effectively evaluate the achievement of affective objectives, their primary concern should still be the cognitive domain.

The dilemma is still very much with us and you, too, will be caught up in it. Both sides have valid points, so reaching a conclusion is not easy. To aid you in your deliberations, we will now look at the five levels of the affective domain.

Receiving

The lowest level in the affective domain is receiving. According to the taxonomy, this is the level at which the learner is sensitized to the existence of certain phenomena and stimuli. At this point, the student is willing to receive or attend to value-laden stimuli. The difficulty of forming behavioral objectives at this level is obvious. The question that must be asked is, "What evidence is there that the student is attending or receiving?" Some individuals may accept the student's posture or the direction in which he or she is facing as evidence of receiving. The assumption, however, is a precarious one. Not only are you unable to tell whether or not the student is listening, but you have no indication regarding his or her level of receiving. It is thus recommended that the teacher accept, as evidence of receiving, verbalizations that show understanding of communicated stimuli. These verbalizations should not be confused with responding behaviors. *At the responding level, students act out behaviors consistent with one holding a particular value.* The value itself begins to become important at the responding level. For example, if the value under consideration is honesty, the student would show evidence at the responding level *by being honest.* Evi-

[6]Krathwohl, ed., *Taxonomy of Educational Objectives, Handbook II.*

dence regarding honesty at the receiving level may be *participating in a discussion about honesty* where an understanding of the rudiments of honesty is emphasized. The point is that the student must engage in some behavior that indicates an increased sensitivity to, awareness of, or attention to affective information. Simply sitting erect or facing the teacher is not an adequate indicator. The following are examples of objectives at the receiving level.

You will:

affect   behavioral

1. Demonstrate a sensitivity to present social problems by contributing to an
       indicator
   introductory discussion on the subject.

affect   behavioral indicator

2. Indicate an interest in good classroom discipline by offering comments about the subject in class.

affect   behavioral indicator

3. Indicate an interest in learning about honesty by bringing relevant articles

   to class on this subject.

Responding

Responding refers to active participation by the student. At this level, students act out behaviors that are consistent with people who hold a particular value. The element of commitment, however, is not present. The student may respond either voluntarily or involuntarily. At the lowest level of this category, the student will not have fully accepted the value even though he or she responds as if this is so. If certain constraints were not present, the student might not elect to conform to the particular value or norm.

At the next higher level of this category, the student must demonstrate willingness to respond. This represents a response based on a voluntary choice. While it is not always easy to determine that a student is responding willingly because he or she holds a particular value, it is not so difficult for a teacher to regulate his or her own behavior so as not to exhibit an expectation of compliance. However, even though the teacher does not display an attitude of expected compliance, there is still no assurance that the student's behaviors are a true indication of his or her accepted values. It can be said, though, that the student is responding voluntarily.

At the highest responding level, students may be observed expressing satisfaction regarding a particular response. They exhibit pleasure, zest, or enjoyment. Generally, at this level, it is said that students have an "interest" or, in other words, that they seek out and enjoy activities of a particular type. The following objectives are written at the responding level. You will:

              affect   behavioral indicator

1. Display a commitment to solving social problems by taking a stand, in class discussions, against drug abuse and by outlining ways of combatting such abuse.

                    affect   behavioral indicator

2. Demonstrate a commitment to good classroom decorum by not disturbing or distracting others during class.

              affect   behavioral indicator

3. Demonstrate a commitment to honesty by not cheating and by not helping others cheat.

Valuing

Valuing refers to the worth or value that someone attaches to an object, phenomenon, or behavior. Valuing develops as a consequence of the individual's own assessment of worth as well as those of society. Through the interaction of personal and social preferences, values are internalized slowly and accepted by the individual as his or her own criterion of worth. Behavior at this level is sufficiently consistent and stable to be considered characteristic of the individual's beliefs. The individual is viewed as holding a particular value because his or her behavior consistently indicates this belief in appropriate situations.

This level is composed of three subcategories that represent increasingly deeper stages of internalization. At the lowest level, there is sufficient acceptance of a value by the student for him or her to prefer being identified with it. However, at this level, the individual still holds out for possible reevaluation of his or her position. Therefore, the student's position is a tentative one.

At the highest level of valuing, the individual exhibits a high degree of certainty with regard to acceptance of a particular value. At this stage, we can say that students are committed. They no longer doubt, but remain firm in their beliefs. A person who displays behaviors at this level is clearly perceived as holding that value. Generally, the student can be observed trying to further the thing valued, to extend his or her own development in terms of it, and to increase his or her involvement with it and things

representing it. Often the student is engaged in the activity to try to convince others or to win converts to his or her cause. Usually there is a zeal associated with this behavior. The following are valuing level objectives.
You will:

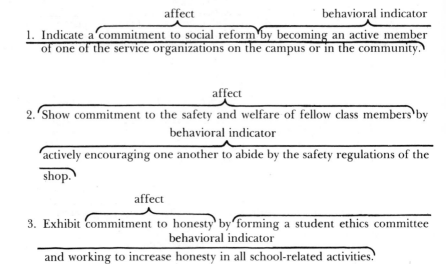

affect   behavioral indicator

1. Indicate a commitment to social reform by becoming an active member of one of the service organizations on the campus or in the community.

affect

2. Show commitment to the safety and welfare of fellow class members by

behavioral indicator

actively encouraging one another to abide by the safety regulations of the shop.

affect

3. Exhibit commitment to honesty by forming a student ethics committee

behavioral indicator

and working to increase honesty in all school-related activities.

Organization

During a student's encounter with possible values, he or she soon recognizes the necessity of organizing several values that are relevant to certain situations. This requires, first, that the student conceptualize the value in a form that permits organization. At this level, then, use is made of higher-level cognitive functioning to deal with affective entities. In other words, at this level there is a necessary interaction between the cognitive and affective domains. Usually, the skills of analysis, synthesis, and evaluation are emphasized. Various values are brought together into an internally consistent system. This is done by comparing the values and their interrelationships. Then values are arranged hierarchically so that the more dominant and pervasive ones are enabled to exhibit the greatest potency.

This level has much possible application in the schools. Emphasizing cognitive value organization aids the student in making conscious choices that can be defended if challenged. Values that are organized with care permit consistent behavior of a permanent nature that is less likely to be weakened by attack. In school, students can engage in learning activities that help them organize their values in a defensible pattern. With values that are organized properly, the student can increase the reliability of his or her behavior and at the same time achieve a greater degree of confidence in the validity of his or her responses.

Even though the organization of a value system is a personal undertaking, it is necessary to help students perform this task with a view toward social reality. Values formed in the absence of social realities lack viability because much behavior must be acted out in social situations and consequently must be at least somewhat consistent with it. Because schools tend to be isolated communities with an excess of artificiality, it is necessary to contrive learning situations with as much realism as possible, given the normal constraints of the classroom. The following are given as examples of organization objectives. You will:

1. Exhibit the organization of the values of honesty and courtesy by making consistent written responses to fifteen situations contrived to require interaction of these two values.
2. Given a series of hypothetical social situations, demonstrate reconciliation of responsibility in yourself and to groups by exhibiting the behaviors that are consistent with your reconciliations.

Characterization

At this level the individual has been controlled long enough by an internally consistent value system to have adapted to behaving in a way consistent with those values. The behavior pattern has become the individual's life-style. Executing appropriate behaviors no longer arouses emotion or affect except at those times when his or her belief system is challenged. Individuals with characterized values are viewed by others as having the characteristics that make up their value pattern. It is relatively easy to predict behavior because it always conforms to the preestablished value pattern. The person simply does not act out of harmony with this "philosophy of life." To have arrived at this level, the individual must have evolved an appropriate balance between affective and cognitive functioning. The individual must understand what he or she is and why he or she has organized his or her life-style in such a way. Ordinarily, such characterization is associated with a high degree of satisfaction. It is likely that the student will leave formal schooling not having characterized his or her values. This is as it should be. Numerous experiences are yet to be encountered that will result in altered perspectives and subsequent reorganization of values. The school's purpose is to initiate the appropriate organization processes and help the student conceptualize the way in which he or she should proceed toward full characterization. Examples of characterization objectives follow. You will:

1. Indicate growth toward characterization of the value of honesty by consistently acting honestly in all your dealings with teachers and fellow students.

2. Exhibit a characterized philosophy of life as indicated by a high degree of correspondence between a written personal philosophy and the actual behaviors engaged in.

Table 2 is included to help you review the characteristics differentiating the various levels of the affective domain.

TABLE 2 Behavioral Terms for Objectives in the Major Categories of the Affective Domain, *Handbook II*

TAXONOMIC CLASSIFICATION	EXAMPLES OF BEHAVIORAL TERMS FOR SPECIFIC LEARNING OUTCOMES
1.0 Receiving	Discusses value concepts, asks questions, takes note of value concepts, differentiates sounds, selects models, identifies sounds.
2.0 Responding	Complies with directions, follows instructions, volunteers to help, practices willingly, applauds performances, reads willingly.
3.0 Valuing	Supports viewpoints, argues against deceptions, helps projects, protests irrelevancies, campaigns actively, espouses the virtues of the library guild, joins and supports the community players, argues for better safety, debates abdications, subsidizes artists.
4.0 Organization	Compares codes of conduct, theorizes on standards, organizes value systems, balances approaches to life, formulates criteria for value determination, defines limits of behaviors.
5.0 Characterization	Changes behavior in light of value reorganization, consistently demonstrates humanitarianism as rated by peers, always listens attentively when spoken to, is judged to be mature by teachers, avoids excesses, manages conflicts consistently.

THE PSYCHOMOTOR DOMAIN

The psychomotor domain is concerned with the development of motor skills and neuromuscular control. Objectives in the psychomotor domain often contain elements of the cognitive and/or affective domains (and vice versa), but the dominant characteristic and intent of the student's response is a physical movement. The curricular areas in which psychomotor skills receive major emphasis include typing, shorthand, home economics, industrial education, art, music, and, of course, physical education. It is important to keep in mind, however, that virtually all other curricular areas depend, to one degree or another, on psychomotor skills because speaking, gesturing, writing, and eye-hand coordination are all examples of psychomotor domain skills.

This psychomotor domain taxonomy, developed by Anita J. Harrow in 1972,[7] represents a model of viewing, explaining, and classifying the neuromuscular development stages through which students pass. As with the cognitive and affective domain taxonomies, this psychomotor domain taxonomy depicts a continuum of simple to complex achievements, and its use can greatly facilitate the conceptualization and sequencing of appropriate objectives and experiences. The levels of the psychomotor domain taxonomy are as follows.

Reflex Movements

Reflex movements are involuntary actions that are elicited ordinarily as a response to some stimulus. Ordinarily educators are not concerned with this level of responding unless a particular student has some impairment that limits proper execution of the movements. These movements are part of the repertoire of all normal children and are developed to a sufficient degree so that more complex psychomotor skills can be developed from them with little difficulty. Consequently, no more time will be devoted to this particular category.

Basic-Fundamental Movements

Basic-fundamental movement patterns are developed in the first year of life. These movements build upon the reflex movements and consist of such behaviors as grasping, reaching, manipulating objects, crawling, creeping, and walking. Ordinarily, basic-fundamental movement patterns are learned naturally, without training. Again the educator need have little concern regarding the formulation of objectives for this level unless a particular student is observed having problems in this area. Special education teachers may be required to provide appropriate activities for their students with regard to basic-fundamental movements, especially where hyperactivity or visual impairment exists.

Perceptual Abilities

In reality, perceptual ability refers essentially to cognitive functioning. Its inclusion in the psychomotor taxonomy is based on the fact that perceptual and motor functions are inseparable. Without proper perceptual skills, students are unable to make adequate motor responses. The taxonomy is divided into the following categories of perception that lead directly to motor behaviors.

Kinesthetic discrimination consists of one's perceptual judgments regarding one's body in relation to surrounding objects in space. It involves the ability to recognize and control the body and its parts in movement while maintaining balance.

[7]Harrow, *A Taxonomy of the Psychomotor Domain.*

Visual discrimination involves a number of components that are necessary for proper psychomotor execution. The first of these is visual acuity. This involves the ability to distinguish form and fine details and to differentiate between various observed objects. Second is visual tracking, which is the ability to follow objects with coordinated eye movements. Following the movement of a ball is an example of this. Third is visual memory. This is the skill to recall from memory past visual experiences or previously observed movement patterns such as dance routines or swinging a baseball bat. Figure-background differentiation is the fourth category of visual discrimination. Here, the learner is able to select the dominant figure from the surrounding background. Evidence that the individual can differentiate figure and background occurs when he or she is able to identify the dominant object and respond to it. Ball catching and hitting thrown balls can be accepted as evidence that the individual can differentiate figure and background. Consistency is the last category of visual discrimination. This is the ability to recognize shapes and forms consistently even though they may have been modified in some way.

Auditory discrimination involves the ability of the learner to receive and differentiate among various sounds and their pitch and intensity, distinguish the direction of sound and follow its movement, and recognize and reproduce postauditory experience such as the notes that can be used to play a song on the piano.

Tactile discrimination is the learner's ability to differentiate between different textures simply by touching. Being able to determine the slickness or smoothness of an object or surface may be essential to properly executing psychomotor movements where the body must come in contact with surfaces in the process.

Coordinated abilities incorporate behaviors that involve two or more of the perceptual abilities and movement patterns. At this level the student is able, for example, to differentiate between the figure and the ground and to coordinate the visually perceived object with a manipulative movement such as in the act of kicking a moving soccer ball. Remember that the actual kicking of the ball is the psychomotor evidence that there is a coordinated discrimination ability.

It should be obvious that perceptual abilities are not actually observable phenomena. Evidence that these abilities exist depends on various movements and cognitive tasks. The following are examples of objectives written at the various levels in the perceptual abilities category:

You will be able to:

1. Without any outside assistance, walk the full distance across a balance beam and back without falling, on each of five tries. (Kinesthetic Discrimination)

2. Given a board that is cut to receive objects of different shapes, place at least 90 percent of the objects in the appropriately shaped cuts. (Visual Acuity).
3. When a soccer ball is rolled along the ground at various angles to you, intercept the ball and kick it while it is moving 90 percent of the time. (Visual Tracking)
4. Observe a demonstration of any of the waltz movements and then perform these movements without error. (Visual Memory)
5. Move to a position on the football field that will permit interception of the ball carrier even though the flow of the play may be in a different direction. (Figure-Ground Differentiation)
6. Given a bag of variously shaped objects, place at least 90 percent of the objects, regardless of size, color, or texture, into groups on the basis of shape alone. (Perceptual Consistency)
7. From an audio recording of a symphony orchestra, list the names of 80 percent of the instruments playing in any 30-second segment of the recording. (Auditory Acuity)
8. While wearing side blinders to prevent visual observation anywhere but in front, and while dribbling a basketball down the court at full speed with a defensive player in pursuit, shift the ball to a position where your body is between the ball and the defensive player as the defensive player moves to intercept the ball. This must be accomplished at least 80 percent of the time. (Auditory Tracking)
9. Given verbal descriptions about how to execute complex pass patterns in football, perform psychomotor movements consistent with those instructions with 100 percent accuracy. (Auditory Memory)
10. Given a bag containing sixteen swatches of cloth of varying textures, group the swatches into four groups by touch alone with 80 percent accuracy. (Tactile Discrimination)
11. Catch 95 percent of the baseballs batted from a distance of approximately fifty yards. (Coordinated Activities)

Physical Abilities

The physical abilities of the learner are essential to efficient execution of psychomotor movements. Physical abilities constitute the foundation for the development of skilled movements because of the demands placed on the various systems of the body during the execution of these psychomotor skills. Underdeveloped physical abilities can be serious limiting factors in developing highly skilled movement. The physical abilities include endurance, strength, flexibility, and agility.

Endurance is the ability of the body to supply and utilize oxygen and to dispose of increased concentrations of lactic acid in the muscles. The lack of endurance reduces the learner's ability to perform movements efficiently over long periods of time. Development of endurance requires strenuous activity on a sustained basis.

Strength is the relative ability to exert tension against resistance. The development of strength is accomplished ordinarily through gradually increasing the extent of the resistance through the use of weights and springs. The student's own body can also be used as a resistance in exercises such as pull-ups and push-ups. Maintenance of strength requires the learner to utilize the muscles continually. Obviously the strength required to perform various psychomotor movements depends upon the nature of these movements as well as on the ability of the learner. For example, a greater amount of strength is required for wrestling than for fencing. In wrestling, strength is developed relative to size. In addition to wrestling, sports that require a good deal of strength include football and gymnastics.

Flexibility refers to the ability of the learner to engage in wide range of motion in his or her joints. Flexibility depends greatly upon the extent to which muscles can be stretched during movement and not result in injury. Hurdlers, gymnasts, and dancers are among those who are most concerned about flexibility.

Agility is the learner's ability to move with dexterity and quickness. Agility is involved with deftness of manipulation, rapid changes of direction, and starting and stopping activities. Typing, playing the piano or other musical instruments, and playing basketball are activities that require a good deal of agility. The following are examples of objectives written at the different levels of the physical abilities category:

You will be able to:

1. Following the Harvard-Step Test, have your recovery period pulse count decrease to a point at or above the next highest classification level when compared with the norms. (Endurance)
2. Execute correctly fifty push-ups and fifteen pull-ups with no more than five minutes' rest between the push-ups and pull-ups. (Strength)
3. While sitting on the ground in the hurdler's position, touch your extended foot with your fingers and hold this position for ten seconds. (Flexibility)
4. Complete the run-and-dodge course in less than twenty seconds. (Agility)

Skilled Movements

A skill is essentially a degree of efficiency in performing a specific but reasonably complex psychomotor behavior. Ordinarily, learning is associated with skill development. The classification of skilled movements consists of two separate continuums, one vertical and one horizontal. The vertical continuum involves the degree of difficulty of the particular movement and is referred to as the levels of skill mastery for each of the levels of complexity. The levels of complexity include simple adaptive, compound adaptive, and complex adaptive. Each of these levels of complexity has the following mastery levels: beginner, intermediate, advanced, and highly skilled.

Activities included in the skilled movement category are those that involve an adaptation of the inherent movement patterns listed in the basic-fundamental movements level. The difference between the two levels is that, with skilled movements, the concern is with evaluating the learner's performance in terms of the degree of proficiency, whereas the basic-fundamental movements level is concerned with whether the learner can simply perform the movement.

Simple adaptive skills refers to those skills that have been adapted from basic-fundamental movements where some learning is involved. For example, dancing is an adaption of walking. Examples of behaviors in this category include typing, playing musical instruments such as piano, hurdling, broad jumping, skating, and sawing wood.

Compound adaptive skills also build up on basic skills, but at this level the learner must incorporate the management of an implement or tool with the execution of the psychomotor movement. Examples of this skill level include tennis, hockey, golf, badminton, and Ping-Pong. It must be pointed out that not all skills involving an implement fit this particular level. It is necessary that the implement be used in some skilled way. Sculling, for example, does not involve skill in using a paddle. It is a basic push-pull movement and thus belongs to the simple adaptive skill category.

Complex adaptive skills are those that require a greater mastery of the body mechanics in executing the skills. In these movements, the performer must judge space and estimate the time necessary to complete the movement. In this category, the movements are very complex, involving the performer, many times, without a base of support, and necessitating the making of a series of delicate adjustments based upon unexpected or uncontrolled cues. Examples of this type of movement include aerial gymnastic stunts, twisting dives, and complicated trampoline stunts.

Remember, in differentiating among the three categories of skilled movements, that the first involves a limited amount of sensory information and only a portion of the performer's body or body parts. The second involves the extension of the body parts through the use of an implement or tool. The third incorporates total body movement, in many instances without a base of support, and necessitates the making of postural adjustments due to the unexpected cues.

With regard to mastery levels in executing skilled movements, there is a horizontal continuum from beginner through intermediate and advanced skill levels to the highly skilled. At the beginner skill level, the learner is able to perform the skill with some degree of confidence and similarity to the movement expected. This stage is somewhat beyond the trial-and-error learning of initial attempts at the learning task. When the learner can minimize the amount of extraneous motion and execute the skill with some proficiency, he or she is categorized as being at the intermediate skill level. Once the individual can perform the skilled movement efficiently and with confidence and achieve almost the same response each time, his or her skill level is judged to be advanced. At this level, the student's performance is usually superior in quality when compared with similar performances of his or her peers. Highly skilled performances are usually limited to those individuals who use their skills professionally. In this case the individual is totally involved in the use of his or her skill. At the highly skilled level, factors such as body structure, body function, and acuity of sensory modalities and perceptual abilities become critical. Proper execution of the skills depends heavily upon each of these components.

The following are examples of behavioral objectives written at the different levels of the skilled movements category.

You will be able to:

1. In a five-minute timed test, type at a rate of forty words per minute and make no more than five errors. (Simple Adaptive Skill)
2. From a distance of twenty feet, putt a golf ball into the cup twenty-five percent of the time. (Compound Adaptive Skill)
3. Execute properly the following dives with a point rating of at least 4.5: forward one and one-half, one-half gainer, and one-and-one-half forward twist. (Complex Adaptive Skill)

Nondiscursive Communication

This category of behaviors consists of nonverbal communications used to convey a message to an observer. These movements involve such nonverbal expressions as facial expressions, postures, and complex dance choreographies. Two subcategories are included: expressive movement and interpretive movement.

Expressive movement is composed of many of the movements that are used in everyday life. The basic types of expressive movement include posture and carriage, gestures, and facial expressions. These means of expression are used to indicate the individual's internal emotional state. Expressive movements as such are not usually incorporated into the formal curriculum. However, they are used in modified form by learners in the area of fine arts and are included in the taxonomy for this reason. The teacher will not ordinarily write behavioral objectives for the purpose of accomplishing expressive movements.

Interpretive movements are art forms. They can either be aesthetic, where the movements are performed for the purpose of creating for the viewer an image of effortless beautiful motion, or they can be creative movements that are designed to communicate some message to the viewer. In both cases, the performer must have a highly developed level of skill in movement with a knowledge of body mechanics and have well-developed physical and perceptual abilities. The following is an objective at the interpretive movements level. You will be able to:

> Create your own movement sequence to a piece of music of your own selection, which contains recognizable rhythmic patterns, keeps time with the music, and communicates a message to the viewer on a contemporary social theme. (Interpretive Movement)

It should be noted that for many movements there are several components. In such cases the learner may be instructed and/or evaluated on either one or all of the components that make up a skill. Dividing the movements into component parts allows for more accurate evaluation and also provides the learner with more specific details that can be used to make movement corrections. Analysis of subcomponent skills is particularly useful for the highly skilled performer. However, for the beginning learner a good deal of confusion may result from two much detailed analysis of inefficient movements. The more advanced learners become, the more they are likely to benefit from detailed analysis.

Table 3 is included to help you review the characteristics differentiating the various levels of the psychomotor domain.

TABLE 3 Behavioral Terms for Objectives in the Major Categories of the Psychomotor Domain

TAXONOMIC CLASSIFICATION	EXAMPLES OF BEHAVIORAL TERMS FOR SPECIFIC LEARNING OUTCOMES
3.00 Perceptual abilities	
3.10 Kinesthetic discrimination	Maintains balance, names body parts, leads with dominant side of body, bounces ball.
3.20 Visual discrimination	
3.21 Visual acuity	Differentiates objects, selects by size, names differences in events
3.22 Visual tracking	Follows ball in flight, follows pendulum movement, reads verbal symbols.
3.23 Visual memory	Draws geometric symbols, writes the alphabet, performs step sequences.
3.24 Figure-ground differentiation	Hits thrown ball, catches thrown ball, shoots clay pigeon.
3.25 Perceptual consistency	Names objects and identifies shapes consistently.
3.30 Auditory discrimination	

Table 3, (continued)

TAXONOMIC CLASSIFICATION	EXAMPLES OF BEHAVIORAL TERMS FOR SPECIFIC LEARNING OUTCOMES
3.31 Auditory acuity	Differentiates pitch and intensity of sounds, differentiates among musical instruments by sound, differentiates among sounds of the alphabet.
3.32 Auditory tracking	Identifies sound direction, follows the movement of sound.
3.33 Auditory memory	Plays piano from memory, repeats poem.
3.40 Tactile discrimination	Differentiates among different textures, names different fabrics by touch, determines smoothness of sanded wood object.
3.50 Coordinated abilities	Kicks a moving soccer ball, hits a tennis ball.
4.00 Physical abilities	
4.10 Endurance	Runs a mile, executes Harvard-Step Test.
4.20 Strength	Grips dynamometer, does push-ups and pull-ups.
4.30 Flexibility	Bends to floor, extends to toe.
4.40 Agility	Dodges obstacles, drives for layup.
5.00 Skilled movement	
5.10 Simple adaptive skills	Dances to music, plays the piano, jumps hurdles, skates on ice.
5.20 Compound adaptive skills	Plays tennis, swings golf club.
5.30 Complex adaptive skills	Executes twisting dive, performs trampoline stunts.
6.00 Nondiscursive communication	
6.10 Expressive movement	Exhibits appropriate carriage, gestures, and facial expressions.
6.20 Interpretive movement	Creates movement sequence, performs original dance.

TESTING OBJECTIVES FOR CLARITY

Once you have ascertained that your objectives are technically correct and provide for student development at a variety of cognitive levels, you should test to see if they communicate the instructional intent clearly. On occasion you may become so involved in the instructional process that the *means* to the ends are communicated to students as objectives rather than the ends themselves. Phrases such as "will read" and "will attend" are almost sure giveaways that the objective is more a learning activity than an objective.

You should remember that objectives do not specify how information or skills will be acquired, only the ultimate behavior sought.

Mager[8] suggests that one way to test the clarity of a precise instructional objective is for the writer to consider whether another competent person could, on the basis of the written objective(s), differentiate among students who can and those who cannot demonstrate the competence described with the same degree of precision as could the writer of the objective(s).

Another way you can test objectives for clarity is to ask other people (co-workers, friends, or students) to read each objective and discern what they think they would have to do to demonstrate the competence. If their interpretation differs from yours or if you find yourself saying, "what I really meant was . . . ," the misleading objective(s) should be rewritten. This second method is particularly useful if students are used as readers, since they will be more representative of the potential "consumers" than anyone else. It may be, for example, that the level of reading difficulty of the objectives is inappropriate for the potential users. If a fellow teacher reads the objectives, this factor may pass unnoticed; if students read the objectives, they will be quick to point out that they simply cannot understand what was written and intended.

For the purpose of clarity, when presenting objectives to students for large units of instruction, it is best to reveal those objectives that describe the ultimate instructional intent rather than the enabling objectives. Consider the following.

You will be able to:

1. Write the definitions of the terms *fact* and *opinion.*
2. When given a series of statements, label, in writing, those that are facts and those that are opinions.
3. When given a newspaper editorial, underline all statements of opinion and explain, in writing, why those statements are opinion.

Of these three objectives, the last best describes the terminal objective. The first two may serve as objectives for individual lesson plans, but the last more accurately reflects the ultimate instructional intent of the teacher. The teacher may well choose to include only the last objective on a list of course objectives given to students. The connection between the first two and the final objective could, and should, be pointed out to students at the time those objectives are used in particular lessons, but the crucial terminal behavior is expressed in the last objective.

[8]Robert F. Mager, *Preparing Instructional Objectives* (Palo Alto, Calif.: Fearson Publishers, 1962), p. 52.

The Use of Precise
Instructional Objectives

It is your task, as the subject-matter specialist, to prepare the basic competencies with which students will deal. Subsequently, it is possible to provide for student participation by handing out the list of objectives, discussing them with students, and asking for suggested additions, deletions, or modifications. It should be impressed upon students that the success of their year or semester will depend, to a large degree, on their involvement in the education process. If they have ideas for things they would like to explore within the framework of the subject area, you may assist them in stating and clarifying those ideas. Your function, as a person with a responsibility for student development, will be to evaluate the ideas contributed and, to the extent possible, include them in the list of objectives following the same procedures followed when the original objectives were written. Individuals in the class should clarify any questions they have concerning the objectives, and each person should understand that it is toward the accomplishment of these goals that all instruction will be aimed. You should point out how particular teaching-learning activities contribute to the eventual achievement of one or another of the agreed-upon objectives.

After putting considerable effort into a set of objectives, you may be reluctant to make changes in them. However, if the teaching-learning situation changes dramatically (the schools are closed for a month during the winter due to a fire, a war is declared, or even something less momentous such as a spontaneous classwide interest in a strike occurs), it may become crucial to reassess and modify the original objectives.

PRACTICE IN CLASSIFYING OBJECTIVES

Practice Exercise 1: The Domains

Classify each objective as belonging to the cognitive (c), affective (a), or psychomotor (p) domain.

You will be able to:

_____ 1. Explain, in writing, which of two possible solutions to the problem of social unrest is most likely to eliminate the problem.

_____ 2. Recite the Emancipation Proclamation from memory with no more than two errors.

_____ 3. Thread a movie projector so that, when the projector is turned on, the film will not flicker.

_____ 4. Show increased interest in band music by attending eight out of the ten concerts offered during the year.

_____ 5. Given thirty quadratic equations, solve correctly, on paper, at least 80 percent of them.

_____ 6. Demonstrate concern for the democratic principles of free enterprise by stating these concerns orally.

_____ 7. Show a growing interest in art by participating extensively in discussions about art forms.

_____ 8. Transfer bacteria from a culture to a petri dish in a manner that produces properly spread colonies and no contamination.

_____ 9. Write an original short story that has appropriate sentence structure and organization and that meets the requirements of heightened action.

_____10. Given a series of paintings, explain, in writing, which one is best, and why.

ANSWERS TO PRACTICE EXERCISE 1

1. C	5. C	8. P
2. C	6. A	9. C
3. P	7. A	10. C
4. A		

Practice Exercise 2: Cognitive Levels

Classify each objective into its level within the cognitive domain. Check your responses against the answers provided. Resolve any discrepancies by further study, analysis, and/or consultation with your instructor and/or peers. Always classify the objectives at the highest level implied.

LEVELS OF THE COGNITIVE DOMAIN

1. Knowledge	4. Analysis
2. Comprehension	5. Synthesis
3. Application	6. Evaluation

You will be able to:

_____ 1. Given three garments of varying prices, choose the garment you consider to be the best buy and give three written reasons for the decision based on the construction of the garment.

_____ 2. List, in writing, at lest five factors that led up to the Spanish-American War.

_____ 3. Given a new list of possible reasons for World War I and World War II, classify them, in writing, under World War I or World War II with no errors.

_____ 4. State, in writing, four common ingredients in pastry.

_____ 5. Given the necessary material, compare, in writing, the state welfare program in Illinois to that in California on at least five points.

_____ 6. Explain, in writing, using at least five examples, why many blacks moved to the North at the end of the Civil War.

_____ 7. Given comprehensive material on the waste of natural resources, write an original legislative bill calling for conservation of natural resources.

___ 8.   Given necessary materials, develop a unique, written ten-year plan for the economic development of a hypothetical country.

___ 9.   On a ten-minute written quiz on ceramics, explain three ways of hand-building a pot.

___10.   Given sculptures done by peers, choose one that you judge to be best and defend that choice by citing, in writing, at least three points of superiority in the selected piece.

___11.   Given the names of two Cubist painters, contrast and compare the styles of each painter in a one-page paper citing at least four similarities and three differences.

___12.   Solve 90 percent of the two-digit multiplication problems on a written math test.

___13.   Calculate and write down how much 1 gram of N HCl will have to be diluted to prepare 500 ml of 0.5N solution.

___14.   Given a list of tasks that must be done during an eight-hour period, create a written work plan that organizes the tasks so that the time will be used efficiently to complete them.

___15.   Use Robert's *Rules of Order* to conduct a class election without any violations of procedure.

ANSWERS TO PRACTICE EXERCISE 2

1. 6	6. 2	11. 4
2. 1	7. 5	12. 3
3. 4	8. 5	13. 3
4. 1	9. 2	14. 5
5. 4	10. 6	15. 3

Practice Exercise 3: Affective Levels

Classify each objective into its level within the affective domain. Check your responses against the answers provided. Resolve any discrepancies by further study, analysis, and/or consultation with your instructor and/or peers.

LEVELS OF THE AFFECTIVE DOMAIN

1. Receiving	4. Organization
2. Responding	5. Characterization
3. Valuing	

You will:

___ 1.   Show a consistent display of ethics by regulating personal and civic life according to a code of behavior based on ethical principles consistent with democratic ideals.

___ 2.   Show an interest in a movie on honesty by taking notes on the film as it is shown.

___ 3. Show a concern for the welfare of others by sharing work materials during class.

___ 4. Show a commitment to artistically appropriate choices and arrangements by decorating your room in relation to these choices.

___ 5. Consistently demonstrate social responsibility by engaging in most available projects for social improvement during the school years.

___ 6. Show your interest in art by visiting museums when assigned to do so.

___ 7. Show an interest in tolerance of other cultures by participating in a discussion of these patterns.

___ 8. Show your appreciation of classical music by listening to classical records whenever there is free time and by encouraging others to listen.

___ 9. Demonstrate that you have balanced properly the consideration of democratic action and the rights of the individual as shown by adhering to group decisions that do not seriously violate defensible personal rights.

___10. Indicate a commitment to the importance of science by checking out and reading at least ten books dealing with science at your level and reporting on these books to the teacher.

ANSWERS TO PRACTICE EXERCISE 3

1. 5	6. 2
2. 1	7. 1
3. 2	8. 3
4. 3	9. 4
5. 5	10. 2

Practice Exercise 4:
Psychomotor Levels

Classify each objective into its level within the psychomotor domain. Check your responses against the answers provided. Resolve any discrepancies by further study, analysis, and/or consultation with your instructor and/or peers.

LEVELS OF THE PSYCHOMOTOR DOMAIN

1. Reflex movements
2. Basic fundamental movements
3. Perceptual abilities
4. Physical abilities
5. Skilled movements
6. Nondiscursive communication

You will be able to:

___ 1. Given bacteria cultures, petri plates, wireloop, and Bunsen burner, transfer bacteria from the culture tubes to the petri dishes using proper streaking techniques and preventing contamination.

___ 2. Type forty words per minute in a three-minute timed test with no errors.

___ 3. Drive an automobile in heavy traffic properly executing a right turn, a left turn, a lane change, a stop, and a parallel park.

___ 4. Draw at least twenty-five Old English letters demonstrating correct proportion and style.

___ 5. Dance the waltz in proper time.

___ 6. Given a series of ten pictures, point to the dominant figure (as opposed to background figures) in at least eight instances.

___ 7. Without any outside assistance, demonstrate a unique dance routine that is coordinated with at least four minutes of music and that communicates the theme of "war."

___ 8. Show an increase in grip strength of five pounds after two weeks of training.

___ 9. Swim 1,000 yards in less than nineteen minutes and have a heart rate of no more than 120 beats per minute after one minute of rest.

___10. While battling against a complete defensive team, hit a pitched baseball safely three out of ten times.

ANSWERS TO PRACTICE EXERCISE 4

1. 5	6. 3
2. 5	7. 6
3. 5	8. 4
4. 5	9. 4
5. 5	10. 5

SUMMARY

The classification of precise instructional objectives into general areas and levels within areas makes it possible to determine what kinds of developmental skills are being emphasized and to shift that emphasis as needed to assure that students develop the more complex human behaviors as well as those that are less complex. Of all current classification schemes, one of the best known was developed by Benjamin S. Bloom and his associates. Bloom's "taxonomy" is divided into three domains. Each domain is divided further into levels and sublevels. Following are the domains and their major levels along with the person most associated with each domain.

I. COGNITIVE DOMAIN—BENJAMIN S. BLOOM (1956)

1.00 Knowledge	Simple recall. No understanding necessary.
2.00 Comprehension	Limited understanding. Demonstrated by translation, interpretation, and extrapolation.

3.00 Application	Utilization of information in new situations and without prompting.
4.00 Analysis	Identification of indistinct components within a whole and the recognition of relationships among those components.
5.00 Synthesis	Combination of parts into a new and unique whole.
6.00 Evaluation	Making, defending, and supporting value judgments.

II. AFFECTIVE DOMAIN—DAVID R. KRATHWOHL (1964)

1.0 Receiving	Sensitization to the existence of certain phenomena and the willingness to direct attention to them.
2.0 Responding	Stage at which students will become sufficiently involved in a subject or activity that they will seek it out and gain satisfaction from working with it or engaging in it.
3.0 Valuing	Stage at which behavior is motivated not by the desire to comply or obey but by the individual's commitment to the underlying value guiding the behavior.
4.0 Organization	Conceptualization of a value system, the placement of values in some hierarchy within that system, and the development of a rationale for the placement of values in the hierarchy.
5.0 Characterization	Stage at which the commitment to particular values has become internalized and thus controls the individual's behavior. The values constitute part of the individual's life-style.

III. PSYCHOMOTOR DOMAIN—ANITA J. HARROW (1972)

1.00 Reflex movements	Movements or actions elicited in response to some stimulus, but without conscious volition on the part of the learner.
2.00 Basic-fundamental movements	Actions such as reaching, crawling, and walking that are inherent motor patterns are based upon the reflex movements of the learner, and that emerge without training.

3.00 Perceptual abilities	Recognition of, and discrimination among, various perceptual modalities such as kinesthetic, visual, auditory, and tactile modes and coordinated abilities such as eye-hand coordination.
4.00 Physical abilities	Functional characteristics of organic vigor (endurance, strength, flexibility, and agility) that when developed provide the learner with a sound, efficiently functioning instrument (his or her body) to be used when making skilled movements.
5.00 Skilled movements	Development of increasing degrees of skill or mastery of movement patterns learned at earlier stages of development.
6.00 Nondiscursive communication	Use of movement to communicate. Includes such movements as facial expressions, postures, gestures, and modern dance choreographies.

After the objectives have been classified and you are satisfied that students will move as quickly as possible from lower- to higher-level objectives, the objectives should be tested for clarity. Procedures for such tests include asking students and peers to read the objectives and report what they think they would have to do to demonstrate competence. If the objectives are not clear to members of the sample population, they should be rewritten.

It is generally a good idea to allow students some input with respect to objectives. A sense of shared ownership may arise from providing input, and such a feeling will contribute to students' desire to achieve the objectives. It is your responsibility to evaluate student contributions and to add appropriate objectives to the original list or to delete or modify the objectives. At this point you will also want to modify objectives, if necessary, to accommodate the needs of any mainstreamed students in your class.

Finally, you will want to make sure that all students have a clear perception of how each objective will help them personally. This understanding is one of the most powerful motivators available—use it. As the class engages in various activities, you should point out how those activities will help students achieve the agreed-upon objectives.

It should be noted that the taxonomy described in this chapter is but one of many. We would like to call to your attention a new classification scheme developed by Walter D. Pierce and Charles E. Gray.[9] The

[9]Walter D. Pierce and Charles E. Gray, *Deciphering the Learning Domains: A Second Generation Classification Model for Educational Objectives* (Washington, D.C.: University Press of America, 1979).

Pierce–Gray classification scheme is unique in that it not only specifies levels within the cognitive, affective, and psychomotor domains, but also shows the correspondence of levels in each domain to levels in the other domains. This correlation of levels among the three domains can help you see clearly how development in one domain correlates with development in the other domains. Perusal of the text will also help you use precise instructional objectives more effectively. We recommend it highly.

FIVE
PREASSESSMENT
The Great Time Saver

It is unfortunate that many teachers consider the time-consuming task of assessing the status of their students at the outset of instruction as burdensome. The time may be rationalized, however, if it is realized that accurately preassessing students can avoid the hours of frustration that often occur when teachers are unaware that a task prerequisite to a particular learning skill was not mastered by students. Preassessment is especially critical when you work with students who have mental or physical disabilities.

In its strictest sense, preassessment within the Logical Instructional Model is an attempt to pinpoint the student's exact developmental status with regard to a specific instructional objective. Besides this precise definition, however, there is the total assessment of the student that may be taken into account as the teacher plans learning activities. This chapter, therefore, is divided into two parts. The first discusses the nature of the adolescent and attempts to familiarize you with certain psychological principles that characterize high school students. It leads you toward the ultimate skills of general psychological student assessment. The second deals with more formal techniques of assessment of pupils in relation to the specific objectives.

Objectives

When you complete this chapter, you will be able to:

1. Write from memory four sources of data useful in an assessment of the psychological position of the student. (Knowledge)

2. When given two sample cumulative records of hypothetical pupils, identify and specify in writing six similarities and six differences in the two students' backgrounds that could be utilized in psychological preassessments of the two students. (Analysis)
3. When given a precise instructional objective for a secondary school course in your major field, describe in writing a preassessment procedure for that objective that would determine each student's status in relation to that objective. (Synthesis)
4. When given a total design for a unit of instruction that follows the Logical Instructional Model, evaluate the preassessment section of that unit and determine if in your opinion it is satisfactory or unsatisfactory, giving at least four reasons for your decision in less than four pages. (Evaluation)

UNDERSTANDING THE ADOLESCENT: PSYCHOLOGICAL PREASSESSMENT

Many personal attributes assist teachers as they work to improve their teaching. One that is extremely helpful is a sincere respect for people. Competence as an instructor involves liking pupils, while at the same time being able to ascertain their relative place in the growth pattern. If these two aspects of teaching can be blended with a realistic assessment of student learning skills, then the production of high-success-probability learning experiences is attainable.

A component helpful in cultivating the attributes of respect and enjoyment of students is the ability to understand the basic influences in their lives. Every student and every class is unique, but certain general characteristics are useful as guiding principles.

Adolescence

The term "adolescence" brings to mind stereotyped images, but it is our best description of a traumatic period in the life of a growing, learning, human being. What is the adolescent circumstance? The average entering age for the intermediate school is about twelve years old. Most twelve-year-olds are considered to be, and behave as, children; yet six years later an eighteen-year-old has completed secondary school and has acquired most of the characteristics of adulthood. He or she can vote, fight in wars, marry and raise children, and, in many states legally purchase and consume alcohol. What of those years of transition? Most of the time the adolescent lived in a state of "betweenness." He or she was too old to be considered and treated as a child and too young to be considered an adult. A period of rapid growth and the trauma of sexual development with all the concomitant problems of adjustment were experienced, for better or worse.

A peculiar dichotomy emerges during adolescence: a preoccupation with "I" that results in a self-centeredness that overpowers reason, accompanied by serious self-doubts. Peer approval becomes a pervasive urge. At the same time, there is a push and pull toward and away from the adult world. Adult parent-teacher approval seems necessary, yet adolescents feel they have "copped out" on goals of self-reliance if this approval smacks of dependence. Concurrently with this period of trauma, the adolescent is surrounded by the "teen" culture—a culture whose fads of dress and social behaviors are often viewed with shock by elders.

Adolescents are the way they are because of the varying sociological influences that surround them. The range of allowable behaviors that the adolescent exhibits must be broad enough so that the perplexities of growth can be solved successfully and narrow enough so that law breaking and antisocial behaviors are inhibited. At the same time, good models of the adult world must be available and commonly accepted values of society exhibited and understood by all. These circumstances add up to no small order for teachers, parents, and school.

Needs of the Adolescent

Teachers are usually aware that people have certain basic needs that must be fulfilled for them to survive. These needs encompass both the physical realm and the psychological realm. Today, fortunately, the majority of students' physical needs have been satisfied; however, educators often ignore physical needs because it is easy to assume that all students have satisfied these needs. Alcorn, Kinder, and Schunert[1] have compiled some statistics that open one's eyes to the problem.

> High school teachers instruct approximately 150 to 200 students each day. Research-based estimates indicate that in an average group of that number:
>
> 1. Five to ten will have speech defects requiring attention if therapy has not been provided in the elementary school.
> 2. Three to six are afflicted with hearing loss sufficient to require medical attention.
> 3. Twenty to fifty require corrective lenses to achieve "normal" vision.
> 4. Ten to fifteen suffer from known allergies, such as eczema, asthma, hay fever, and hives.
> 5. One to ten have epilepsy, diabetes, or cardiac disability.

And this does not include the students who come to school hungry, not necessarily because there was no food in the house but because negative home conditions precluded meal planning.

You are not expected to be able to identify instantly all cases of physical deficiencies, but teachers do vary in their sensitivity. In an investigation of

---

[1]Marvin D. Alcorn, James S. Kinder, and Jim R. Schunart, *Better Teaching in Secondary Schools* (New York: Holt, Rinehart and Winston, 1970), p. 21.

a case of a high school student's poor vision, it was discovered that two teachers out of six had recognized the problem in the youngster and had adjusted seating arrangements to put her close to the chalkboard. In one class she was close to the front by "the luck of the draw," and in her other two classroom-oriented subjects she was in the back or middle. And this case was not difficult to spot because the student's glasses were referred to as being like the "bottoms of coke bottles." How many difficult-to-spot cases go undetected?

The psychological needs of the adolescent are just as important as the physical needs, but even more difficult to spot. Many teachers have found it useful to combine the many views of needs into one category: self-concept. There are widely differing definitions for the term *self-concept*, but they generally focus upon how people view themselves, for example, well liked versus not well liked, attractive versus unattractive, able versus unable. The actions of people are governed, to one extent or another, by their self-concepts, and many acts in which people engage are aimed directly at trying to improve self-concepts. In school, when students cannot engage in "acceptable" acts to acquire praise, success, recognition, or even a sense of accomplishment, they may well turn to "unacceptable" acts and become "discipline problems." It must be remembered that students usually prefer to engage in "acceptable" acts since such acts tend to produce more widely valued positive feedback, but if these actions are beyond their capabilities or are scorned by those whose opinion they value, other, less acceptable actions *will* be taken. An important part of your role as a teacher is to help all students, the able and the not so able, to find acceptable ways to build and continually improve a favorable self-concept.

Many sociologists have pointed out that an obvious place for fulfillment of the satisfaction of needs has been the family, but with the loosening of this unit in our society has come an increasing pressure on other institutions to accept more responsibility for ensuring such satisfaction. Regardless of many educators' reservations, the fulfillment of needs is now becoming a task for both home and school. But at the same time that adolescents are attempting to satisfy felt needs, they are preparing to move to adulthood, and this growth of independence can conflict with need satisfaction.

SOURCES OF INFORMATION
IN ASSESSING STUDENTS

Some teachers excuse themselves from doing any kind of assessment of their students with such comments as, "Oh, I don't want to prejudge" or "Everyone starts with a clean slate in my class." However, students are not the same, and their records can assist in indicating their status in relation to many objectives. If teachers are not going to use the data that have been gathered, then there has been a considerable waste of time and effort. An analogy could be made to the physician who does not use medical records in his or her diagnosis because he or she does not wish to prejudice a medical judgment. Such a procedure would be considered unthinkable.

Cumulative Records

Every school system seems to have its own record-keeping system. In larger schools, the cumulative records of students are usually kept in the counseling office. In smaller schools, they may be in the principal's office. Often they are in the hands of the elementary teacher or, at the secondary level, in the hands of the homeroom teacher.

The cumulative records of any student may include any or all of the following:

1. The academic grades received throughout the educational career.
2. Intelligence test scores at various grade levels (usually including the tests taken).
3. Achievement test scores in various subjects at different grade levels.
4. Vocational preference tests results.
5. Aptitude test scores.
6. Anecdotal records by teachers, principals, counselors, coaches, or other staff members.
7. Records of conferences held about, or with, the student between any of the staff, perhaps including parents.
8. Doctors' records of physical examinations, illnesses, and sometimes attendance records.
9. Self-portraits and autobiographies.
10. Copies of letters from or to the school about the student.
11. Comments by teachers about techniques that assisted in teaching the student.
12. Records of transcripts or other information sent to or received from other schools.
13. Records of police inquiries or information released to prospective employers or responses to other legal inquiries.

Record-Keeping Ethics   There are two main problems connected with the maintenance of records, especially since the use of computers is making it possible to collect and store large amounts of information and retrieve it more and more rapidly.[2] The first question is "What kinds of information about pupils should be maintained in schools?" This question has an obvious answer: only those data should be kept that are pertinent to the learning

---

[2]V.S. Teitelborum, "School Records Can Be an Invasion of Privacy," *Today's Education,* *60,* no. 5 (May 1971), 43–45.

situation. However, the school has accepted more and more responsibility for the development of not only the intellectual aspects of the personality but also the emotional growth of the individual. In this context, the rationale for collecting any bits of information that could help students make personal adjustments is supplied. The terminal point in collecting information has yet to be defined.

A second question that needs attention is, "Who should have access to this information?" Present school law in various states differs somewhat on this point, but in general only the students, their parents or legal guardians, and school personnel have access to confidential records, and after students are eighteen, even parents must have their child's permission.

With recent federal legislation that allows parents of pupils less than eighteen years of age legal access to such records, and pupils over eighteen personal access when they formally request it, some schools are formulating new policies that restrict the information that may be accumulated. The full ramifications of the legislation have not yet been felt, but it appears that parents and students may demand removal of anecdotal records they perceive as being negative and that such demands must be complied with.

Teachers must exhibit the highest degree of professionalism when dealing with school records. This means you are charged with the responsibility of gathering all information available, applying high evaluative skills to analyze it, and then using the information for diagnostic purposes. At the same time, however, such information must be treated as private. This delicate use of professional judgment is more difficult than one would suppose.

Teachers can be held legally responsible for statements and comments they make about students. It would be extremely unwise, for example, to write (or say) that "Johnny steals" or that "Johnny seems to have homosexual tendencies." Cumulative records can be helpful, but they *can* be misleading. Anecdotes, opinions, and similar "soft" data must not be taken as gospel. Students' opinions, attitudes, and feelings change rapidly during adolescence, and "soft" data may easily be outdated and no longer applicable.

The Student as a Source

Besides access to the records available in the office, an eqully important source for information about students is the students themselves. At the beginning of the school year, asking students to respond to questionnaires or open-ended sentences can tangibly help the teacher assess the status of his or her pupils. Samples of categories of inquiry that are important to the teacher in assessment are the following:

1. Students' perception of their previous background in the subject.
2. Types of classroom activities they think they like best.

3. Their perceptions of benefits they will receive from the class.
4. Their expectations for liking or disliking the subject.
5. Their study areas at home.

As long as the information obtained is defensible in terms of the educational process, the teacher should encounter little friction. Be cautious, however, about a question such as "Do you have a set of reference encyclopedias at home?" The question seems to be acceptable educationally, but if its purpose is to gather the names of prospective customers for a part-time sales venture, it becomes highly unethical.

STRATEGIES FOR BLENDING PSYCHOLOGICAL PREASSESSMENT AND INSTRUCTION

Many teachers who make a conscientious effort to gather information about their students from cumulative records and student self-reporting devices fall short when it comes to the actual use of this information in planning for instruction. There has been a general "impression" of the student planted in the brain of the teacher, and it may alter teacher behavior at times, but not in any formalized fashion.

Better educationally is the use of a strategy for data gathering and review that leads the teacher logically to decisions regarding the types of activities and teacher reactions that will maximize learning and psychological growth.

For example, suppose you find a student with two evident needs. Entries in the cumulative folder and input from staff and your own observations identify a problem in the affective domain and a strength in the cognitive domain. The student is self-conscious and has a tendency to self-isolation but, at the same time, exhibits a strength in the writing of papers. You could make a note to attempt to have the student share quality papers with the class and then look for opportunities to do so.

PREASSESSMENT PROCEDURES FOR SPECIFIC INSTRUCTIONAL OBJECTIVES

After preassessment of the relative psychological status of the students, you are ready to check the students' abilities as they relate to specific objectives. You may find yourself in one of several positions when it comes to the objectives of the course or courses you teach. In some cases you may have the flexibility to adjust your objectives after preassessment; that is, in extreme cases an objective decided on may be abandoned completely after preassessment because it had been found to be inappropriate. A better approach would be to specify whatever remedial objectives and activities were necessary to provide the background needed for success. This raises the question of how much "catching up" a teacher can engage students in without totally ignoring mandates to prepare them for entry into subsequent courses.

In many situations you will, in fact, have restricted freedom to abandon objectives or to add remedial objectives even though it would be logical to do so. In the foreign languages and mathematics programs in many schools, the teacher is committed to bringing the students to a certain point so that they may proceed to the next course. In these instances, preassessment does not necessarily lead to the abandonment of the terminal behavior but rather to adjustments in en-route objectives to reach the terminal objective in the most expedient way. It is in such situations that the need for a self-paced, competency-based approach to education is most obvious.

Cognitive domain objectives can be classified into several categories for preassessment purposes. First, many objectives lend themselves to formal preassessment procedures that can be checked with paper-and-pencil tests. It is obvious that you must ensure that your students understand some basic areas of information before higher-level objectives are attempted in which that information is manipulated. When the objective is of a higher order, the preassessment may be a search-and-find mission to uncover a set of data that will serve as the vehicle for practicing some particular analytical skill. In this case, you can choose a content topic that the preassessment has shown to be already familiar to the members of the class and spend the time organizing, classifying, comparing, or in other ways analyzing and manipulating the data.

Of course, there are many instances in which the objective for a class is the simple acquisition of knowledge. Here the pretest may be a sampling of the same types of items that will be found on the final test. It may also be in situations such as this that the teacher will be preassessing only at the beginning of a course to determine the initial entry points for the class members because the nature of the subject makes it highly unlikely that any students can already achieve the terminal objectives.

Other types of objectives do not imply an evaluation through the use of paper-and-pencil tests. This leads to a basic principle to follow when dealing with preassessment: approach any preassessment in the most direct, expedient way. There is no need to conceal or be overly subtle about preassessment. If the terminal behavior desired is the student's ability to discern fact from opinion in editorials, you should make your preassessment a sample of that skill. Leading a discussion about a TV editorial seen in class and attempting to assess each student's ability in this skill from his or her responses is inefficient and unnecessary.

If the behavior being preassessed is a skill that cannot be measured through paper-and-pencil tests, then the teacher must work to structure the classroom activities in such a way as to check each student's ability without "losing" the rest of the class. If, for instance, the skill being preassessed is the ability to give a five-minute extemporaneous speech, it would be possible in a thirty-student class to completely inhibit students' intrinsic motivation through a string of poorly done five-minute speeches that would last for three or four days. Preassessment, in this case, might consist of having a randomly selected group of students deliver two-minute speeches. This would give you a reasonably sound basis for modifying (if needed) your planned instructional activities.

Another approach may be necessary for preassessment of objectives that utilize psychomotor skills. An art instructor may preassess and determine that a student possesses the necessary prerequisite skills to produce a unique piece of jewelry. Some of these prerequisites will already be known because of their use in prior projects. Preassessment in this case may be as simple as asking students whether they are familiar with the operation of a new tool necessary to construct a new project. If the new tool involves factors of safety, preassessment may of necessity be much more formal.

Another preassessment situation may allow you to choose paper-and-pencil procedures or to use alternatives. When dealing with higher-order cognitive objectives, many may be stated in a way that permits paper-and-pencil tests for preassessment, and you may wish to use such tests. In some instances, preassessment through the use of paper-and-pencil tests is possible even though the terminal behavior is not stated in a way that implies a paper-and-pencil evaluation. For instance, if a terminal behavior in a general business class is written as "You will be able to compare three products in a grocery store for price and quality and choose the best buy," a preassessment might describe the situation hypothetically and the students' responses would still give the instructor reliable information as to the areas of instruction that need emphasis. Conversely, the teacher may be able to determine, through a series of direct questions, the relative student ability for an objective that will ultimately be evaluated through a paper-and-pencil test.

STUDENT REACTION
TO PREASSESSMENT TESTS

Many times students feel threatened by tests. You can make your preassessment tests less threatening if you explain fully how the test results will be used and if you assure students that the results will not affect their final grades. There are also other points about which you should be aware.

Popham and Baker[3] point out, for example, that "Another pretesting consideration is whether the student will come to feel frustrated if he scores poorly on the test. This is a factor to consider, and may suggest that pretesting be conducted in small pieces rather than in one overwhelming course covering session."

There are several reasons for avoiding very large preassessment sessions. One is the frustration that some students may feel if they know nothing about the material at all. At worst, they will not only be agitated during the test itself, but they may also build a resistance to learning the material. Another reason for preassessing for the upcoming objectives as they are approached is that there will be some student change. A preassessment for many objectives at the beginning of a course may no longer be valid several weeks later. Students who have since learned prerequisite tasks through classroom instruction may now see relationships that need not be emphasized, whereas a preassessment given too early may indicate that they do need emphasis.

It sometimes happens that the preassessment will reveal that students are already able to demonstrate the bulk of the terminal behaviors sought. This situation may be painful for the teacher because many planned lessons may have to be put aside and new ones generated. The extra effort will be well worth the trouble, however, since any other course of action will result in boredom for many of the students.

PREASSESSMENT
AND MAINSTREAMED STUDENTS

It should be clear that all that has been said concerning preassessment applies in full measure to mainstreamed students. In fact, preassessment is even more crucial for mainstreamed students than for regular students.

If you have mainstreamed students in your class, you should make a special effort to talk with the special education teachers and/or the guidance counselors to determine the specific nature and extent of the students' disabilities, what has been done up to this point to help the student, and most important, what you can do to help the student(s) succeed.

In proceeding with your preassessment activities, it is advisable to keep complete records of the performance of all students but particularly those of mainstreamed students. These records may provide the baseline data against which the progress of mainstreamed students is measured in the event they achieve few of the regular objectives. In any event, the preassessment data you collect can become part of the student's achievement record and will undoubtedly help others to help the student.

[3]James Popham and Eva Baker, *Systematic Instruction* (Englewood Cliffs, N.J.: Prentice-Hall, 1970), p. 74.

SUMMARY

This chapter describes two basic types of preassessment important in attempts to maximize pupil learning: the student's psychological status and the student's intellectual position in relation to a specific objective.

Every human has basic needs, and at the age of adolescence these needs are crucial and powerful. They involve both the physical and emotional realms and drive the adolescent to test his or her independence against a dependence upon family, teachers, and other adults.

To adjust the classroom to the needs of the students, the teacher must gather data from an assortment of sources. The professional teacher handles these data so as to make an accurate diagnosis of the status and needs of the student and always treats the data in a confidential manner. The teacher should recognize adolescents need to be supported as they struggle to gain full independence in a partially independent setting. As much as possible, adolescents need to be treated as adults.

SIX
SELECTING INSTRUCTIONAL PROCEDURES

There are three basic principles underlying the discussion of instructional procedures in this chapter. The first is that the vast majority of instructional procedures should be planned with care. While it is true that extemporaneous experiences are occasionally both enjoyable and valuable, it is more often the case that they are simply time-fillers resulting from inadequate planning. Since time is a valuable commodity to both you and your students, careful planning of instructional experiences can maximize the effective utilization of class time by minimizing essentially nonproductive activities.

Among the factors to be considered when planning instructional procedures are (1) the particular instructional objectives to be achieved, (2) the time available, (3) the materials available, (4) the background of the student, and (5) the size and physical arrangement of the group of students.

The second principle is that instructional experiences should be varied. A steady diet of any one approach, no matter how successful it may have been originally, will ultimately pale with continued use. Interest can best be stimulated and maintained if change in instructional procedures is frequent and meaningful. Using a variety of procedures will facilitate the achievement of specified objectives. The variety of terminal behaviors stipulated in almost any list of instructional objectives can be viewed as a mandate for a variety of instructional experiences. This analysis is deliberate since there is a tendency for teachers to find an approach that seems to work well and then to become resistant to change. They become unsure about alternatives and unwilling to attempt anything new. A lack of teacher enthusiasm results from seldom attempting or experiencing a new pattern, and students detect this lack of enthusiasm and react similarly. On the other hand, if a teacher becomes enthusiastic and interested in "doing something different," students will tend to reflect that excitement or interest. Just as variety in instructional experiences can help maintain the interest, vitality, and morale of the students, it can do the same for the teacher.

The third principle involves the organization of instructional activities to move students from teacher-controlled to student-controlled activities as quickly as possible. The more students are working on their own using the skills and information they learned to solve problems of importance to themselves, the more they are becoming independent individuals able to live and succeed in our society.

OBJECTIVES

When you complete this chapter, you will be able to:

1. When given, on a multiple-choice test, a series of instructional objectives and/or situations and a series of instructional procedures, match the most appropriate experience with the objective or situation in at least 80 percent of the cases. (Application, Analysis)
2. When shown a film, videotape recording, or demonstration of any instructional procedure, describe, in less than two pages, at least one strong point and one weak point in its use and prescribe corrective measures (if any). (Evaluation, Synthesis)
3. Write two precise instructional objectives (one reflecting lower-level cognitive skills and the other higher-level cognitive skills) and develop, in less than two pages, at least a two-point rationale supporting your choice of particular instructional procedures most likely to help students achieve the stated objectives. (Synthesis, Evaluation)

TYPES OF INSTRUCTIONAL EXPERIENCES

Formal and Informal Lectures

Lectures at the secondary level have fallen into some disrepute, simply because too many lectures were poorly done by too many teachers. A good lecture—one that is well planned and delivered smoothly and with conviction—can be an exciting learning experience and will be perceived as such by students. The line between such a lecture and an artistic performance is very fine indeed, and the extensive use of lectures must be reserved for the teacher with the personality and ability to do such work. It is possible for almost any teacher to plan and orchestrate a lecture that is cohesive and polished and that will capture the interest of all but the most reluctant student. The time spent in planning such a lecture, however, precludes all but an occasional use of this experience by most teachers.

Rather than striving for the perfect "formal" lecture, that is, a lecture in which students do little except listen to a virtuoso performance, it is better for most teachers to concentrate on identifying those points, skills, and procedures that will enable them to deliver an "informal" lecture, that is, one that provides for student participation rather than passive student reception. This approach has the advantages of being well within the capabilities of most teachers, ensuring student interest, and thus being more useful. From this point on, the term *lecture* refers to the informal lecture unless stipulated otherwise.

Uses of Lectures   Lectures are used appropriately to (1) quickly and concisely present a great deal of new and integrated information, (2) clarify relationships among general points or between specific causes and effects, (3) explain procedures, and (4) summarize information. It is reasonable to ask why you should not simply use handouts to convey this information, since most students can read and comprehend at a rate of about 250 words per minute whereas most can listen and comprehend at a rate of only 150 per minute. In many situations in which lectures are used, a handout *would* be as appropriate or even more appropriate; however, there are other situations, particularly those in which you may wish to add emphasis by inflecting your voice or to make instant modifications on the basis of student reactions, in which lectures are clearly an appropriate instructional experience. Additionally, the informal lecture allows for spontaneous student response and questions, and thus points can be clarified as they are raised by the students.

Planning Lectures   There are a number of appropriate lecture-planning procedures. Perhaps the most common is to construct a word or phrase outline. As the first step in this process, you describe the specific instructional objective students will be able to achieve after listening to, and participating in, the lecture.

The kinds of objectives for which lectures are most appropriate are generally those at the low cognitive levels. For example, you will be able to:

1. Explain in writing six causes of World War I.
2. Write, in your own words, the definition of ethnocentrism and illustrate it with at least two examples.

The objectives are appropriate to lectures since their terminal behaviors are not time consuming (and thus do not infringe on the time available for the lecture) and do not require much, if any, student practice. With such objectives, students can be expected to demonstrate successfully the desired behavior simply by virtue of having been exposed to the information.

The objective will serve as the standard against which all prospective constituent elements of the lecture will be compared. Those elements that contribute clearly to student achievement of the objective will find their way into the word or phrase outline, whereas those that contribute little or nothing will be discarded. This procedure assures cohesiveness in the lecture and facilitates evaluation of the lecture's effectiveness. The outline may consist of short sentences, phrases, or even single words. Many teachers have found that they can lecture most effectively if they reduce their notes to a minimum. Voluminous notes, either in the form of lengthy outlines on sheets of paper or many brief items on index cards, tend to inhibit rather than to help the lecturer. Faced with detailed notes, many beginning teachers tend to refer to the notes more often than necessary, simply because they are there. In some cases the referrals become so frequent that the lecturer is, in effect, reading the notes. Additionally, voluminous notes tend to tie the lecturer to the podium, increase the probability of losing one's place, and decrease the opportunities the lecturer has to look at the audience while speaking. Extensive notes, in most cases, simply do not add to the smoothness and polish of a final delivery.

Your lecture outline should serve to spark your memory, not as a source of new information. The outline contains the key phrases, facts, figures, names, dates, and so on that are at the heart of the material and should help you to organize the material into logical blocks and to subdivide these blocks into manageable sizes to facilitate student learning. When giving an initial lecture, you may find it helpful to make notes concerning the approximate length of time each part of the lecture should take.

Another part of planning concerns checking the content for its suitability for the student's level. It is easy to make notes without realizing that the students may not be familiar with certain terms, especially those that are technical or complex. If such terms are used in the outline they should be starred or otherwise noted to remind the teacher to define and explain them.

During the planning of lectures, you should consider the use of appropriate instructional aids. Almost any lecture will hold student attention longer when the lecturer includes pictures, maps, graphs, cartoons, or similar support materials. The time to consider the use of such aids is when the lecture is being planned, and appropriate steps in ordering should be taken early.

There are two parties in an informal lecture: the students and the lecturer. Teachers who use this learning mode can often increase their effectiveness by working with students to ensure that common-sense note-taking procedures are used. For example, you can instruct students that

1. Each set of lecture notes should start on a separate page and carry the date and title of the lecture (as well as the lecturer's name if a guest is presenting the lecture).

2. A consistent outline format should be used, such as the following:

    I. Major topic (the purpose of outlining)
        A. Subheading (logical organization of content)
            1. Explanations (sequential steps: causes and effects, etc.)
                a. Further explanations

3. Notes tend to be more useful if the students attempt to write down only major ideas and points rather than to copy the lecture word for word.
4. They should look for techniques such as the restating, rephrasing, and listing of points on the board or overhead projector as clues that these are major points.
5. Contextual clues such as "There are *three* main facts here . . ." are often used at the beginning of a series of points and can facilitate the outlining of the information.
6. The development of a personal shorthand system for abbreviating frequently used words and phrases can save considerable time.
7. There are advantages to writing neatly enough that recopying the notes is not necessary. Students can read and study neatly written notes in less time than it takes to recopy them. Some students, however, find that the act of recopying or rephasing notes assists in learning.
8. Space may be allowed, as the notes are being taken, to add personal thoughts, comments, questions, and reactions.
9. Some students, particularly handicapped students, may benefit from taping the lectures.

Delivering the Lecture   After considerable effort has been made to prepare material for a lecture, you may find that the students will deem the mode ineffective because of delivery or style. Lectures, as with any other instructional procedure, are enhanced by the stimulation of student interest *at the very beginning*. Student interest and student involvement are closely tied. Useful techniques for establishing motivation include (1) asking a question or posing a pertinent problem and eliciting student responses, (2) asking students to respond to a graphic situation, picture, or quotation, (3) asking a student to recount briefly personal experiences relevant to the lecture material, or (4) revealing related startling facts. This initial interest arousement is enhanced by involving students as directly as possible and should "tune them in" to what the lecture is about. There is some evidence that teachers who can initiate lessons well can elicit more learning than teachers who do not concentrate on the initial stages of a presentation.[1]

Language usage can also contribute to, or detract from, the effectiveness of a lecture. Using language of appropriate complexity and formality is an art worth practicing. If new words are to be introduced, clear definitions should be made so that students will understand their meanings

[1]Robert F. Schuck, "The Effect of Set Induction upon Pupil Achievement, Retention and Assessment of Effective Teaching in a Unit on Respiration in the BSCS Curricula," *Educational Leadership Research Supplement*, 2, no. 5 (May 1969), 785–793.

in the context in which they are used. Language complexity early in the lecture will cause students to "tune out" because they feel the lecture is going to be "over their heads," making it difficult to recapture their interest.

Good lecturers will often explain to students how the lecture is organized (cause-effect relationships, chronological order, easy-to-difficult, concrete-to-abstract, rule-example-rule, etc.). This helps students orient their thinking and organize their notes.

The effectiveness of lecturers is increased by visual reinforcement of verbal information. If students *see* important facts, figures, names, and dates as well as *hear* them, the probability of their being remembered increases. Furthermore, varying the stimulus can, in itself, be a device helpful in refocusing the attention of students whose interest may be wavering. Among the most common kinds of visual aids are prepared posters, chalkboards, overhead projectors, and opaque projectors. These devices are easy to use and provide sufficient latitude for creative utilization.

The ways in which you use your voice also influences effectiveness. Voice inflections, for example, can place emphasis on particular points and can dramatize quotations and asides. By varying the pitch and volume of the voice, lecturers add the variety necessary to capture the interest of the students. Rate, too, is important. Although most people can listen and comprehend from about 125 to 150 words per minute, a lecture is intended to instruct, and to do so properly, the rate at which the lecture is delivered should be slower, from 110 to 130 words per minute. The rate of delivery depends on the purpose and complexity of the material. In the case of most lectures, you should allow time for students to listen to what is being said, comprehend what they hear, and relate new information to what is already known. This last step cannot be done when the material is complex or if it is delivered at too fast a rate.

You *can* improve your own lecture delivery techniques. By taping segments of your own speech and dividing the number of words spoken by the number of minutes elapsed, the words per minute can be calculated. It will also become apparent if there is a tendency to vary delivery rate. If there is a tendency to mispronounce particular words, to use personal pronouns, or insert phrases such as "you know" or "uh," listening to recorded lectures will make it immediately apparent. Teachers simply do not realize their own idiosyncracies until they listen to themselves and analyze what they hear.

Just as the use of formal visual aids adds to the interest of a lecture, so do your physical movements. Appropriate hand and arm movements can help punctuate sentences and emphasize important points. Moving from behind the desk or podium and walking about can provide visual stimulation, but all these movements must stop short of being distracting. The use of a videotape recorder to detect and correct inappropriate physical movements can be revealing and beneficial.

The use of numerous and relevant examples has been shown to facilitate student understanding of content. Generous use of examples, nonexamples, analogies, and illustrations will help to keep student interest high and produce more learning.

When students are involved actively, their interest is higher and you can assess responses for students' understanding. Student participation is best encouraged by careful planning. Procedures found helpful to many teachers include preparing sets of key questions to be asked at appropriate places in the lecture. The experienced teacher makes maximum use of nonverbal clues and student behaviors that indicate confusion. The use of students in the class to reiterate points by answering questions will often clarify important points for students who are still struggling with a new idea.

A good lecture concludes with a summary and review of the main points. While this activity can be done verbally, it may be helpful to students if you make use of visual aids. Visual reinforcement helps to emphasize important points, and it gives students a chance to double-check notes, fill in points they may have missed, and correct errors.

In summary, the lecture is one of the most often used instructional procedures. Lectures have the advantage of enabling you to present to students a large body of information in a relatively short period of time, and they are relatively easy to direct and control.

Possible disadvantages are that lectures can encourage passive, rather than active, student participation; that they may not provide much of the student-teacher interaction needed for proper evaluation of the instructional process; that they can foster unquestioning acceptance of presented material; that they may not capitalize on student curiosity or creativity; and that they tend to center more on the content than on what the student is to do with the content.

Questioning

The judicious use of questions can be the basis for valuable instructional experiences. Questions can be used to find out how well students understand a particular block of information, to shift student attention from one point to another, to increase retention of important points by isolating and emphasizing them, and to point students in the right direction before starting assignments. Perhaps their most valuable use, however, is to elicit high-order thinking on the part of students as questions are asked that call for analysis, synthesis, and evaluation skills and to provide practice for students in formulating and orally communicating specific answers to specific questions.

Using the following steps of the "overhead" questioning technique may prove helpful in increasing the effectiveness of questions:

1. *State the question clearly and precisely.* A question such as, "What about microcomputers?", for example, gives the student little direction for an answer. You will find it necessary to ask a follow-up question to clarify your first question. It would be better to ask, "How does a microcomputer differ from a large computer?" or "How could a microcomputer be used in this class?"

2. *Pause after asking the question and allow it to "hang overhead."* When you ask questions in a classroom, it is beneficial for all students to think about the answer. To encourage this kind of attention, ask the question clearly and then pause before calling on someone. The pause gives students a chance to think about the question and encourages all students to do so since they do not yet know who is to answer.

3. *Call upon your students at random.* Since it is desirable for all students to think about the questions, you should not follow any pattern when calling on students. Any pattern, be it a seating arrangement, an alphabetical arrangement, or any other kind of sequence, has the effect of reducing attention on the part of those students who feel they will not be called upon.

4. *Provide immediate feedback to students.* You should indicate the appropriateness of student answers. If an answer is not wholly correct, try to use the part that is correct or state the question to which the given answer would have been appropriate. If students are assured that their responses have value, active participation will continue.

Categorization of Questions   The nature of questions may be varied to ensure differing types of responses from students. One convenient way of categorizing questions to see the frequency of a particular type is to compare them with the divisions of the cognitive domain. The following examples may be helpful in placing questions into appropriate categories and are also indicative of the types of objectives for which this procedure is appropriate:

1. *Knowledge (or simple recall).* "What are the three basic parts of a precise instructional objective?"
2. *Comprehension (or understanding).* "What is meant by the term *in loco parentis?*"
3. *Application (for using information).* "Traveling at 55 miles per hour, how long would it take to get from New York to Los Angeles?"
4. *Analysis (or pulling an idea apart).* "What words or phrases does the author of this article use that cause the article to be biased?"
5. *Synthesis (putting together something new).* "How would you have improved upon Germany's strategy during the Battle of Britain?"
6. *Evaluation (or making and defending a judgment).* "Who do you think our best president was, and why?"

Another way to categorize questions is according to their essential function.

1. *First-order questions.* A first-order question may be defined as any question that has served its purpose as soon as an acceptable answer is given. Any of the six categories of questions described earlier can be considered first-order questions if their answers are clear cut and if no further elaboration is elicited or desired.

2. *Probing questions.* A probing question is asked to encourage students to go beyond their initial responses to explain themselves further. An example of the use of a probing style might be, "Good, you're right so far, now can you give us an illustration . . . ?" By asking students to provide examples, illustrations, rationales, and so on, teachers can frequently determine the depth of students' understanding of material more accurately than by using first-order questions alone. A follow-up probing question often begins with "why"

3. *Open-ended questions.* An open-ended question has no definite right or wrong answer. A question such as "What do you think about the probability of extraterrestial life forms?" is asked to encourage students to go beyond the recollection or explanation or previously acquired information and to hypothesize, project, and infer. Such questions are particularly well suited to the initiation of discussions.

4. *Convergent questions.* Convergent questions are arranged in a series and are designed to "converge" on a particular point or idea. For example, questions such as "Are there fewer or more farmers now than twenty years ago?" and "How do farm subsidies affect consumer prices?" could be used to help students focus attention on the issue of government farm subsidies. Convergent questions may be used to induce a principle or deduce an answer.

5. *Divergent questions.* Divergent questions, as the name implies, are asked to draw a student's attention away from one point and allow it creative freedom to settle on a different but related point. Divergent questions are particularly useful in inspiring student discovery of analogous situations. "What present-day parallels do we have, if any, to the Athenian agora?" is an example of an analysis-level question being used to stimulate divergent thinking.

Encouraging students to ask questions is a skill that can be manifested in numerous ways. You can assist students in phrasing questions and you can make it clear that you feel questions indicate a willingness to learn, not ignorance, on the part of students. You can respond to students' questions thoroughly, courteously, and in a friendly manner and indicate the importance of students' questions by comments such as "That was a good question because . . . " Finally, you must be certain that you never humiliate a student who gives a wrong answer.

Discussions

Discussions, in one form or another, are among the most commonly used instructional experiences. A discussion differs from usual conversation in that the intent and content of discussions are more carefully delineated and structured. Conversations that occur spontaneously are usually not intended to achieve specific objectives and are therefore essentially random. Instructional discussions have a specific purpose and direction. Their function is to help students acquire the information and skills necessary to achieve specific objectives. Typical of objectives calling for one or another kind of discussion are the following:
  You will be able to:

1. Describe, in writing, the contents of a survival kit to be taken into the mountains by hikers planning a two-week camping trip.
2. Describe orally either a strength or a weakness in a given political system and explain why it is a strength or a weakness.

The skills and information necessary to achieve these two objectives can be acquired by students in a number of ways, one of which is the discussion. For example, using a discussion to give students practice in analyzing the components of survival kits in general will directly contribute to their ability to compile such components into a kit for any given situation later. The second objective can be achieved directly in a discussion since each student can be given the opportunity to participate and hence demonstrate the required behavior.

General Discussions The least specific of the discussion types is the general discussion. As in the other kinds of discussions, the purpose of general discussion is to give students practice in on-the-spot thinking, clear oral expression, and posing and responding to questions. Such discussions are also useful for assessing the diversification of views and exploring ideas.

As with any discussion, your initial step is to gather together and make available to students appropriate background information, materials, and sources. The success of a discussion as an instructional experience depends upon the degree to which students are informed and prepared. Without background in the topic, students will be unlikely to make good contributions to a discussion. Proper procedure often leads to the recording of key questions for use in stimulating or changing the direction of the discussion. By using key questions, discussions can be guided along those lines most likely to contribute to student achievement of the instructional objectives.

Since one of the aims in discussions is to encourage student-to-student communication, it can be helpful to arrange desks or chairs in such a way that students can comfortably see each other. Circular, semicircular, or horseshoe arrangements are useful.

It is necessary to agree, with students, on certain discussion ground rules. Some of these ground rules may be that contributions will be impersonal; that ideas, not the people who suggest them, will be the focus of the discussion; and that common social courtesies will be observed. If there are consistent violations of the rules, students may wish to establish a process for helping their peers who are lax in proper participation procedures.

It is common for teachers unconsciously to allow one or two students to monopolize the discussions. This problem can be avoided by asking for the comments and opinions of those students who do not volunteer to participate, but care should be taken not to force such participation. If students feel threatened, their participation will decrease rather than increase. Asking for opinions rather for than specific facts is a good way to encourage participation without posing a threat.

The problem of digression often emerges in general discussions. Some digressions that lead away from the objective may deal with information that has meaning and relevance for the students. It is up to you to decide whether the digression is important enough in its own right to allow it to continue.

Guided or Directed Discussions   A directed discussion is appropriate if students are to be guided through a series of questions to the discovery of some principle, formula, relationship, or other specific preselected result. In guided discussions students are given practice in inductive or deductive, step-by-step thinking, and since the thinking is convergent, the net result is to lead the students toward a common revelation of a major principle or conclusion.

There is some danger in using directed discussions because you will have determined what it is that the students are to discover. If students become too frustrated in the chain of logic leading to the discovery, they may react with the attitude. "Why didn't you just say so in the first place?" and the value of the experience will be lost. Many teachers who use this technique feel that using it for only ten-or fifteen-minute blocks of time works best. Once the conclusion is reached or the principle is discovered, a shift to another instructional experience to utilize that conclusion or principle logically follows. It has also been found helpful to begin guided discussions with a statement such as, "There is an underlying point here . . . " or "Let's see if we can reach a conclusion concerning . . ." Statements such as these help set the stage for the guided discussion and minimize the possibility of students seeing the experience as guesswork.

An analogy might be made between a guided discussion and a computer-assisted instruction program. In each case the most likely student responses to questions must be anticipated and appropriate questions (or instruction) planned. Both are designed to provide reinforcement to the student for correct answers and are built around a series of sequential steps. The important difference is that in a guided discussion the teacher very closely monitors the interaction and can modify the remaining questions to capitalize on some unexpected student response.

If used cogently, guided discussions can provide an additional rich instructional experience. Students enjoy discovering and solving, and once they have "discovered" a principle, they remember it longer than if it is simply explained to them.

Reflective Discussions   Reflective discussions are used to assist students in developing analytical skills, arriving at alternative explanations, finding solutions to selected problems, and classifying ideas into major categories. These skills relate directly to objectives at the higher cognitive levels (i.e., analysis, synthesis, and evaluation). A typical objective for a reflective discussion might be, "You will explain orally how some aspect of daily life would differ if we lived under a socialistic government."

When using reflective discussions you should define a particular problem relative to the instructional objective. Then devise a series of open-ended questions to encourage a variety of possible responses. Additional specific questions will be generated and asked spontaneously during the discussion.

To help maximize the benefit from reflective discussions, you can delegate one student to list the identified main points of each response on the chalkboard. To supplement this listing, you can elicit from the class appropriate headings for clusters of responses that have points in common. In this way as students are given practice in classifying ideas and in analysis skills, a basis is provided for predicting and hypothesizing solutions to the original problem.

Unlike guided discussions, which can often be conducted at a rapid rate since the teacher has prior knowledge of the result, reflective discussions should be conducted at a relatively slow pace and include periods of silence. Time must be allowed for students to consider alternate possibilities and to think about the ramifications of those possibilities. Many teachers complain that the slowness of reflective discussions is a serious drawback and that the discussions take time that can be used in more valuable ways. Other teachers feel the "thinking" time required is one of the strongest attributes of reflective discussions and use the discussions frequently. In deciding how often to use them, you must weigh these factors and balance time used against the opportunities for divergent responses, large-scale student participation, practice in classification, and reflection.

Inquiry Discussions and the Scientific Method   Inquiry discussions are used to provide students with opportunities to use an analytical approach for reasoning and acquire new information with a minimum of help from the teacher. In inquiry discussions students practice critical thinking, gathering and analyzing data, and drawing conclusions on the basis of evidence rather than intuition.

It is vital that students have access to appropriate resources (books, maps, instruments, graphs, etc.) if inquiry discussions are to be worthwhile. Such materials are used most effectively if they are available in the classroom, but if this is not practical, they could be placed on reserve in the school library or in other central locations.

Inquiry discussion is often used in conjunction with what is called the *scientific method*. The steps of the scientific method are usually stated in a form such as the following:

1. Identify the problem.
2. Formulate a hypothesis (a probable solution or explanation).
3. Gather, evaluate, and categorize available data.
4. Reach some conclusion (either reject or support the hypothesis) on the basis of the evidence acquired.
5. Take some action appropriate to the results (write a letter to an appropriate party concerning the implications of the conclusions, let other interested parties know of the results, etc.) so that students will be reinforced for their efforts.

When used as part of the scientific method, most inquiry discussions will be but one part of an overall scheme including several types of instructional experiences. An inquiry discussion will prove valuable at each of the five phases of the scientific method, but using the method itself could occupy a widely varying amount of class time. To facilitate utilization of this method, you can establish a timetable with the class, assuring that the investigation will move along smoothly and will conclude by a certain date. Time is allowed for consolidation sessions during which progress to date can be evaluated and future plans refined.

When used as a single-period experience, an inquiry discussion follows the same scientific method used in longer-term investigations, but the data-gathering process is abbreviated, with all information coming directly from the students (usually based on their experience and their assigned reading). To keep this process from deteriorating, you must be alert for incorrect, incomplete, or misleading student input. When misinformation is detected, you may be able to use the instance to generate students' interest in finding out more from sources at hand or from sources available for an out-of-class venture. For purposes of inquiry discussions, it is usually inappropriate for you to act as a major source of information. Your role is that of resource person—one who helps point students to the sources of information—rather than as a supplier of data. This is in contrast to guided discussions in which teachers not only provide information but also direct students to predetermined outcomes.

For example, assume that you adopted the objective, "Each student will describe, in writing, at least five sources of information needed by a modern world leader to function effectively." This objective might be achieved partially by providing students practice in determining what kinds of information the president of the United States needs and how that information is, or might be, acquired. This session lends itself to an inquiry discussion. Consider the following steps.

1. *Identify the problem.* As a beginning point you could ask students how they think the President gets information relevant to decisions he makes. This line of questioning usually results in a number of ideas, but the need to pinpoint more specifically the kind of information being discussed will almost certainly emerge. The type of information available from newspapers, for example, is different from that available from top-secret dispatches. Once the problem is restated precisely, the second step can be taken.

2. *Formulate a hypothesis.* Through the use of questions some probable hypothesis can be structured. You should not leave the impression that all possibilities are equally valid, thus precluding the need for further analysis. All ideas concerning a hypothesis may be accepted, but the class should decide on a limited number for further investigation.

3. *Gather, evaluate, and categorize available data.* It is at this point that inquiry discussions may prove difficult to complete within a single class period. Ideally, students should search out all types of data and subject them to a detailed analysis. If only a single class period is to be used, you must make extensive use of questions and clues and must encourage students to analyze their own answers. By questioning, sufficient data can often be acquired and analyzed. If sufficient data are not acquired after questioning, data-gathering teams may be necessary and analysis postponed for a subsequent time.

4. *Reach some conclusion.* Once the data are gathered and analyzed, the class is ready to reach a conclusion. The acquired facts are related to original hypothesis. Properly handled, the facts should support or reject the hypothesis. In the process, students will have acquired practice in the skill of applying the scientific method to a problem and they will have engaged in analytical thought.

5. *Take some action.* A logical application of the practice just engaged in would be to have students demonstrate the lesson's objective by casting it

in a hypothetical situation. (For example, "You are now the president of the United States. How will you organize your information-gathering machine and of what will it consist?")

If, when an inquiry discussion is initiated, students realize they do not have sufficient information to reach intelligent conclusions, intervening plans for obtaining additional data emerge. Once the data have been acquired, the class reviews the initial steps and proceeds through the remaining steps. For teachers who utilize the scientific method inquiry approach, acquisition of the data is as important as producing the result.

Exploratory Discussions   Exploratory discussions have almost as unstructured a framework as general discussions, but there are some important differences. Exploratory discussions are intended to enable students to discuss controversial issues (such as premarital sex, use of illegal drugs, and abortion) without fear of censure. Such discussions help make students aware of the other students' views and can thus help them become more tolerant of differing notions.

When exploratory discussions are conducted, you must define the topic clearly with the understanding that there will be no negative criticism of other student views during the discussion. That does not preclude disagreement and alternative views, but if a tone of ridicule emerges, students will become reluctant to voice further opinions, thus defeating the purpose of the discussion. While the later scrutinizing of a general class feeling is not threatening to individuals and can cause little harm, the scrutinizing of a particular student's opinion or comment may cause negative attention to be focused on him or her and may thus cause an unintended and undesirable reaction.

One of the problems of exploratory discussions is that they are often explorations into the affective domain, and a precise definition of what was gained by students is difficult. Students may feel that little was accomplished. To minimize these difficulties, you can synthesize the various contributions and use them as a basis for further instructional experiences that are more precisely defined. There may be few concrete accomplishments directly attributable to an exploratory discussion, but there may be many students who are enlightened by the variety of opinions held by their peers and who are thus given new insights.

Exploratory discussions may also be used in conjunction with a resource person knowledgeable in the area to be studied. The function of such a person would be to present new ideas and opinions to which students could respond.

Evaluation of Discussions   Discussions are time-consuming instructional procedures in relation to content gained by students, especially in comparison with experiences such as reading assignments or lectures. The advantage most forms of discussion have over information-gathering procedures, however, is that they capitalize upon student curiosity and creativity, encourage participation, and allow for development of higher-level thought processes.

Discussions, like all instructional procedures, must be evaluated to determine effectiveness. The best way to judge a discussion is to determine if students can achieve the instructional objective for which the discussion was chosen as the learning activity.

Practicing teachers find it useful to note which students do or do not contribute to discussions and what types of contributions are made by individuals, for comparision with evaluation results. It is sometimes found, for instance, that, even though students did not participate vocally in a discussion they were involved mentally and developed analytical skills. Nonparticipation may indicate that the student needs special, individualized help, but it may also mean that these students are simply thinking about what is being said. By comparing evaluation results with patterns of participation, with it may be possible to determine which students need the maximum amount of encouragement to participate, since participation, in their case, aids learning.

The quality of students' responses is a valid indicator of the effectiveness of discussions. When students make comments indicative of muddled thinking or misconceptions you should be alert to a need to clear up the confusing points or misconceptions. On occasion, however, students make such comments purely for effect—to impress their peers or to elicit special attention from you. If it becomes clear that a student is engaging in "artificial" participation, attempting to take care of the problem during the ongoing discussion is likely to produce denials or challenges by the concerned student and should be avoided. A private conference is usually more fruitful.

Effective evaluation of discussions takes thought, but the potential for improvement makes the effort worthwhile. The more discussions are used and evaluated, the more polished you will become in their use. By providing for student demonstrations of instructional objectives, and by keeping track of participation, you can polish their ability in this instructional procedure.

Brainstorming

Brainstorming is an instructional procedure similar in many ways to an exploratory discussion. Brainstorming is used to generate a wide variety of creative ideas concerning a problem in a short period of time.

To conduct a brainstorming session, you must act as a facilitator. The facilitator's primary responsibility is to see that proper procedures are followed. Brainstorming uses relatively few, but crucial, rules. After the problem is identified, the facilitator explains that the point of the brainstorming session is to acquire as many creative ideas as possible. Everyone is encouraged to contribute any idea regardless of how "far out" it may seem. The facilitator makes it clear that no idea or contribution is to be discussed, evaluated, or criticized during the brainstorming session and that each idea suggested will be added to a written list of ideas that will be compiled.

The effectiveness of brainstorming session depends on rapid pace, short duration, and close adherence to the rule that no idea or contribution during the brainstorming is to be discussed. At the end of the session the class will have a number of suggestions written down relating to the central topic. The facilitator then helps the class divide the ideas into general categories and move into an exploratory discussion in which the various ideas are discussed. If such discussion is allowed to interrupt the brainstorming session itself, the necessary freewheeling atmosphere is inhibited.

One common use for brainstorming sessions is to acquire seed material for more complex tasks, such as synthesizing. Thus, you might use a brainstorming session to help students generate ideas with which to build a rationale for or against suggested governmental legislation.

Demonstrations

Demonstrations have the unique advantage of enabling students to observe the demonstrator engage in a learning task rather than simply talking about it. A correctly conducted demonstration, whether of some laboratory procedure, physical skill, or other action, is often a stimulating instructional experience because it demonstrates a living model. A typical objective calling for a demonstration might be, "You will apply an arm splint, which meets Red Cross requirements, to a 'subject' within three minutes."

To make demonstrations effective, you must often break down entire processes into component parts and decide what aspect of the skill, process, or procedure will be demonstrated in the time available. This is necessary because most demonstrations are a part of a larger task that cannot be demonstrated in its entirety during usual school time allotments. For instance, one demonstration in home economics may include the selection of a dessert, say, a cake, and include the exact choice of type of cake, possible substitutions of ingredients, proper blending procedures, and possible pitfalls. Including baking time and frosting may not be possible in the usual time allotment.

Having decided what can adequately be demonstrated within the time allowed, you should then proceed to plan the component parts of the demonstration. Depending upon the nature of the demonstration, initial steps may include an overview description of the skill, process, or procedure. If machinery or equipment of any kind is to be used, the safety aspects are stressed. An outline of main points is often written on the chalkboard for quick reference, or students may be given handouts containing this information. Very detailed descriptions are often not necessary because students are able to understand terms, labels, and relationships easily as they view the demonstration.

During planning for the actual demonstration, you will need to test all the equipment to be used to be sure it functions properly. Before the demonstration is conducted, the environment is arranged so that all students can see what is happening. If small instruments or fine manipulations are called for, schools so equipped often use a closed-circuit TV camera or videotape equipment. Many classrooms in which large numbers of demonstrations take place are equipped with overhead mirrors above demonstration tables. Effective demonstrations blend your verbal skills with accompanying psychomotor skills. Gifted demonstrators are able to use the full range of questioning skills, drawing students' attention to crucial steps and to the way in which various steps are carried out. Exaggerated movements are to be avoided since they might confuse or mislead students as they attempt to practice the movements later.

Demonstrations that can be followed by immediate student practice appear to have maxium effectiveness. If it is not possible to provide for immediate practice, a review is necessary before delayed practice is begun. If no student practice is available, it may be possible that an alternative experience would be as effective as a fully prepared demonstration. If the length or complexity of the demonstration prohibits immediate practice, it may be possible to divide the demonstration into two parts. The biggest asset of a demonstration is its ability to guide and precede students' actual involvement in a similar experience.

When the demonstration involves valuable or potentially dangerous material or equipment, you must weigh carefully the dangers and benefits involved. If material or equipment is too dangerous or too valuable, it may be wise to choose a different procedure. Students are in school to learn, but not in an environment where they take unnecessary risks.

As students practice the skill or procedure, you should provide individual corrective feedback and encourage students to assess their own performances. This is particularly important when dealing with mainstreamed students. Good teaching demands, of course, that allowances be made for individual differences that may affect the way in which instructions are carried out. For example, if the instructions begin, "Using your right hand . . . ," left-handed students may find such a movement awkward. In addition, allowance must be made for deviation among students' approaches. All students do not exhibit the same techniques in practice, and for some students certain procedures may come easily. If a particular student's idiosyncrasy is deemed detrimental to later performance, however, it warrants early correction.

One effectvie way to conclude a demonstration is to conduct a short questioning session covering specific procedures, terms, labels, and cause-effect relationships. If the practice of the demonstrated skill or procedure is to result in some product (as opposed to resulting in the improvement of some process), examples of satisfactory and unsatisfactory products should be made available so students can compare and contrast their own products with the models. Opportunities for creative responses in the product's development should be encouraged as long as established standards are maintained.

Panel Discussions

An instructional procedure in which the teacher plays a reduced role is the panel discussion. Panel discussions permit a small group of students to delve deeply into an area of interest and then to act as a source of information for the rest of the class.

To arrange a panel discussion, a small group of students (six or fewer) is identified as participants on the panel, and one student acts as chairperson. If needed, assistance is provided in dividing up research responsibilities and setting up a time schedule. Responsibilities on the panel are assigned commensurate with the abilities of the students. For some students, providing specific references and sources may be necessary.

When the panel is ready to act as an authority, the chairperson or other moderator may follow several courses of action. One common approach is for the moderator or chairperson to explain briefly what the panel is prepared to discuss with the class, to introduce each of the panel members and identify his or her special areas of interest, and begin accepting questions from the class.

An alternative approach uses the moderator or chairperson to introduce briefly the topic to be discussed and then to introduce each of the panel members, allowing each about five minutes to discuss or explain his or her particular area of interest. The moderator or chairperson then summarizes the findings and opens the panel to questions and comments from the class. This procedure has the benefit of providing the rest of the students with information upon which to base questions.

In both approaches the moderator or chairperson ensures that all panel members participate on an equal basis and that sufficient time is left for a final summation. Time is also allowed for the teacher to bring the panel discussion to a close near the end of the class period and establish the relationship of the discussion to the instructional objective.

Sociodramas

Sociodramas are useful for dramatizing particular social problems and for increasing student empathy for the feelings, viewpoints, and problems of other members of society. Teachers who use sociodramas success-fully find they are most useful when working to help students achieve various affective domain objectives. Typical of such objectives might be the following.

You will be able to:

1. Identify and explain the cause for your reaction to the statement, "Homo-sexuality is normal."
2. Add or eliminate at least one rationale used to defend your attitude about abortion.

To conduct a sociodrama successfully, you must make certain that all students understand that participants will be acting out roles as they believe people would actually behave. Participants, therefore, theoretically do not act out their *own* feelings, but what they perceive the feelings of others to be. It is made clear that the sociodrama will be stopped if students step out of their roles or begin to get too emotionally involved.

Once the ground rules are understood, the class proceeds to identify a situation in which two or more people interact and the specific roles and "positions" of the participants. After this is done students are encouraged to volunteer to play each of the roles. No one should be forced to participate.

Participants are allowed to confer briefly about how they intend to act out the situation (not to rehearse) and should then act it out. Usually two or three minutes is sufficient for students to decide how they intend to present the situation and another ten minutes for the actual sociodrama.

Before any discussion of the sociodrama takes place, it is sometimes worthwhile to have a second set of students confer and act out the same situation. After the second sociodrama, students can compare and contrast pertinent points in the dramatizations. No effort is made to evaluate the performance level of students. The focus of the discussion after a socio-drama is on the differing perceptions of the roles by the participants and nonparticipants, on an attempt to understand the probable feelings and beliefs of the person(s) in the real situation, and on an examination of personal rationales for values held.

Guest Speakers

The chief purposes of inviting guest speakers into the classroom are to expose students to experts in particular fields, especially individuals who may have views different from those already explored in class, and to help motivate students. Taking advantage of such people in the classroom—a controlled situation—establishes a direct contact between the classroom and the real world.

To maximize the usefulness of guest speakers as an instructional ex-perience, you should involve students in organizing to obtain and utilize the guest speaker. When the class identifies a need in a particular area in which a speaker can provide a unique contribution, a list of potential speakers is compiled. The names of the prospective speakers are then cleared through the principal or other appropriate administrator, and permission is obtained to invite them to speak to the class. On the list should be persons who can fit such a visit into their schedule. Administrators may be able to suggest individuals who are willing to speak to classes and who have been well received in the past.

It is a good learning experience for students when they can be used to contact the prospective speaker. Among the things the prospective speaker may wish to know will be the age and grade level of the students, the topic being studied, how much the students already know about the topic, what type of unique contribution he or she might make, and the specific time, date, and topic.

It requires effort to prepare students for a guest speaker. If the speaker is to discuss a relatively new topic, it is usually possible to have students read available relevant information and/or discuss the topic. This gives students a matrix in which to work, thereby increasing their interest and enabling them to ask more intelligent questions. Some speakers prefer to respond to questions written by students before the talk. The quality of such questions depends upon the students' having experience in the content area prior to the speaker's visit.

On the appointed day the speaker will appreciate a student escort, who will meet the speaker at the entrance to the school and guide him or her to the classroom. In the few moments before introducing the speaker, you can determine the approach the speaker will take. It is proper to suggest that time be left for a question-and-answer period after the presentation. If you wish to make a tape recording of the presentation be sure to obtain the permission of the speaker.

After the presentation is complete, you should tie the loose strands together and bring about closure. Points may have been made that will require further study and aspects of the content presented may need to be related to previously learned material and to the instructional objective underlying the presentation. If students do not suggest a thank-you note, you will want to remind them and discuss a procedure for writing it.

Field Trips

The logical extension of bringing part of the world into the classroom is taking the class into the "real" world. Field trips are useful not only because they give students firsthand knowledge and enable them to see how a number of skills, processes, and so forth, blend into a whole, but also because they can be used to provide students with cultural experiences available in no other way. Many students, for example, would never get to see the printing of a newspaper from start to finish unless they saw it on a school field trip. Similarly, many students might never go to an art museum, concert, or professional play unless they were introduced to them on a field trip.

Field trips should be related directly to an ongoing unit of work. When possible, it is desirable to capitalize on a perceived student need for a field trip, but if you know that long-range planning is a necessity for a particular trip, you should take the initiative. Once it has been decided that a field trip is useful or desirable, specific objectives to be achieved by the trip can be shared with, or generated by, the class. Of course, you may have determined beforehand that such a trip is an instructional experience that can help to achieve some of the objectives on the list handed out at the beginning of the term. In either case, the objectives can be used as a springboard to produce specific questions to be answered by students while they are on the field trip or upon their return. During a trip there will be many activities and new experiences competing or the students' attention, and the questions will help focus their attention on the most important activities and experiences.

Student involvement during each step of planning a field trip helps generate interest and make the trips more worthwhile. For example, while some students are building questions that focus attention on important aspects, others may gather information about the facilities at the site of the field trip. This latter group may wish to write for information on the availability of guided tours, admission costs, dates and times the facility is open, specific clothing requirements, and the availability of eating facilities. Still another group may obtain information about transportation. Even though you will probably be familiar with bus use, it is instructive to students to discover for themselves whether school district regulations allow classes to use school buses for field trips and whether this use is dependent upon the buses being returned before they are needed to transport students home from school at the end of the day; whether the distance is such that students will have to leave particularly early or get back after school hours; how to charter a bus if necessary; and the importance of school insurance policies that cover field trips and their ramifications for the use of private automobiles.

If chartered transportation is needed, it must be paid for, which may be an inhibiting factor. Depending on the student population, it may be unfair to expect parents to contribute enough money to cover both the incidental expenses of their children and transportation costs. If such is the case, the class may decide to raise the necessary money. Regardless of how the money is raised or collected, it is important to keep accurate and public records. The procedures adopted should coincide exactly with those advocated by the school.

Most schools require that the parents or guardians of students going on a field trip sign permission slips. These slips are *not* legal documents meant to protect you from a lawsuit; they are simply devices to assure the school that parents know where the students will be going that day and approve of the trip. You can extend the utility of permission slips by including on them details parents would wish to know, such as departure and arrival times, whether students are to bring food with them or purchase it, and special clothing requirements.

All these considerations are influenced by board and administrative policies. You must cooperate with the school administration to ensure that policies are followed concerning absences from other classes, providing for students who are unwilling or unable to go, securing sufficient chaperonage, special cases such as financially or physically handicapped students or students with particular religious or dietary restrictions. There may also be regulations concerning taking along a first-aid kit or extra cash. Students, of course, should be asked to demonstrate that they know where the bus will be waiting for the group should they get separated, and what time it is scheduled to leave the field trip site.

Proper follow-up activities are particularly important with respect to field trips. Unlike other instructional activities, field trips involve staff members outside of the class. If, after disturbing the instructional plans of other teachers and perhaps keeping students from attending other classes, the field trip does not yield worthwhile results, you may find it difficult to secure permission for other trips. This possibility, coupled with financial problems, has caused many boards of education to prohibit field trips completely. When the field trip has focused on specific objectives and students are given adequate preparation, follow-up discussions and evaluations do not prove difficult. General and ambiguous reactions to the trip, while perhaps of passing interest, are not the main concern. The experience should be evaluated primarily on the basis of how well the instructional objective was achieved, how well the newly acquired information was related to previously learned information, and how well the experience can serve as the basis for future instructional experiences.

School-community relations tend to improve as interaction between the two increases. Field trips and the use of outside speakers both provide interaction and thus help to improve school-community relations.

Small-Group Activities

A number of instructional situations will lead you to decide to use small-group activities. Such activities are useful for increasing social interaction and thereby maximizing social development: They make efficient use of limited materials and resources; they allow complex problems and tasks to be divided into less complex components; they provide opportunities for peer-to-peer tutoring situations to arise; and they enable students to take more responsibility for planning and carrying out educational tasks.

Depending upon the situation, you may choose any one of several procedures to determine group makeup. Simple random assignment or alphabetical arrangement is useful when no homogeneity is desired. Social development is maximized by such grouping since students will interact with other people with whom they may or may not have much in common.

Another procedure for the grouping of students is on the basis of friendship. When students are motivated, an advantage to this grouping pattern is that since the students are already on a friendly basis they tend to get to work more quickly. Digression, when not purposefully motivated, however, is a potential hazard.

Groups can also be formed on the basis of interest. The main advantage to this pattern is that productivity is usually high since students are intrinsically motivated and the motivation of each reinforces the motivation of the group.

A fourth grouping pattern is by achievement. In this pattern, no one individual overshadows all the rest and the work load can be divided equally. Progress is usually rapid because the group is not held back by one or two members who work at a different pace. This type of grouping is ueful if there are a few slower students who seem to be on the fringe of the class activities. Grouping these students together and providing them with special help makes it possible for them to make a significant contribution to the class and to build up their own self-concepts.

Still another way to group students is heterogeneously. By deliberately putting students with varying abilities and interests in the same group, you can increase social interaction and development and provide opportunities for slower students to receive spontaneous help from brighter students. It is crucial, however, to consider very carefully the personalities of the students in the group, to be sure the slower students will be helped and not ridiculed.

Once the group is formed you must ensure that the group realizes how their work will fit into the ongoing class activities. You should stress that each of the four, five, or six members will have a specific job to do by prearranged deadlines if the class as a whole is to accomplish its task. The students may be encouraged to write out an operating plan.

When the small-group activities are completed, the results are brought to the attention of the entire class. This not only enables the class to benefit from the work of the small groups, but it also provides you with an opportunity to commend publicly the members of the groups for their efforts. Frequently panel discussions and/or modified debates provide appropriate vehicles for the dissemination of the results of such efforts.

You should be aware of groups in which one or two members are being "carried" by the rest. Assisting in decisions about what each member is to do helps to minimize this problem, but evaluation of individual contributions is still difficult, especially when students of differing abilities and interests are assigned to the same group.

Out-of-Class Assignments

Among the possible instructional procedures available, the use of individual or whole-class "homework' assignments creates more than its share of controversy. The opponents of such assignments point out that many students have neither the time nor the environment in which to complete such assignments. They point out, too, that once students leave the classroom there is no assurance that they will be ones actually doing the assignment. Friends, relatives, or parents may do the actual work and the students may then pass it in as their own. Finally, many question the justification of asking students to continue doing formal schoolwork on their own time.

Proponents of out-off-class assignments, on the other hand, point out that a student's chief responsibility should be to schoolwork, that formal learning should not be restricted to particular school hours, and that many valuable instructional experiences cannot easily be engaged in within the four walls of the classroom or within the usual class meetings. For these reasons the proponents claim that out-of-class assignments are absolutely necessary.

As with most controversial issues concerning education, there is no one right or wrong position that is valid for all situations. If you attempt to eliminate mundane out-of-class assignments, the probability of other assignments being completed, and being completed properly, increases. As with any other instructional procedure, overuse is counterproductive.

Some of the purposes appropriate for out-of-class assignments include the following.

1. *Helping students to acquire new information.* When you assign a section of a textbook to be read as a basis for a future discussion, or ask students to view a particular TV program or listen to a particular tape-slide sequence, you are asking students to acquire new information. These new data will be dealt with in class, but they are to be acquired outside of class.

2. *Providing practice in particular skills.* Some skills, such as typing, solving mathematical problems, and so forth, can be polished by repeated practice. Since you may be reluctant to use class time for extended periods of such practice, ask students to engage in such practice out of class.

3. *Giving students practice in long-term planning.* Some assignments, such as term papers and correspondence-type projects, require a good deal of

student planning. The fact that students must allocate time to achieve the long-term objective is, in itself, a valuable experience that you may consider sufficient justification for such assignments. In this case the process and the product are of equal, or nearly equal, importance.

4. *Providing for student creativity and particular student needs.* In-class activities generally force students to be one of a group and leave little opportunity for them to demonstrate skill unique to them as individuals or to engage in instructional activities they feel are of particular interest to them personally. By working with individuals in planning out-of-class assignments, you can do much to make school relevant and interesting.

For whatever reasons you may make out-of-class assignments, there are certain steps that help to make those assignments more effective and valuable. If the assignment is one in which all students are going to engage, you must ensure that all students understand the exact nature of the assignment. Such assurance can be gained by writing the assignment on the board and/or duplicating it and handing it to each student. A verbal explanation may accompany the written directions, and questions concerning the assignment may be elicited from the students. If the assignment is one designed to help students acquire new information, guided questions may be utilized profitably. If the assignment is one in which a product is generated, students should have a clear idea of the qualities necessary for minimum acceptability of that product. If the assignment is long term in nature, a final deadline should be determined and students should be encouraged to bring in drafts, partially completed work, and so forth for periodic appraisal. If the assignment is individualized, you should make sure there is agreement on exactly what is to be done and what the final product is to be. You can facilitate student accomplishment of out-of-class assignments by making sure that required instructional materials are available. Placing needed books, magazines, film strips, and so forth on reserve in the library is one step in this direction; providing worksheets is another.

If an assignment is worth making, it is worthy of careful evaluation and student feedback. If students perceive that their work is being ignored or dealt with lightly, a large incentive for continuing such efforts will be lost. In addition, you lose an excellent opportunity to detect students' problems and determine the effectiveness of instruction.

One useful out-of-class assignment procedure is the self-instructional package. Self-instructional packages can be used for any of the purposes mentioned earlier and have a number of advantages. They are built around specific instructional objectives, all the information or sources the student needs to achieve the objective have been included or specified, preassessment and self-assessment instruments are included, and practice exercises are provided. Even more important, self-instructional packages can be self-paced and are designed with this goal in mind. This means that students receive the benefit of a carefully sequenced set of learning activities and are at the same time being given the freedom to learn at their own rates. Self-instructional packages constitute an ideal intermediary between whole-class, teacher-dominated experiences such as lectures and questioning, and experiences such as individual projects in which individual students design and carry out instructional projects reflecting their own needs and desires with guidance from the teacher only when perceived necessary by the student (see Chapter 11).

SUMMARY

In this chapter a number of instructional procedures that you can use to improve the teaching-learning process have been surveyed. It is important to vary instructional experiences not only to stimulate and maintain interest and vitality but also to facilitate achievement of various types of objectives. Differing objectives require differing instructional experiences if they are to be achieved expeditiously, and the selection of an inappropriate instructional experience can prove frustrating to both you and your students.

Some procedures, such as discussions and debates, require extensive preparation by students before their initial utilization. Other procedures require more extensive preparation, but their benefits can counteract the extra preparation time.

Procedures that allow active student participation generate more student learning than do those that require students to sit passively. Some procedures, such as lectures and demonstrations, minimize this participation whereas others, such as brainstorming and exploratory discussions, maximize it.

All instructional procedures need evaluation. Some procedures (such as lectures, speakers, and field trips), lend themselves to evaluation through the use of formal paper-and-pencil tests. Other procedures (such as exploratory discussion, brainstorming, and sociodramas) are more difficult to evaluate, and you must rely on such factors as the extent of student participation, the degree of interest apparently generated by the experience, and the degree to which students express a desire for additional similar experiences.

Instructional procedures should be evaluated in terms of how well they have helped students to achieve specific objectives. Good procedures are usually more effective when they provide analogous and/or equivalent practice. If practice was effective, students will be better able to perform with the competence specified in the objectives. When you plan instructional procedures with regard to specific instructional objectives and are willing to use a variety of instructional experiences, you will provide environments that have the potential to maximize learning.

SEVEN
INSTRUCTIONAL MEDIA
AND MATERIALS

For many educators, it is somehow unsettling to realize that in a techno-logically advanced country such as ours, much instruction is still conducted in the same manner it was twenty-four hundred years ago. When Socrates, Plato, and Aristotle were helping students to learn at about 400 B.C., they did so by asking questions, by telling, and by discussing. Most students today learn in school in the same way. While it is not the intention of the authors to downgrade the value of lectures or discussions, it is important that you recognize the unique and valuable contributions to the teaching-learning process that can be made by alternative instructional forms.

There is an ancient proverb that says, "A picture is worth a thousand words." One wonders then what the "exchange rate" would be for a time-lapse motion picture that enables students to watch a rosebud as it unfolds into full bloom or a motion picture that gives students an idea of the drama and mindless passions aroused by one of Hitler's torchlight parades. How does one calculate an "exchange rate" when a student makes a mistake in an auto simulator rather than in a real car? Without the use of mediated instruction, many valuable and interesting learning experiences would be either impossible or impractical, and the students' education would be that much poorer.

Since virtually all teachers find themselves using mediated instruction at one time or another (with varying degrees of effectiveness), this chapter will be devoted to familiarizing you with a variety of alternative instructional forms. Such a familiarity will increase the probability of alternatives being used intelligently to enhance and enrich the learning experiences of students.

When you complete this chapter, you will be able to:

1. List, in writing, three forms of mediated instruction. (Knowledge)
2. Given the names of three forms of mediated instruction, write at least one example of how each could be used to enhance learning in your own subject area. (Comprehension)
3. Given an example of one utilization of a mediated instruction form (such as a microcomputer), describe at least one other way the same device could be used to aid learning. (Application)
4. Given hypothetical situations calling for the use of mediated instruction and a list of mediated instruction forms, select the most appropriate form for each situation. (Analysis)
5. Write a lesson plan for a fifty-minute lesson in which the use of some form of mediated instruction plays a central part. (Synthesis)
6. Take a position for or against the use of mediated instruction by classroom teachers and defend that position by citing specific facts or examples in a paper of less than three pages. (Evaluation)

GENERAL UTILIZATION FACTORS

Mediated instruction, by definition, includes any instruction that makes use of some device (mechanical or otherwise) to facilitate learning.

Although there is tremendous variety in the forms of mediated instruction available to teachers, some utilization procedures are generally applicable to all forms. Among these are the following.

1. *Select mediated instruction for specific instructional objectives.* To be of maximum effectiveness, mediated instruction should be an integral part of the instructional procedures; its use should not be an afterthought. Familiarity with a variety of forms of instruction enhances learning by enabling you to:

   a. Obtain an overview of the types of mediated instruction you intend to use and thus provide for greater variety.
   b. Order materials well in advance.
   c. Use material effectively.

When mediated instruction is used on the spur of the moment, without relationship to specific objectives, students will realize that it is being misused, probably as a time-filler or diversion. If the medium contains a message, do not let the message be, "I did not have anything else planned, so we will try this."

2. *Become familiar with the material or device prior to using it with students.* Depending on the form of mediated instruction being considered, you

should read it, view it, handle it, and otherwise use it prior to exposing students to it. This procedure not only provides assurance that the instructional aid is exactly what was expected, but it also enables you to estimate how much time to allow for correct use and to pinpoint specific strengths and weaknesses and thus better prepare students. When mechanical devices are involved, you will become more proficient in the operation of the device and thus avoid the potential loss of attention that accompanies the misuse of equipment.

3. *Prepare the students.* If students are to derive the full benefit of mediated instruction, they should be given some idea of its general content or purpose beforehand so they will know what to emphasize. Usually a brief description is sufficient to orient students, but some teachers find it useful to formulate a set of guide questions for students to answer. This helps further to focus student attention on important points.

4. *Use the mediated instruction correctly.* There is little value in attempting to use a form of mediated instruction if there is insufficient time for its proper use or if other conditions are not appropriate. While most forms of mediated instruction have utilization factors unique to them, common sense will dictate acceptable procedures. For example, if the device being used has a volume control, remember that it controls only the machine's volume, not students. If students are noisy, raising the volume on the device will not necessarily cause them to quiet down; in fact it may have just the opposite effect. Establishing the proper motivational set is a function of preparation of activities, and it is often difficult to use the mediated instruction itself for this purpose.

Among other common sense considerations is the problem of light. In most classrooms there is sufficient light control for all activities, but many teachers find it difficult to get their rooms dark enough to use some forms of mediated instruction, particularly film projectors and opaque projectors. Light control should be checked before materials are ordered.

5. *Conduct follow-up activities.* Follow-up activities provide an opportunity to clarify confusing points, answer questions, discuss interesting points, and integrate the new information with previous learning. The need for follow-up activites varies with the form of mediated instruction being used, but it is most crucial when aids such as films or broadcasts have been used. Since it is inconvenient or impossible to interrupt these types of aids while they are in use, students may misinterpret some point or miss subtle points altogether because of lack of teacher emphasis. Follow-up activities enable you to correct misconceptions and tie up loose ends. As with all instruction, follow-up activities should be planned in advance and ensure student participation.

6. *Evaluate the mediated instruction.* After using any form of mediated instruction, it is helpful to write a short evaluation of how effectively it helped students achieve the specified objectives. As these evaluations accumulate, they can be used to help you select the most appropriate and effective form of mediated instruction for each type of objective.

AIDS TO TEACHING

Materials That Are Read

Textbooks (Traditional)   Ever since the mid-1400s when Johann Gutenberg developed movable type, educators have made increasing use of books as instructional aids. Today books are by far the most common aid to instruction available to teachers and, surprisingly, they can be one of the most powerful.

Textbooks have a number of sometimes forgotten advantages. Most people, for example, can read and comprehend at least twice as fast as they can listen and comprehend. Students without reading problems can acquire information from texts quickly and efficiently. Textbooks also provide students with a common body of information arranged in some logical order. It is possible to base discussions on commonly available data and to help students perceive cause-effect relationships. Most texts also include chapter summaries, questions to be answered, and associated learning activities that provide guides for studying the information. Considering that most textbooks can be used repeatedly and that many contain pictures, charts, graphs, and maps, they are relatively inexpensive. Finally, textbooks can be adapted to individualization and self-pacing if you choose to use them in this way.

As with any instructional aid, textbooks can be misused, and most of the disadvantages associated with them stem from such misuses. Perhaps the greatest single misuse of texts is allowing them to dictate what will be taught. While textbook authors may be specialists in their fields, they are unlikely to be familiar with your particular group of students or with your particular instructional objectives. In some cases, especially in those that involve older texts, the information may not be up to date.

Often teachers are guilty of using the "chapter a week" approach; sometimes teachers assume that because they are using a text they must teach the contents from cover to cover before the last day of school. If you adopt this approach you will tend to find the slower readers in the class falling farther and farther behind as the rest of the class members lockstep their way through the material. This in itself will cause problems, but more important, more emphasis is being placed on how many pages are being turned than on how much is being learned. Such an approach also stifles the creativity of you and your students and can discourage full utilization of some of the text's built-in features.

The often-neglected first step in using a textbook is for the teacher to review it. While you will have a grasp of the material you intend to teach, the approach of the text may be unique. Textbook authors include what they feel is important and exclude whatever they feel is less important. A careful perusal of the text will enable you to capitalize on the author's particular insights.

The next step is to help students acquire an overview of the text. Many teachers have found that students at all levels can benefit from a short lesson on using the textbook. Good teachers will often include a survey of the table of contents with comments concerning what will and will not be emphasized, a discussion of the author's intent, an explanation of how the index is organized, and a survey of a representative chapter.

When surveying the representative chapter, it is helpful to encourage students to convert the chapter title and headings to questions and then read to find the answers. Encouraging students to look at the chapter summary and the questions at the end of the chapter before reading it is profitable. Perusing boldface type, italics, maps, charts, and so forth will help later in locating major points. Some teachers find it useful to teach students the skill of skimming, with particular emphasis on the importance of introductory and culminating sentences. Still others find it useful to encourage students to write out answers to teacher-posed questions pertaining to, and reinforcing, important points in the chapter.

Textbooks (Programmed)   Programmed instruction began as an attempt to make learning more efficient by applying what was known about reinforcement and animal behavior to the teaching-learning process. Programmed instruction did not gain broad attention, however, until 1954, when B. F. Skinner published an article entitled "The Science of Learning and the Art of Teaching."[1] This article gave major impetus to the programmed learning movement.

Programmed instruction presents information to students in a series of very carefully planned sequential steps. As students move from step to step, they receive immediate feedback concerning learning progress and in some programs, are "branched" to review remedial or enrichment information depending on the response made to a given question. Active student participation in the learning process (students are forced to construct or select a response) makes up one of the major differences between

[1]B. F. Skinner, "The Science of Learning and the Art of Teaching," *The Harvard Educational Review*, 24 (Spring 1954), 86–97.

programmed and traditional texts and instruction. A second difference is that the formation of misconceptions is reduced (or eliminated entirely) because the sequential nature of the program carefully relates each new piece of information to the one immediately preceding it.

There are two basic kinds of strategies for all programmed materials whether they are presented through the use of programmed texts, teaching machines, or computers. These are linear and nonlinear strategies.

Linear Programs   Linear programs are most closely associated with B. F. Skinner.[2] The following are some of the characteristics most closely associated with such programs:

1. Each student is required to go through *an identical sequence* of small steps.
2. Each student *constructs responses,* usually by writing a word or a number, from recalled information.
3. Via the *liberal use of cues* such as boldface type, italics, and underlining, an attempt is made to keep each student's performance as error-free as possible. Usually an error rate of less than 5 percent is sought by authors of programmed materials.
4. *No remedial steps are taken when a student makes an error.* Except with slightly modified, quasi-linear programs, the student simply sees the correct response and moves on.

Nonlinear Programs   Nonlinear (or branching, or intrinsic) programs are associated most closely with Norman Crowder.[3] The following are some of the characteristics most closely associated with such programs.

1. Each student *selects* responses to multiple-choice questions and those responses determine the *unique path* that student will follow through the material, that is, whether the student goes on to new material or is given review or enrichment material.
2. *Little, if any, use of cues* is made since errors are anticipated and remedial instruction is provided to deal with the specific weakness disclosed by the student's choice of response.

Another kind of "programming" has been advocated by Sidney L. Pressey.[4] It was Pressey's work in 1924 that served as a basis for the later development of sophisticated teaching machines, but although he himself was a strong advocate of programmed learning, he saw it as an adjunct to

---

[2]B. F. Skinner, *The Technology of Teaching* (Englewood Cliffs, N.J.: Prentice-Hall, 1968).

[3]Norman A. Crowder, "Automatic Tutoring by Means of Intrinsic Programming," in *Automatic Teaching: The State of the Art,* ed., Eugene Gatanter (New York: John Wiley, 1959), pp. 109–110.

[4]Sidney L. Pressey, "A Machine for Automatic Teaching of Drill Material," *School and Society,* 25, no. 645 (May 7, 1927), pp 549–592.

more traditional kinds of instruction. He felt that information should first be acquired in some traditional manner and then reinforced via programmed techniques. The term "adjunct programming" is therefore sometimes used to label Pressey's view.

It is not likely, however,[5] that students of the future will find themselves following a programmed test as the exclusive learning mode. Most programmed texts available today deal with basic, concrete facts, and this situation is not likely to change in the near future. By its very nature, noncomputerized programmed instruction virtually eliminates student creativity. All acceptable responses are already programmed, and divergent thinking is, in terms of the program, incorrect thinking. There are many who believe that for basic, sequential kinds of material, programmed materials will eventually replace traditional kinds of instruction and that it is in the integration and application of knowledge that human teachers are most needed.

Since the use of texts, whether programmed or not, requires students to read, their use must be limited to students who exhibit this skill with a competence commensurate with the materials used. This limitation inhibits their use.

All the forms of mediated instruction surveyed in the balance of this chapter are useful as adjuncts to more traditional kinds of instruction.

Audio Aids

Radios, Record Players, and Tape Recorders   Radios, record players, and audio tape recorders all utilize a single input sense, that of sound. With the advent of films, television, and videotapes, purely auditory devices are being used less frequently, but they still have their place.

Radios, for example, are still a convenient means for getting up-to-the minute news reports for class analysis. Record players make it possible to listen conveniently to plays, operas, concerts, and speeches, while tape recorders make it possible to record broadcast material or live performances of guest speakers, class debates, and so forth for later use and analysis. These forms of mediated instruction are also used extensively as audio models for students, and the audio tape recorder provides an added dimension by enabling students to record and then listen to their own voices for diagnostic, developmental, or remedial purposes.

As young people have increased their leisure-time use of films and television, they have become accustomed to having a visual point on which to focus their attention. When using audio aids, students may literally not know what to look at. You may take the position that learning to use straight

---

[5]See Leslie J. Briggs et al., *Instructional Media: A Procedure for the Design of Multi-Media Instruction. A Critical Review of Research, and Suggestions for Future Research* (Pittsburgh, Pa.: American Institutes for Research, 1967), p. 116, for further discussion.

audio inputs is a skill that needs development or that appropriate visual aids (pictures, maps, etc.) that relate to what the students are listening to, and that can serve as visual focal points, should be supplied.

Research in the area of listening is enlightening. It is estimated, for example, that approximately 45 percent of the average adult's working day is spent listening and that this figure rises to 60 percent for elementary school students and to 90 percent for high school and college students.[6] Unfortunately, the research also shows that, even if students are concentrating on what they hear, they will retain only about 50 percent and within two months will be able to recall less than half of that.[7] Obviously students can use additional practice in the frequently overlooked skill of effective listening. Radios, record players, and audio tape recorders can be used to provide that practice.

Telephones   Telephones represent yet another purely auditory form of mediated instruction. Although the telephone was invented in 1876 and the radio in 1895, the telephone's nineteen-year advantage has not been reflected in its significantly greater use by educators. This is unfortunate because the telephone companies have much to offer and they are generally quite willing to work with educators.

One unique application of telephone technology is the "teleinterview." Upon request, most telephone companies will rent to schools equipment that makes it possible to set up two-way communication between a whole class and a speaker at some distant point. The equipment is relatively inexpensive (especially when compared with the costs of bringing the speaker physically to the class), yet it has many of the advantages of actually having the speaker there. All students can listen at the same time, ask questions, and receive answers.

Although student preparation is important with all forms of mediated instruction, it is particularly important when teleinterviews are used, since the charges are calculated according to the time for which the telephone line is in use. Adequate preparation in this case would include preparing the speaker by involving him or her in the objectives of the telelecture. Preparation of the students should include the formulation of specific questions to ask the speaker.

In 1971 the American Telephone & Telegraph Company developed a device called a Variable Speech Control (VSC). The purpose of the VSC is to change the rate at which speech can be understood by omitting pauses and shortening vowel sounds. The practical applications of the device include enabling blind people to listen to, and comprehend, spoken words nearly as quickly as sighted people can read and comprehend written words,

---

[6]James W. Brown, Richard B. Lewis, and Fred F. Harcleroad, *A V Instruction—Media and Methods*, 3rd ed. (New York: McGraw-Hill, 1969), p. 327.

[7]Ibid., p. 327.

and enabling teachers and students to make greater use of taped materials by allowing them to listen to extensive recorded tapes in shorter periods of time.

Visual Aids

Pictures   Still pictures, whether in the form of paintings, magazine clippings, photographs, slides, or filmstrips, have unique properties that make them extremely valuable as instructional aids. Among these properties is their ability to convey abstractions powerfully without depending on verbal descriptions, their ability to focus attention on a characteristic situation or on a particular step in a process, and their ability to allow students to study a picture at length, to refer back to it conveniently, and to make side-by-side comparisons. The combination of these properties is not available in many other forms of mediated instruction.

Pictures, such as those available from magazines, travel bureaus, and commercial concerns, represent one of the easiest to acquire, and least expensive, forms of mediated instruction available to teachers. You can increase the instructional value of pictures if common-sense principles are followed. For instance, you should be sure that the picture selected is appropriate for the students who will see it. Very complex pictures, for example, are not well suited for younger students regardless of how attractive they may be otherwise. Colored pictures can usually attract and hold students' attention better than can black-and-white pictures, and all pictures must be large enough to be seen easily. Ensuring that the picture is relevant to what will be studied and that it does not present a biased view (unless such a view is intended) is important.

Opaque Projectors   It sometimes happens that a picture is of particular benefit but is too small to be seen by the entire class at one time. In such instances, the opaque projector may be useful. The "opaque" will project and enlarge any flat picture whether it is a single sheet or a page bound in a book. Furthermore, most opaque projectors come equipped with a built-in light arrow, which can be used to draw students' attention to particular points on the projected image. Many teachers have also found the "opaque" useful for projecting images on chalkboards so they can be traced.

Opaque projectors make use of a large and powerful bulb as a light source, and this bulb gets hot. Most "opaques," therefore, include a built-in, heat-absorbing glass plate between the bulb and the projection stage. In spite of this precaution, thin materials sometimes curl or scorch. Proper use would then include checking prior to using an "opaque" to make sure there is a heat-absorbing glass plate and checking material periodically during use.

Although opaque projectors generate a lot of heat, they do not project a lot of light. Opaque projectors use a reflected light source rather than a direct light source such as that found in film projectors. Less light reaches the screen than with other kinds of projectors, and unless the room is reasonably dark students may have difficulty seeing the projection. Check to see if the room can be darkened sufficiently before using the "opaque" with students. Because the room must be darkened, students may be unable to take notes. For this reason most teachers do not use opaque projectors for extended periods of time.

Slides and Filmstrips   Slides and filmstrips have all the advantages of pictures and the added advantage of increased realism. Because slides are actual photographs and are shown via a bright light source, the scenes they portray appear more "real" than printed pictures and the colors appear more brilliant. These factors appeal to students. In addition, it is much easier to store a set of slides than to store a set of large, mounted pictures.

A more significant advantage associated with slides is the opportunity they provide for you to create your own instructional aids. Many teachers make it a point to take along a camera and slide film (rather than print film) when encountering circumstances pertinent to their teaching area, and many have thus compiled an impressive set of slides that are useful in stimulating and maintaining students' interest. Many teachers have also initiated class projects wherein students organize a slide program complete with an accompanying tape recording. Such projects have the dual advantages of being useful, interesting learning activities, and increasing the teacher's store of instructional aids.

A filmstrip is essentially a series of connected slides. Most filmstrips are prepared commercially and many have brief captions printed on each frame. A recent development is the sprocketless filmstrip projector, which should result in longer life for a filmstrip. As the filmstrip is advanced and each frame is discussed by the teacher, various procedures may be used to enrich the experience. Besides a basic approach, such as asking students to read the captions out loud, teachers have discovered that teacher and student comments and discussion are possible and profitable while the filmstrip is being shown as well as afterward.

Bulletin Boards   Bulletin boards are ideally suited for the display of visual materials such as pictures, cartoons, postcards, newspaper clippings, outstanding papers, and student-made collages and montages. Common sense will dictate procedures for the use of bulletin boards. You will find, for instance, that bulletin boards promote learning best when they concern a single idea or topic. They should also be neat and uncluttered, make use of bright colors and attention-getting materials such as colored yarn and plastics, and they should be oriented pictorially rather than verbally. The instructional value of bulletin boards can be increased further by building into the display participation devices, such as questions with the answers covered by flaps, or manipulative devices.

A bulletin board's instructional value lasts a relatively short time, in some cases not more than a few days. Once you go to the trouble to construct an exceptional bulletin board, you may be reluctant to take it down. There is certainly no reason to take down a display that students still find useful, but once students stop paying attention to the display or the class moves on to some other topic, the bulletin board display needs replacement.

Teachers have found that some groups of students enjoy the responsibility for putting up new displays periodically throughout the year. This helps to increase students' interest in the display and can lead to increased learning as groups find that research in the area will assist in developing an attractive and interesting display. You can provide advice and assistance in the form of suggesting sources for, and providing, actual materials.

Maps and Globes, Charts and Graphs   Maps, globes, charts, and graphs are grouped together because each of these forms of mediated instruction may require increased student preparation. Students may have difficulty interpreting maps, globes, charts, and graphs unless you make a special effort to help them.

Maps and globes are used to show portions of the earth's surface in a less than life-sized scale. Cartographers have constructed maps and globes to emphasize political, geographic, and climatic divisions and have developed a number of different map projections. You will find it useful to draw students' attention to the particular kind of projection being used and to discuss the way it distorts the real size and shape of particular geographic features. Without an understanding of projection, students may have misconceptions about maps.

Efforts to draw students' attention to the legend of the map or globe will reap dividends. It is here that the cartographer explains the meanings of the symbols used on the map or globe, gives the scale to which features are drawn, and provides additional information such as the meanings of particular colors.

You should study maps and globes before using them. Political divisions, particularly boundaries and names, change more often than is suspected, and it is not uncommon for a map or globe in a classroom to be out of date. If so, this fact should be made known to students and, if possible, transparencies and overlays should be used to emphasize the changes.

Charts differ from graphs and diagrams in that they may include a wider variety of pictorial forms. Graphs and diagrams generally have only simple lines or bars. The most common kinds of charts are flow charts (showing sequential steps), process charts (showing some process from start to finish), and time charts (showing developments over a period of time). The instructional value of charts is maximized when you take the time to make sure students can read and interpret the data presented. A special lesson devoted to reading all types of charts is time well invested.

Graphs are used primarily to condense and convey numerical data in visual form. The most common kinds are the circle graph (useful for showing the relationship of parts to the whole), bar graphs (useful for showing comparative data such as the changes in unemployment from year to year), and line graphs (useful for plotting profiles of patterns).

Although students should be given special instruction in the use of maps, globes, charts, and graphs, teachers should obtain the least complicated aid that will serve their immediate purpose. Trying to select an aid that can be used in a variety of lessons will be a false economy if students have difficulty interpreting the aid or are confused by it.

Chalkboards   Chalkboards are available in almost every classroom and most teachers use them frequently. Chalkboards are used to display instructions, diagrams, examples, and other information that is subject to frequent change. Board work also gives students the chance to demonstrate their abilities and allows active student participation.

There are a number of ways you can utilize chalkboards to make them more valuable to students. One is not to talk to the board. Students may have difficulty hearing teachers who insist on trying to face the board and talk to students at the same time. Teachers who make frequent use of the board often construct, or invest in, templates to facilitate the drawing of frequently used shapes. This not only saves time, but allows more consistency. An inexpensive form of template can be made by simply tracing a design and punching holes along the traced lines. Brushing a dusty chalk eraser across the template while it is held to the board will create a dotted outline. As was mentioned earlier, pictures can also be traced on the board from projected images.

When using the chalkboard, you should avoid cluttering. Once an item written on the board has served its purpose, it is best to erase it so students will not be distracted by it. Certain types of colored chalk are intended for use on paper, not on chalkboards. If the wrong kind of chalk is used, it may stain the chalkboard permanently. Finally, lettering must be large enough to be seen easily. Usually letters that are about two and a half inches high can be seen easily from a distance up to thirty feet.

Overhead Projectors   Of the types of projectors available to teachers, overhead projectors are easily the most common. Overhead projectors can project any material that is drawn, written, or printed on transparent film. They are often used instead of the chalkboard because they allow you to write and at the same time face the students. Enabling you to maintain eye contact with your students is one of the greatest advantages of the overhead. Another advantage is to be able to use the machine without darkening the room, which facilitates note taking and, more important, student interaction.

The use of overlays with base transparencies is a particularly effective instructional tool. A typical overlay package might contain a base map of the United States, a transparency to go over the base outline to show major river systems, a third transparency to depict major cities and to show their relationship to rivers, and a fourth transparency to show railroad development.

To use an overhead projector as an "electric chalkboard," you need only a sheet of clear plastic (usually acetate, but cellophane or even a commercial plastic wrap will do) to protect the glass projection plate and a grease pencil, china marker, crayon, or felt-tipped pen. Grease pencils are usually filled with a wax-based material and generally project black lines. Grease pencils can project colors, but if color is desired (and it does make the projections more attractive), felt-tipped pens are less expensive and work just as well. Crayons and china markers will project black lines regardless of their color but they have the advantage, along with grease pencils, of being erased by light rubbing with a soft cloth or tissue. To remove transparent ink it is often necessary to use a cleaner or even a solvent, depending on the kind of ink in the pen. Some overheads come equipped with a roll of acetate. You write on the acetate and then simply roll up the used surface to expose an unused portion, thus temporarily eliminating the need to erase. You may construct your own transparencies by simply drawing them, but if better quality or permanency is desired, one of a number of heat processes, or an ammonia process known as "diazo," may be used. Most school librarians have sources of information concerning these processes, or the audiovisual department in the school or a nearby college or university may offer assistance.

As you become experienced in the making of transparencies and overlays, you will find that the use of color can add interest and emphasis, that printed (manuscript) characters are easier to form and read than are cursive characters, and that typing (especially when done with a primary typewriter) adds to the neatness and legibility of the finished product. Including too much on one transparency can inhibit use by learners; about twenty lines seem to be optimum. Typewriters with pica or elite type are not commonly used for transparency work since the projected image is usually too small to be read easily.

It is often possible to acquire commercially prepared transparencies and overlays made by experts with a wealth of materials to work with, and thus, are usually more polished than teacher-made materials. But they may also involve more expense.[8]

Most overhead projectors have a thermostatically controlled switch that permits the fan to continue operating until the interior of the projector is cool. Do not be upset if the machine does not stop when it is turned off, and do not pull the plug. It will stop automatically when it has cooled down.

Realia The term "realia" refers to any specimens, models, mock-ups, or artifacts that can be used to help students learn. Depending on what is being taught, teachers and students may display living animals, coin collections, insects, or dozens of others. The list is as limitless and as varied as there are real things in the world that may be displayed without danger or great expense. Modified representations of real things, such as cut-away or "exploded" models are also helpful. In the latter, the whole is broken into segments and each segment is held apart from the others, while the pieces still maintain the same relative positions as in the unexploded model. Other good teaching tools are models that students can assemble and disassemble,[9] and dioramas, which are three-dimensional scenes that students can construct.

Audiovisual Combinations

Multimedia Kits As an increasing number of schools adopt a systems approach to education, many educators are finding multimedia kits helpful. Multimedia kits are compilations of instructional materials that include a variety of mediated instruction forms designed to help students achieve a specific instructional objective by exposing them to different types of closely integrated educational experiences.

A typical multimedia kit may contain, for example, booklets, filmstrips, a loop film, audio tapes, and artifacts. All the components are selected with a single purpose in mind—to generate and maintain students' interest in a particular topic or subject while at the same time providing them with as much pertinent information as possible.

Multimedia kits can be used with excellent results for groups, but perhaps their greatest utilization is found when they are used as self-in-

[8]Among the many sources of commercially prepared transparencies are the following: Encyclopedia Britannica Films, Inc., 1150 Wilmette Ave., Wilmette, Ill. 60091; Instructo Products Company, 1635 N. 55th St., Philadelphia, Pa. 19131; and 3M Company, Visual Products, 2501 Hudson Road, St. Paul, Minn. 55119.

[9]Although most realia are brought to the classroom from the collections of either the students or the teacher, there is a wealth of models available commercially. Two of the many sources are Models of Industry, 2804 Tenth St., Berkeley, Calif. 74710; and W. M. Welch Scientific Co., 1515 Sedgwick St., Chicago, Ill. 60610.

structional devices for students to use at their own convenience and at their own rate. As with most other forms of mediated instruction, multimedia kits may be prepared by teachers themselves or can be purchased ready made.[10]

Films and Television   Films and television provide students with more of a "you are there" feeling than do most other forms of mediated instruction. They also enable students to view demonstrations (both scientific and social), experiments, natural phenomena, and other events that would be too difficult, dangerous, or even impossible to view otherwise (for instance, moon walks and erupting volcanoes).

Techniques such as time-lapse photography, microphotography, long-range photography, animation, and slow-motion projection offer unique approaches for students' exploration. Students may watch as a flower unfolds into full bloom or as a single cell divides. They can see the earth as an astronaut would see it or gain an understanding of the phenomenon of nuclear fission. Infrared photography, "zoom-ins," and even X-ray photography are also possible through films and television.

Proper preparation of students and good planning in the use of films can enhance learning. One researcher has found that students who are well prepared for a film (by being given such things as questions to be answered, study guides, and explanations of new or difficult words) experience a learning gain 20 percent greater than do students who are not so prepared.[11] Other researchers have found that periodically stopping a film to provide time for active student participation, or splicing into the film questions for discussion, can also increase student learning.[12]

Teachers are often pleasantly surprised at the ease with which films can be borrowed. Most universities and state departments of education maintain extensive film libraries, as do many businesses and public utilities. A check with the audiovisual department in any public school or with a school librarian can result in the acquisition of good sources of free or inexpensive films.[13]

In addition to 16mm films, educators are also finding that 8mm, single-concept or single-skill continuous-loop films are very useful. Like the larger 16mm films, 8mm films can be used for large groups, but they are especially well suited for individual use and can thus play an important

---

[10]Two sources of multimedia kits are American Telephone & Telegraph Co., 195 Broadway, New York, N.Y. 10007; and Westinghouse Electric Corp., P.O. Box J, Sea Cliff, N.Y. 11579. (See Chapter 11.)

[11]Briggs et al., *Instructional Media*, p. 112.

[12]Ibid., p. 114.

[13]Some excellent sources include the local telephone company; American Iron and Steel Institute, 150 E. 42nd St., New York, N.Y. 10017; General Motors Corp., General Motors Building, Detroit, Mich. 48202; and Coronet Films, 65 E. South Water St., Chicago, Ill. 60601.

part in individualization and self-pacing of instruction. Most 8mm loop films are silent, but that has not detracted from their popularity.

An advantage of television over film is that of immediacy. Via television, students can watch events as they are actually happening. In effect they are seeing for themselves, but the TV camera can even improve on personal presence by providing each student with a clear, unobstructed, and close-up view.

Television has been used effectively in a variety of ways. The first, and most common, is the use of commercial programs. Although often thought of only in terms of its entertainment value, commercial television frequently broadcasts special programs and documentaries that have significant instructional value.

Another type of broadcast television is educational television, or ETV. ETV broadcasts are primarily instructional but they are aimed at a broad, public audience and, therefore, attempt to meet a variety of needs. Typical ETV programs include discussions with industrial, political, and social leaders, "how-to-do-it" courses, and nonviolent children's programs. One of the most famous of the ETV children's programs is *Sesame Street*.[14]

A third type of broadcast television is instructional television, or ITV. The distinctions between ETV and ITV are considered to be both in programming intent and in program financing. ETV programs, such as *Sesame Street*, are not intended for specific and formal instruction; ITV programs generally are. ETV programs are frequently sponsored by commercial concerns, whereas ITV programs are financed most often by governmental grants, private foundations, individual school systems, and colleges and universities.

Closed-circuit television represents a fourth way to use the medium. In closed-circuit television, only TV sets connected directly to a transmitter, or adapted to receive the 2500 mHz (megaHertz) wavelength reserved for closed-circuit television, can receive the programs. Closed-circuit television is most often used on an "in-house" basis to televise meetings and debates, demonstrations and experiments, and even regular classes. Because it is an in-house operation students can participate in the actual program development and televising, thus adding yet another dimension to their educational experience.

A fifth way to use television is via videotape recorders, or (VTR). Videotape recorders are directly analogous to audio tape recorders, with the obvious difference that the former provides a visual, as well as an audio, record. More and more schools are acquiring VTR equipment, not only for taping and saving lectures, demonstrations, and theatrical presenta-

[14]For further information concerning ETV, you can write to either the National Association of Educational Broadcasters, 1346 Connecticut Ave., N.W., Washington, D.C., 20036, or NET Film Service, Indiana University, Bloomington, Ind. 47401. Nearby colleges and universities are also likely sources of information about ETV.

tions, but also for use in everyday teaching situations. As a way of enabling both teachers and students to see themselves as others see them, VTR equipment has found increasing use. Coaches, for instance, have found VTR equipment invaluable for instant feedback of student psychomotor skills.

Computers as the Tools for Learning

Most early "teaching machines" did not do much more than control the actions of the learner. The machines kept the student from skipping ahead or going back to change answers. With the advent of computers, however, it became possible to design truly sophisticated teaching machines.

Computer-assisted instruction (CAI) is, without doubt, the single most complex and sophisticated form of mediated instruction yet developed. As the name implies, computer-assisted instruction makes use of a computer and a computer program to assist students in the acquisition of skills and information. Because CAI programs are written to react to student responses, it is possible to design exercises specifically for individual needs and ability levels and to present new information at a rate and degree of complexity compatible with the student's ability. Computers are also useful in providing students with practice in responding to lifelike situations without the hazards associated with the actual endeavor and in automatically keeping accurate records of students' performances in any or all of these activities. In addition, the computer does not get tired or short tempered. It is willing and able to work twenty-four hours a day, has infinite patience, and when properly used does not threaten students personally. It is not hard to see why some educators feel that extensive use of computers can improve the teaching-learning process.

There are four principal kinds of CAI programs. *Drill-and-practice* programs are probably the most common. They are usually branching programs and can thus vary the complexity of the material to keep it commensurate with the proficiency demonstrated by the student. If students have difficulty with one level of problems, for example, CAI drill-and-practice programs can shift them automatically to less complex levels and then, as they become more proficient, shift them back automatically through successively more complex levels. To date, most drill-and-practice programs focus on mathematical or language skills.

A second type of CAI program is the *tutorial* program. Unlike drill-and-practice programs, tutorial programs present students with new information and then, on the basis of student responses to questions or problems, provide further new information, or supplemental information.

A third type of CAI programming is known as *simulation*. The function of simulations is usually to provide a "real-life" situation to which the student can react. Depending on the programming strategy used, simulated situations can change on the basis of sequentially or randomly occurring variables or solely on the basis of student input.

Simulation programs have been used at a number of medical schools. At one school, prospective doctors are presented, via a CAI terminal, with a patient and a set of symptoms. The student prescribes treatment via the terminal and the computer acts upon this input. After an appropriate length of time has elapsed (that length of time that would have elapsed in real life), the terminal prints out the patient's reaction to the treatment. Variables such as allergic reactions and unexpected complications can also be programmed to test the student's abilities further.

The fourth kind of CAI programming is simple *problem solving*. Here the student can capitalize on the power of the computer to compute. Students can try out complex mathematical solutions without hours of stultifying work with a pencil and paper. They can make projections and change variables without regard to the difficulty of the computations. The computer is able to do it all virtually instantaneously.

Kinds of Computing Systems

The kinds of programs (software) described can be run on different kinds of computers (hardware). The earliest computer applications simply involved submitting a computing job to a large computer and letting it "crunch" the numbers. As technology progressed, ways were found to take advantage of the computer's speed and share its power among a number of users, each one of which would get responses from the computer so fast that it would seem that the computer was dealing only with that one user. One of the largest time-sharing projects in the country is the Programmed Logic for Automatic Teaching Operation (PLATO) project at the University of Illinois. This project was designed to enable thousands of computer terminals at widely separated sites to be connected to a single large computer (mainframe). The speed of the computer would enable each user to receive "individual" attention, and the sophistication of the terminals would enable students to receive visual auditory feedback, view data stored on microfiche, and with some terminals, communicate with the computer simply by touching their fingers to the display panel.

Since the mid-1970s there has been a revolution in the computer industry caused by breakthroughs in the miniaturization of computer circuitry. This miniaturization has made possible the microcomputer, which although small in size, parallels in power the large mainframes of just a few years age. The microcomputer explosion has had a dramatic impact on education. "Between 1970 and 1980, the best estimates of instructional usage of the computer showed increases from 13% in 1970 to 74% in 1980. Instructional usage is anticipated to reach 87% by 1985.[15] Most of the microcomputers sold to date are the Radio Shack TRS80s and, in terms

[15]Jack Chambers and Alfred Bork, "Computer Assisted Learning," Topics, joint issue by Education Board (New York: Association for Computing Machinery, 1981), p. 10.

of numbers, these are followed closely by Apple IIs and Commodore PETs. In addition, there are at least seventy other brands of computers. Regardless of the kind of microcomputer in your school, you will be able to provide new and exciting instructional activities if you learn to use it.

The programs (software) for microcomputers fall into the same categories of programs already described for programmed materials (drill and practice, tutorial, simulation, and problem solving). The big difference between the use of these programs with noncomputerized devices and their use with microcomputers is that the student is placed in a much more lifelike situation. The feedback provided in drill-and-practice programs, for example, can contain animated scenes and be personalized with the student's name as well as providing the student with a complete summary and analysis of his or her performance immediately upon completion of the work. Likewise, tutorial programs can use animated scenes to help teach new information and can enable the student to change the animation on the basis of immediate input.

Perhaps the greatest advantage of the microcomputer is with respect to its use for simulation. In addition to the unique qualities mentioned in conjunction with drill-and-practice and tutorial programs, simulation programs on the microcomputer open new possibilities for students to express their creativity. One example of such a program is called "Dancing Demon,"[16] which allows students who know nothing about reading or writing music or about choreography to write a tune and a dance routine and then watch a "Demon" perform it. This kind of creative endeavor was impossible without computers but is now becoming commonplace.

Aside from greatly enhancing your opportunities for creative and effective instruction in the classroom, familiarity with microcomputers can also help you to get into the classroom in the first place. Many personnel recruiters are now looking for teachers who can help administrators find new applications for the microcomputers currently in the schools and/or on the way. If you can demonstrate that you have used computers and have some ideas of how microcomputers could be used in your classroom, you are a better job candidate than one who knows little or nothing about computers.

Fortunately, it is relatively easy to become familiar with microcomputers. Simply walk into the computer lab at your school or into any commercial computer outlet and ask to see how a microcomputer can be used for instruction. Once you are introduced to the basic operation of the machine, it is simply a matter of taking the time to try a number of programs to familiarize yourself with the capabilities of the hardware and software. After that you may find it hard to walk away—the fascination power of the computer is almost irresistible.

---

[16]"Dancing Demon," copyright by Tandy Corp., 1980.

Biofeedback and the Chemical Transfer of Knowledge

Since this chapter began with an examination of one of the oldest forms of instructional aids, it is fitting that we conclude with a look at some forms possible in the future.

Biofeedback is the process whereby people may be made aware of body and mental processes that are normally unobservable and learn to control these processes to their own advantage. By using a device known as an electroencephalograph (EEG), scientists have been able to identify those brainwave patterns generated when people are relaxed (Alpha waves—8 to 12 cycles per second) and when they are concentrating (Theta waves— 3 to 7 cycles per second). In one experiment involving the monitoring of radar screens, individuals given feedback concerning their brainwave patterns outperformed individuals who were not given such feedback.[17] It is possible that further work in this area will result in students being able to monitor their own brainwaves and thus increase their powers of concentration.

In an experiment conducted at the Stanford Research Institute, a subject was able to control the action of a computer by simply "thinking at it" and having it monitor, and react to, specific brainwave patterns.[18] With such direct communication possible between human and electronic "brains," it may become possible to program computers simply by "thinking" the program at them or, conversely, to learn from computers by allowing them to "think" at people.

Chemists have not been idle either, and in one experiment rats trained to prefer a particular size of circle were killed and extracts of their brains were fed to a second group of rats. The second group of rats were trained to prefer circles of the same size in much less time than an "untreated" control group.[19] As further experimentation in the chemical transfer of learning is conducted, it may become possible literally to bottle knowledge.[20]

The possible ramifications of biofeedback and the chemical transfer of learning for the teaching-learning process boggle the imagination. Will devices such as electroencephalographs or bottles of "knowledge" become the mediated instructional devices of tomorrow? Predictions are dangerous, but the possibility exists.

[17]Jackson Beatty et al., "Operant Control of Occipital Theta Rhythm Affects Performance in a Radar Monitoring Task," *Science*, 183, no. 4127 (March 1, 1974), 871.

[18]"Mind-Reading Computer," *Time*, July 1, 1974, p. 67.

[19]Lendell W. Braud and William G. Braud, "Biochemical Transfer of Relational Responding (Transposition)." *Science*, 176, no. 4037 (May 26, 1972), 942.

[20]Nikolaus R. Hansi and Adele B. Hansi, "Learning and Memory Improvement Through Chemistry: Dream or Reality in the Offing?" *Phi Delta Kappan*, 16, no. 4 (December 1979), 264.

SUMMARY

Aids to instruction range from simple forms such as textbooks and radios to moderately complex forms such as films and television to very complex forms such as multimedia kits and computer-assisted instruction, and even to problematical forms such as electroencephalographs and chemicals. Mediated instructional aids in their many forms provide teachers with unique instructional tools and with alternatives to the common sit-and-listen-to-the-teacher instruction.

Regardless of the kind of mediated instruction considered, particular forms must be selected in relation to specific instructional objectives. For maximum effectiveness, good teaching requires that you be thoroughly familiar with the material or device before using it with students. Proper preparation of students for the mediated instruction is also crucial. Follow-up activities are important, paricularly when a one-way communicator such as radio, television, or film has been used. A file of evaluations of the mediated instructional materials used will facilitate decisions regarding the inclusion or exclusion of the media in future learning activities.

Although this chapter has dealt with many of the forms of mediated instruction that most teachers will find commonly available, no attempt has been made to make the chapter all inclusive. Other forms of mediated instruction (such as magazines and posters) are equally valid and useful. Experienced teachers strive to increase their familiarity with as many forms of mediated instruction as possible. The more variety teachers include in their instructional activities, the more their students will learn, and the more they will enjoy learning. We do suggest, however, that all prospective teachers become familiar with microcomputers. Such familiarity will help them to get a teaching position and be more effective in it.

EIGHT
EVALUATION

Most conscientious teachers spend considerable time planning lessons and helping their students to learn. Undoubtedly you will do the same, and, like other conscientious teachers, you will want to know how effective you have been and how you might become even more effective. This chapter will help you to find answers to those concerns.

The first part of this chapter concerns student evaluation. In this section we will look at some fundamental points you will want to consider as you plan your evaluation procedures; the construction and utilization of paper-and-pencil tests including teacher-made objective tests, teacher-made essay tests, and standardized tests; alternatives to formal paper-and-pencil tests; and the calculation and reporting of grades.

In the second part of the chapter we will explore various ways of assessing your own performance including teacher performance tests; student, peer, and administrative evaluations; and interaction analysis.

OBJECTIVES

When you complete this chapter, you will be able to:

1. Explain in writing at least three basic considerations that should be dealt with when planning an evaluation procedure. (Comprehension)
2. Construct two types of objective tests (twenty items each) and two essay tests (three items each) that meet the standards described for such tests in this chapter. (Synthesis)

3. When given a series of test scores, assign grades to the scores using a systematic procedure and explain the procedure and a rationale for its use. (Synthesis)
4. Describe a procedure you believe would be helpful in both evaluating and improving your own instructional techniques and explain, in less than four pages, why you believe your procedure would be at least as effective as any other(s). (Synthesis, Evaluation)

THE GRADING DICHOTOMY

The evaluation of a student's performance often poses painful problems for teachers. Most teachers recognize the need for precise and objective data for evaluation of students. Besides being a prerequisite for assigning grades, evaluations are often the basis for important decisions concerning educational and vocational plans. Inaccurate data can cause misdirection in those plans. In addition, data concerning students' performance also serve as a partial measure of teacher effectiveness. Accurate knowledge of what students can and cannot do, coupled with knowledge of the instructional intent, provides you with a sound basis for evaluating your own instructional strengths and weaknesses.

On the other hand, most teachers are aware of ethical considerations often associated with grading students. Is one morally justified in applying any absolute standards to twenty or thirty human beings when one realizes that each of those individuals is unique in terms of background, aspirations, and degree of personal effort? Is it fair, for example, to reward a bright student who does well even though he or she is working at minimal effort, and at the same time fail to reward a slower student who does not do well but exhibits maximum effort?

The need to provide accurate data concerning students' performance must be balanced against the fact that you are dealing with human beings and not machined products. In efforts to acquire such data, care must be exercised not to trample the feelings and values of students—to do so might well impede or even destroy the potential love for learning within students. It would be a hollow victory to obtain accurate evaluation data only to find that the evaluation process itself has made students cynical and contemptuous of learning as a worthwhile activity.

Unfortunately, there is no single evaluation or grading technique that can simultaneously solve all the problems associated with the evaluation and grading of students. It is possible, however, to acquire a number of basic evaluation criteria and a variety of grading techniques that, when used in combination, may enable you to synthesize evaluation and grading procedures with which you feel comfortable.

BASIC EVALUATION CONSIDERATIONS

Honesty

It is assumed that all teachers approach the evaluation of students with ethical intentions. Certainly, no professional teacher would deliberately set out to fail a student or to punish a class by misgrading a test. It does happen, however, that evaluation problems arise because of unintentional acts by the teacher. These acts often take the form of misleading students concerning the basis upon which they will be graded or of failing to state explicitly the objectives of the course. For example, students in a writing class may be told to concentrate upon developing clear and logical arguments only to find that their grades depend, to a large degree, upon the grammatical correctness of their papers.

In terms of being honest with students regarding evaluation criteria, there are few substitutes for properly written precise instructional objectives. If you specify exactly what is expected of students, and go over those expectations so that everyone has the same interpretation of what they mean, a substantial portion of this criterion has been met. When the targets and standards are known, students are more able to focus their efforts on acquiring those skills without hesitation. When you are consistent in evaluating students on the basis of stated objectives, the procedure will be deemed "honest" by students.

Variety

Currently, a high percentage of academic evaluation programs rely heavily upon paper-and-pencil tests. This phenomenon is not predominant by chance but, rather, has evolved over the years as an expedient way to assess the achievements of large numbers of students. Many of the arguments that have been used successfully to defend paper-and-pencil tests are still valid and powerful. Among these arguments are the following.

1. Paper-and-pencil tests can be used to pose the same problems to all students under the same test conditions and can therefore provide a reasonable basis for comparison.
2. Paper-and-pencil tests generate products (student responses) that are easily stored and are therefore readily accessible for later analysis or review, if and when marking procedures are questioned.
3. Paper-and-pencil tests can be used equally well to sample a broad scope of a student's knowledge or to probe deeply into a single area.

These advantages have made many teachers reluctant to deviate from this form of evaluation, even when legitimate alternatives exist. It is true that paper-and-pencil tests can provide reliable and objective evaluation data. It is equally true, however, that you must attempt to evaluate a whole that is greater than the sum of a series of test scores.

Alternatives to paper-and-pencil tests include more frequent use of demonstrations and products. If you devise activities that call for the synthesis and application of a number of subsidiary skills, and if students can demonstrate those skills through the construction of a product, sound evidence has been produced to evaluate required objectives. In addition to skill-oriented classes—sewing, for instance, in which each student constructs a garment—academic classes offer unique opportunities for such efforts; for example, an economics class might offer an opportunity for students to build and manipulate their own hypothetical stock portfolio. Student development of tape-slide programs, booklets, instructional packages, school-to-school projects, community projects, models, and class presentations are other possibilities.

It is apparent that it is easier to use demonstrations and products to evaluate student efforts in some courses than it is in others. Remember, however, that demonstrations and products represent ways for students to begin to apply what they have learned. If you cannot suggest practical applications for many of the skills you expect students to master, then a reconsideration of those skills may be in order. No teacher wishes to be accused of teaching content and skills that are irrelevant.

Frequency

The optimum frequency for evaluation varies with specific circumstances. The reliability of grades is endangered if decisions are based on only one or two evaluations. Giving too many tests, however, has the effect of emphasizing the wrong aspect of the teaching-learning process. A balance between too few evaluations and too many is necessary. Using a variety of evaluation forms (paper-and-pencil tests, demonstrations, and products) helps provide students with the information they need to guide their learning and can also provide you with the information needed to plan future lessons without upsetting the balance.

In addition to formal evaluations, it is important to provide students with informal evaluations (such as comments, corrected homework, and self-assessable activities) to provide feedback as often as possible. The more input students receive as they practice skills, the more able they are to correct errors. These informal evaluations can assist in the task of student assessment without alienating the student, especially if students are provided with positive reinforcement for good points in their work.

Purpose

One basic reason for evaluating students is to acquire accurate data concerning the skills and knowledge they have acquired and the proficiency with which they can demonstrate that skill and knowledge. Besides the teacher, students, parents, administrators, counselors, prospective employers, and admissions officers of colleges and universities may, at one time or another, need such data. If you bias those data for any reason, they become invalid and discredit the whole evaluation program. The potential anger, frustration, and heartache that students might undergo because you failed to evaluate their achievements, or lack of achievements, accurately is cause enough to insist that evaluations be conducted with rigor and professionalism.

If a fundamental purpose of evaluation programs is to acquire accurate data concerning students' achievements, this implies not only scholastic achievements, but improvements (or regression) in other areas such as dependability, honesty, effort, and citizenship. An often-neglected point is the importance of evaluating each characteristic or achievement separately and not clouding the issue by allowing one variable to bias another. If you intend to evaluate achievement, then you should evaluate achievement; if the area of concern is effort or dependability, then the focus should be on those things. *One judgment should not influence the other.* Attempting to use any evaluation procedure for something other than what it was designed for specifically is a misuse of that procedure and will yield little, if any, useful information; it can, however, do a great deal of harm.

When dealing with the problem of how to reward the bright but lazy students or the slow but hardworking students, you must be completely honest with each student concerning his or her actual achievements. At the same time, however, you can be equally honest in conveying your perceptions of the amount of effort each put forth and the effect that attitude can have on future undertakings. If each student must be given an achievement grade, the grading should be done on the basis of demonstrated achievement alone, but you need not hesitate to supplement that grade with additional, relevant data concerning demonstrated effort and/or possibilities for profitable remedial instruction.

Throughout this chapter the term "evaluation" is meant to include not only the computation of a student's test scores but also more nebulous factors, such as effort, dependability, and so on. The crucial point to remember is that the grade must reflect *only* the student's demonstrated achievements; the other aspects (e.g., effort, dependability) that make up the total evaluation must be reported as the separate factors they are.

Review

When thinking about the evaluation and grading of students, you should consider at least these four essentials:

1. *Honesty.* Both you and your students should know, prior to the beginning of instruction, the exact basis upon which they will be evaluated. This knowledge will enable students to focus their efforts on the most important matters and will help keep extraneous factors from clouding evaluation data.

2. *Variety.* Students should be given the opportunity to demonstrate their achievements not only by means of paper-and-pencil tests, but by other means as well, particularly by the accomplishment of those culminating activities that synthesize subsidiary skills and knowledge.

3. *Frequency.* All students need formal feedback concerning their progress given at logical intervals as close to the practice period as possible. The more feedback students receive, the more likely they are to improve their skills and finally to succeed.

4. *Purpose.* All students have the right to receive accurate evaluation data concerning their achievements and equally accurate data concerning your perceptions of other variables such as effort, dependability, and citizenship. Each variable, however, should be evaluated and reported as the separate and distinct entity it is.

These principles are most effective when you are able to construct, administer, interpret, and report the results of evaluation instruments properly.

RELIABILITY AND VALIDITY

There are two terms with which you should become familiar when dealing with evaluation: *reliability* and *validity*. They are referred to throughout this chapter with the specific definitions that follow in mind.

Reliability is an index of how consistently a device measures whatever it measures. Elaborate statistical procedures have been developed for determining the reliability of norm-referenced paper-and-pencil tests. It is useful to think of reliability as a measure of the probability that a student would achieve the same score if he or she were to repeat a particular test, or how close the two scores would be if the student took two equivalent forms of a test. Another way of viewing reliability is to think of test results for a class of students with the scores ordered from best to worst. If, after some time elapsed, all the students were to retake the test and receive a score placing them in the same relative order, the test would be reliable. The key to reliability is how *consistently* students score on similar forms or repeated tests, or how consistently they score in relation to each other.

There are several types of validity. The validity with which classroom teachers are most concerned is *content validity*. This simply means that the evaluation instrument is valid when it measures what the teacher wishes it to measure, namely the amount of content or the proficiency of skills learned in class. Many extraneous factors can cloud the determination of content validity. For example, if you have engaged in straight lecture and have then asked the class to answer rigorous analytical questions on an essay test, the students may do poorly. Since there was no practice of analytic skill (only the giving of information during the lecture), the content validity of the test may be in question.[1]

Predictive validity is a measure of how well a student will do on a later task or on a test based upon his or her score on a preliminary measure. The higher the correlation between the two measures, the higher the predictive validity.

CRITERION- VERSUS NORM-REFERENCED TESTS

Evaluating students to determine their abilities relative to objectives involves comparing each student's performance with certain preset standards or criteria. This kind of evaluation is known as *criterion-referenced evaluation* and is an integral part of the use of precise instructional objectives. Because the purpose of this evaluation is to determine who can demonstrate specific competencies, precise instructional objectives are stated, and these objectives include the evaluation criteria. The evaluation becomes a matter of observing who can and who cannot achieve the minimum acceptable standards.

Criterion-referenced evaluation usually does not provide *comparative* evaluation data, however, and these data are often desired. Ours is largely a competitive society, and it is commonly asked not only what people can do, but also how well they can do it in comparison with others. To get these kinds of data each student's performance must be compared with the average performance of those students with whom he or she has certain similarities (such as age or grade level). This comparison group is known as a norming group, and this type of evaluation is known as *norm-referenced evaluation*.

Much might be said about norm-referenced tests. Their reliability, for instance, tends to increase with the size of the norming group and with the generality of the skills and knowledge being evaluated. Norm-referenced and criterion-referenced tests may often seem to be almost identical. There is, however, a subtle difference. Norm-referenced tests are most powerful when there is a wide disparity among the test scores. To achieve this, norm-referenced tests contain items that range in difficulty from the nearly impossible to the very simple, and it often happens that the items at both extremes have little relationship to the original instructional intent.

[1]See Walter Pierce and Howard Getz, "Relationships Among Teaching, Cognitive Levels, Testing and IQ," *Illinois School Research*, 6, no. 2 (Winter 1973), 27–31.

Many such items are included more to differentiate between students than to differentiate between those who can and cannot demonstrate specified competencies. In criterion-referenced tests there is no attempt to achieve a spread in the test scores, so items tend to be of equal difficulty and the focus is on validity so as to obtain an accurate reflection of the original instructional intent.

PAPER-AND-PENCIL TESTS

Teacher-Made Objective Tests

Perhaps the most popular form of teacher-made paper-and-pencil tests is the objective test. Multiple-choice, true-false, matching, and completion items are all varieties of a basic test form that requires students to select or construct a response from a given, or very limited, range of options.

One of the many reasons for the popularity of objective tests is their ability to sample a broad range of knowledge at one time. Rather than concentrating on just one or two questions (which might be the "wrong" questions for a particular student), objective tests ask a relatively large number of questions about a number of different aspects of any given topic. The larger the number of questions and the range of the information covered, the higher the chance to obtain reliable test scores. Proponents of objective tests also point out that they are relatively easy to score and minimize the number of value judgments teachers have to make when assigning grades.

There are also a number of disadvantages associated with objective tests. Some educators point out that objective tests can emphasize the memorization of bits and pieces of information. They claim that students often do very well on the basis of memorizing and recognizing these bits and pieces even though they may have no idea of the relationship of the parts to a larger whole. In addition, constructing items for objective tests is time consuming, and even though you may work hard to construct good items, it is not uncommon to find that some questions still confuse students.

Considering all the pros and cons, many teachers have concluded that their own objective tests meet some of their evaluation needs better than any other means, especially when they wish to sample students' general knowledge about some topic. Typical objectives for objective tests might include the following.

1. You will recall and apply information about the steel industry, from mining through smelting and product production, well enough to achieve a score of at least 80 percent on a multiple-choice test dealing with this information.

2. You will, given a wiring diagram containing numbered connections, place a check before the numbers of all incorrect or superfluous connections.

Important general rules can be followed that will help you to build and administer valid and reliable objective tests.

1. *Keep the language simple.* Unless the purpose of the test is to survey the extent of students' vocabularies, there is no point in using words that are unfamiliar to students or in phrasing questions so they are difficult to understand. Students will be justifiably angry and frustrated if they get answers wrong because they could not understand what was being asked rather than because they did not know the right answer. Compare the following two examples:

A. The physical relationship between most petroleum products and most purely aqueous solutions is generally such that physical interaction and diffusion of the two is severely limited. (1) True, (2) False.

B. As a general rule, oil and water do not mix. (1) True, (2) False.

The only justifiable reason for using example A is if you were attempting to check students' vocabulary. Ask questions as simply and concisely as possible to help ensure valid and reliable test results.

2. *Ask students to apply, rather than simply to recall, information.* If students can apply the information they learned, it is a safe bet they have committed it to memory. It does not follow, however, that simply because students have memorized information they can also apply it. This being the case, you would be wise to aim questions at application rather than simple recall. Consider the following two examples:

C. The area of a rectangle is found by multiplying the length by the width. (1) True, (2) False.

D. A rectangle 2′ × 4′ has an area of 8 square feet. (1) True, (2) False.

The computation involved in example B is not difficult, and yet it enables students to apply what they learned and thus emphasizes learning for the sake of practical application rather than learning for the sake of passing tests.

3. *Make sure that each item is independent.* Check questions to be sure that one question does not provide a clue to some other question or that the answer to one question is not crucial to the answer of another. Both situations decrease the reliability of the test results. For example,

E. The number of square feet in a room 9′ × 12′ is (1) 3, (2) 21, (3) 81, (4) 108, (5) 144.

F.   At $2 a square foot, what would it cost to carpet the room described in question E? (1) $6, (2) $42, (3) $162, (4) $216, (5) $288.

Given these two questions, any student who missed E would almost certainly miss F. Other than having the student miss two items instead of just one, nothing was gained by linking the questions. It would have been more advantageous if questions E and F had been combined, for example, "How much would it cost to carpet a room 9′ × 12′ if carpeting costs $2 a square foot?" and the extra space used for a separate and distinct item.

4. *Do not establish or follow a pattern for correct responses.* Regardless of how clever an answer pattern is, some student will eventually discover it and compromise the test results. The problems involved with detecting compromised tests and doing something about them are far greater than any possible advantage to patterning responses.

5. *Do not include trick or trivial questions on tests.* Sometimes teachers are tempted to ask questions that require extended effort for correct interpretation or that deal with unimportant points. This temptation may stem from being unable to build items as quickly as one would like or from a desire to assure a wide spread among test scores. Trick or trivial questions not only reduce the validity and reliability of tests, but they may have a powerful negative effect if they antagonize students.

6. *Do not answer questions after the test has started unless it is done publicly.* Sometimes individual students will seek further clarification of a question as they work through the test. If additional information is provided to that student, the test results may be biased since that student will have had access to direct help when others did not. It is wise to make a general announcement prior to each test concerning your reluctance to answer questions during a test. This, plus careful proofreading of tests prior to their administration, should forestall most questions. If it does become necessary to answer a question about some test item, assume that other students may be equally confused about it and call everyone's attention to the clarification. Remember, however, that interrupting students during a test destroys their train of thought and thus should be avoided whenever possible.

In addition to these few general rules, other considerations relevant to the construction of specific kinds of objective test items are presented in the paragraphs that follow.

Multiple-Choice Items   Multiple-choice items are particularly useful because they can be used easily to sample cognitive skills ranging from simple recall through analysis. The following examples illustrate several levels of cognitive thought:

G. Which should have the ultimate responsibility for adapting precise instructional objectives?
   (1)   Curriculum specialists
   (2)   Teachers
   (3)   Principals
   (4)   Textbook publishers
   (5)   Student/administration committees

APPLICATION SAMPLE

H. The scores on a test were 95, 90, 90, 85, 70, 60, 0. What is the mode?
   (1)   90
   (2)   85
   (3)   81.66
   (4)   70
   (5)   47.5

ANALYSIS SAMPLE

I. A teacher suspected a particular student of storing drugs in his locker. Staying late one day the teacher forced open the student's locker, found drugs, and turned them over to the principal. In a later trial, the case against the student was dismissed because the evidence (the drugs) had been acquired illegally. What *should* the teacher have done?
   (1)   Gotten a key to open the student's locker.
   (2)   Turned the drugs over to the police.
   (3)   Searched the locker and then, if he found drugs, called the police immediately.
   (4)   Asked the principal, student, student's parents, and the police to be present when the locker was opened.
   (5)   Asked the principal and another teacher to be present when the locker was opened and photographed its contents immediately.

PRINCIPLES FOR BUILDING MULTIPLE-CHOICE ITEMS

1. *Put as much of the item as possible into the stem.* The "stem" of a multiple-choice question is that part that asks the question or states the problem. If the stem does its job properly, it gives the student an idea of what is sought before reading the options. Consider the following two examples.

   J. John Adams was
      (1)   the second president of the United States.
      (2)   the third president of the United States.
      (3)   the fourth president of the United States.
      (4)   none of the above.
   K. The second president of the United States was
      (1)   John Adams.
      (2)   Thomas Jefferson.
      (3)   James Madison.
      (4)   none of the above.

In example J, the students do not know what is sought until they have read the options. Furthermore, because it is necessary to repeat the same words in each option, the student must spend more time reading. Both points make for inefficient testing.

In example K, the options are shorter than the stem (which is, in itself, a good guide), the stem clearly and concisely asks the question, and it provides sufficient data to help the student start thinking about the correct answer.

2. *Make options reasonable.* In norm-referenced tests, the teacher attempts to discriminate among students. This discrimination process is facilitated by ensuring that all options seem reasonable to someone who is unsure of the exact information. Option 4 in example J and K, for instance, may not be very useful since most students are aware that John Adams was one of our early presidents. Even though students may not be sure just which president Adams was, they could still eliminate option 4 and thus increase the chance of guessing correctly from among the remaining options. One way to construct good options is based on the type of error students are most likely to make. In the application sample on page 137, for instance, the second option is the median, the third is the mean of the three middle scores, the fourth is the mean, and the fifth is the mean of the highest and lowest scores. To someone who was unclear about measures of central tendency, any of these options might seem reasonable. The advantage to this tactic is that the student's *incorrect* response can be used to diagnose the source of difficulties.

3. *Make sure that unintentional clues are not provided.* It sometimes happens that an option can be eliminated simply because it is grammatically incorrect. If, for example, the stem of an item is of the completion variety, and the last word is "an," students can safely ignore any option beginning with a consonant. Similarly, incorrect tenses or forms of words can provide clues, as can correct options that are consistently longer or shorter than the incorrect options. The use of "always" or "never" is frequently a giveaway, as is the use of "all of the above" or "none of the above" if they are used simply as fillers. Careful proofreading of each stem along with each of its options can eliminate many of these unintentional clues and help make tests more reliable. The following item is an example of a grammatical giveaway.

L. Factual recall is best checked through the use of an
   (1) objective test.
   (2) short-answer test.
   (3) matching text.
   (4) subjective test.

Multiple-choice items lend themselves particularly well to improvement via a technique known as an item analysis. To use this technique, first make a count of how many times each foil (possible answer) was selected and then look at the response pattern. If more than 60 percent of your students got a particular item wrong, it is likely that you failed to make that particular point clear or failed to stress it enough. This is especially true if the majority of students selected the same incorrect foil. You would probably want to go back and reemphasize the correct information. On the other hand, if more than 60 percent of your students got an item right, you could congratulate yourself on some well-done instruction and then consider replacing the question with one of greater complexity.

The item analysis will also tell you if some of your foils are ineffective. Ideally, each foil should look equally appealing to a student who is just guessing at the correct answer. If the item analysis reveals that some foils are never selected by any students, then those foils are useless and should be replaced by others that will appear more reasonable and therefore more appealing.

True-False Items   True-false items are often singled out as prime examples of the superficiality of objective testing, and often they stand justly accused. Because true-false items seem so easy to write, many teachers rely heavily upon them and forget that they are most appropriate for the lower-level cognitive skills. Keep in mind that a student who has no idea of the correct answer still has a 50:50 chance of guessing correctly. Although true-false items are often misused, it is possible to exercise the needed care to construct true-false items that sample cognitive skills as high as the analysis level. Consider the following examples.

RECALL SAMPLE

M. In the United States, FORTRAN is one of the most common computer programming languages. (1) True, (2) False.

APPLICATION SAMPLE

N. A man earning $250 a week would earn $13,000 a year if he worked each week. (1) True, (2) False.

ANALYSIS SAMPLE

O. If every school system were given its own computer, the most difficult problems currently limiting wider use of computer-assisted instruction would be solved. (1) True, (2) False.

Even though it is possible to write true-false items at various levels of the cognitive domain, it is still questionable whether the time required to write such items is well spent considering that other kinds of items could sample the same cognitive levels without requiring as much preparation time. Here are a few points to keep in mind when writing true-false items.

1. *Be sure that every item is definitely true or definitely false.*
2. *Whenever possible, avoid terms such as "generally" and "usually."* These terms, while not as obvious giveaways as "always" and "never," are still open to varying interpretations.
3. *Be sure that items are not dependent upon insignificant facts.* Make sure that each item asks something of importance and worth remembering.
4. *Be sure that correct items are not consistently longer or shorter than incorrect items.*
5. *Avoid the use of double negatives, but if you use any negative at all, call attention to it by underlining or capitalizing it.*

Matching Items   Matching items are used most easily to measure low-level cognitive skills such as recall and comprehension. A typical matching test might ask students to link people with events or dates. Variations include asking students to match terms with numbers on a diagram or to match labels for a chart, graph, or map in which such labels have been replaced by letters or numbers. Guidelines for the construction of matching items follow.

1. *Keep the number of items to be matched short.* If students are required to search through more than ten or so items as they respond to each question, they will spend valuable time just searching. Their time would be better spent responding to another series of items in another question.

2. *Make sure that all items concern one topic.* Unless all items are concerned with one topic, students can simply eliminate some options as being irrelevant to some questions. This reduces the reliability of the test.

3. *Include more possible answers than questions and/or stipulate that some answers can be used more than once.* These steps will also help prevent students from getting right answers purely by eliminating some options.

4. *Arrange the options in some logical order such as chronological or alphabetical.* This will make it easier for students to search through the options and will help avoid providing unintentional clues.

Completion Items   Completion items depend almost entirely upon the student's ability to recall a key word or phrase. Since most secondary school teachers are after more than rote memorization, generally completion items are not used as frequently as are other kinds of objectives test items. Here are some points to keep in mind if completion items are written.

1. *Write items that can be completed with a single word or a short phrase.* There is a difference between a completion item and an essay exam. When students are required to "fill in" more than a few words, the grading of the item is complicated and it ceases to be a completion item.

2. *Be sure that only one word or phrase can correctly complete the sentence.* In a phrase such as, "The first World War began in _____" either a date or the name of a country could correctly be used. Guard against this common error by trying different words or phrases to see if there are correct alternatives. Revise each item until only the one word or phrase sought can be used correctly.

3. *Put the blanks near the end of the sentence so the student is guided toward the correct response.*

4. *Make all the blanks the same length.* Sometimes unintentional clues are provided when teachers try to make the size of the blanks correspond to the size of the word or phrase to be inserted. The items should be clear enough to make this kind of clue unnecessary.

5. *Do not put more than two blanks in any one item.* The more blanks in the item, the greater the chance the student will be unable to determine just what is sought.

Although there is considerable overlap, the following chart helps to illustrate the types of test items that are usually most appropriate with specific types of precise instructional objectives. Keep in mind that the overlap exists because different kinds of test items *can* be written to sample almost any behavior. The following chart is simply illustrative.

OBJECTIVE	POSSIBLE TEST ITEM
1. List, in writing, two distinguishing characteristics of a republic. (Knowledge)	1. Two distinguishing characteristics of a republic are (1) _____, (2) _____.
2. Given a graph and a series of statements relating to the data presented, label all the incorrect statements. (Comprehension)	2. According to graph A, the greatest production of thingamagigs occurred in 1783. (1) True, (2) False.
3. Given word problems involving the derivation of cost per yard, label the correct solution to at least 80 percent of the problems. (Application)	3. At $10 per square yard, how much will it cost to carpet a room 9' × 9'? (a) $810 (b) $90 (c) $890 (d) $270 (e) none of the above
4. Given a wiring diagram with various circuits showing specific colors, match the outcome of power input to any given circuit and its result. (Analysis)	4. Power input in this circuit (input column) will cause this output (output column).

	Input	*Output*
	red	ring bell
	blue	blow horn
	green	light bulb
	yellow	turn on fan, start motor

Objective Tests—A Final Word   This section has outlined procedures helpful in the construction of objective tests. Of particular importance is the fact that objective test items should be constructed so they are stated clearly and concisely. Item construction time tends to increase as items are designed to measure successively higher levels of cognitive skills.

Although they are called "objective" tests because of the objectivity inherent in their grading, it would be foolish to maintain that objective tests are as objective as the term implies. You still make important subjective decisions about what questions to ask and how to ask them, and unless those decisions are based on the originally stated instructional objectives, "objective" tests will not be very objective.

Teacher-Made Essay Tests

Essay tests represent a second kind of teacher-made evaluation device. The greatest single advantage of essay tests is that they require students to synthesize a response and, in so doing, to demonstrate not only their understanding of the relationships among bits and pieces of information but also their understanding of the body of information as a whole. Essays allow you to call upon students to interpret, evaluate, and organize data; draw conclusions; make inferences; and express their thoughts coherently. This makes the essay test useful in assessing higher-level cognitive skills such as synthesis and evaluation.

Offsetting these strong points are a number of disadvantages.

1.   Teacher fatigue, subconscious biases, and other extraneous variables can affect students' grades.
2.   Essay tests are inherently biased in favor of those students who can write quickly, neatly, and effectively.
3.   Essay tests are often low in reliability and validity since only a few questions are asked and a student may, by chance, be asked questions about which he or she happens to know a great deal (or very little).
4.   Essay tests take a longer time to grade than do other types of evaluations.

Other problems, particularly those concerning reliable grading, can be avoided or minimized by following definite procedures in the construction and grading of the tests.

1. *Be definitive about what is expected from students.* As test items are formulated, keep in mind the types of thought processes in which students are to engage, and the types of points that should be included in their responses. Consider the following two examples.

P.   Describe the "water cycle," including the cause-effect relationships among the various phases.
Q.   Identify three problems associated with mandatory public education and explain how these problems might be eliminated or lessened.

Example P requires more precise information than does example Q and may only be checking student comprehension. It may be more efficient to check student comprehension by an objective test.

In example Q, students are expected to demonstrate greater originality than in example P, so this item is better suited for an essay test.

2. *Describe the task clearly.* Examples P and Q describe clearly what the student is to do. They provide sufficient direction so that if the student has the necessary information he or she would be able to formulate acceptable answers. Compare the preceding two examples with the following two examples.

R.   Discuss the effects of World War II.
S.   State your opinion concerning East-West détente.

Example R provides so little direction that students would not be able to formulate precise answers. Some students might concentrate upon the military effects, others on the social effects, others on the technological effects. The structure of the question is too broad. Depending upon the teacher's intent, some students would find they had included some of the appropriate information while others would find they had not—even though all might have been able to formulate acceptable answers had they known more precisely what the teacher wished.

Example S presents a similar problem. Unless you specify prior to the test the exact grading criteria, you should give full credit for any given answer. How can it be argued, for example, that a student's answer did not represent an opinion? When you ask general questions you must be prepared to accept general answers.

3. *Make sure that students have sufficient time and materials to do the job.* One strength of essay tests is the opportunity they provide to students to analyze relationships among points within a topic or problem and then formulate responses by synthesizing the information they possess. This process is much more time consuming than responding to objective test items, and students must have sufficient time to analyze the items, perhaps outline their answer, and then write it legibly. If students are unduly pressed for time, their responses may not be as true a reflection of their abilities as they might otherwise have been.

A practical way to estimate the amount of time to allow students for each item is for you to time yourself as you write an acceptable response and use this base to allow students additional time. This procedure provides not only a good estimate of how many items to which students can reasonably be expected to respond but also a model response against which student responses can be compared.

Many teachers find it easier to read responses that are written in ink on lined paper. Other teachers prefer to have students write their answers on the same sheet containing the questions.

4. *Grade papers anonymously.* Sometimes, when evaluators know the author of a paper, it can bias the evaluation. Conscientious teachers for example, may often be able to identify many students from handwriting samples. This possibility can be minimized by using procedures that make it possible to ignore the names on the papers, one of which is to use code numbers on papers rather than names.

5. *Compare each response with a model or a list of crucial points.* There is a tendency, after having graded a few responses, to begin comparing those read later with those read previously, rather than comparing them with the model answer or to a list of important points. This tendency can be minimized by making continuous references to the model response or list of crucial points. This is essential when using the essay test as a criterion-referenced measure.

6. *When possible, use more than one evaluator and then average the grades.* Greater reliability can be achieved if more than one evaluator is used and the separate evaluations are averaged.

7. *Avoid mixing essay items and objective tests items on the same test.* The intellectual operations required to synthesize a response to an essay item are significantly different from those required to select a response to an objective test item, and to expect students to demonstrate both kinds of cognitive skills within a single class period may be expecting too much.

Quick Reference Guidelines— Teacher-Made Tests

OBJECTIVE TESTS

  I. Advantages
   A. Provide a broad sampling of students' knowledge.
   B. Present the same problems and the same alternatives to each student.
   C. Minimize the chance of student bluffing.
   D. Permit rapid scoring with little or no need for subjective decisions.
   E. Permit items to be improved on the basis of item analysis.
   F. Permit increased reliability through item improvement.
 II. Disadvantages
   A. Present difficulties in assessing some cognitive skills, such as synthesis and creativity.
   B. Increase the possibility of guessing.
   C. Require a relatively long time to construct items.
III. Utilization Factors
   A. Construction and administration
    1. Keep the language simple.
    2. Ask students to apply rather than simply recall information.
    3. Make sure that each item is independent.
    4. Do not establish or follow a pattern for correct responses.
    5. Do not include trick or trivial questions.

      6. Do not answer questions after the test has started unless you do so publicly.
- B. Multiple-choice items
  1. Put as much of the item as possible into the stem.
  2. Make all options reasonable.
  3. Do not provide unintentional clues.
  4. Avoid the use of all-inclusive or all-exclusive terms.
- C. True-false items
  1. Be sure that each item is definitely true or definitely false.
  2. Avoid the use of all-inclusive or all-exclusive terms.
  3. Be sure that items are not dependent upon insignificant facts.
  4. Be sure that true items are not consistently longer or shorter than false items.
  5. Avoid the use of double negatives and call attention to single negatives by underlining or capitalizing the negative word.
- D. Matching items
  1. Limit the number of items to be matched to ten or less.
  2. Make sure that all items concern one topic.
  3. Have more answers than questions or stipulate that some answers can be used more than once.
  4. Arrange options in some logical order.
- E. Completion Items
  1. Write items that can be completed with a single word or a short phrase.
  2. Be sure that only one word or phrase can correctly complete the sentence.
  3. Put the blanks near the end of the sentences.
  4. Make all blanks the same length.
  5. Do not put more than two blanks in any one item.

ESSAY TESTS

- I. Advantages
  - A. Emphasize high-level cognitive skills, such as synthesis and evaluation.
  - B. Provide an in-depth sampling of students' knowledge of a specific topic.
  - C. Allow for student creativity, analysis, and synthesis skill assessment.
  - D. Easier to construct than objective tests.
- II. Disadvantages
  - A. Reduce reliability and validity compared with objective tests.
  - B. Create bias in favor of those students who write well.
  - C. Make grading time-consuming.
  - D. Increase possibility of bluffing.
- III. Utilization Factors
  - A. Be definitive about what you expect from students.
  - B. Make sure that students have sufficient time and materials to do the job.
  - C. Grade papers as anonymously as possible.
  - D. Compare each response with a model response or a list of crucial points.
  - E. When possible, have tests checked by more than one evaluator and average the grades.
  - F. Do not mix essay items and objective items on the same test.

Validity and Use
of Teacher-Made Tests

Teacher-made essay and objective tests deserve emphasis because you, better than anyone else, know what the instructional objectives were and what kinds of questions need to be asked to determine whether the objectives have been achieved. Hence, you determine whether content validity of the evaluation exists.

Both essay tests and objective tests can be used prior to instruction (to determine students' existing abilities), during instruction (to check on progress and determine areas of strengths and weaknesses), and after instruction (to determine final achievement). Well-constructed teacher-made tests, if tailored to precise needs, can be a key tool to help improve the teaching-learning process.

STANDARDIZED TESTS

Standardized tests are usually constructed by commercial test producers. Each item that appears on a standardized test has generally been checked carefully to assure that it (1) is appropriate in difficulty for a particular, described population, (2) has high discrimination power (spreads the scores), (3) has a high reliability index, and (4) has a good biserial correlation (students who score well on the test tend to get any given item correct, and students who score low tend to get any given item wrong). Standardized tests usually come with a detailed set of instructions for administration and can often be machine scored.

Appropriate "norms" are included to facilitate the interpretation of scores. Test "norms" are averages against which individual scores can be compared. In the case of most standardized tests, these norms are derived by averaging the scores of a wide sampling of students all having in common some characteristic such as age or grade level. The large size of the norming groups helps eliminate gross distortions caused by extreme scores, thus making the norms rather stable measures. Additional information relevant to the norms (such as the test's standard error, standard deviation, and standard scores) also help make score interpretation more valid.

For test manufacturers to stay in business, they must produce tests that are not only reliable but also attractive to large numbers of prospective users. One characteristic of standardized tests that contributes to their reliability and attractiveness is their generality. Most standardized tests concern themselves with general kinds of skills and knowledge, thereby enabling measurement experts to construct items that provide a reliable survey of that skill or topic as a whole.

Since standardized tests are *general* measures, they are often not appropriate for use in measuring achievement of specific instructional objectives. It is unlikely that a standardized test will emphasize the exact content you are emphasizing, and therefore the test's content validity may be questioned. It would be foolish for you to assume that your efforts were wasted simply because your students did not do well on a standardized test. To determine whether students achieved stated objectives, it is usually necessary to use teacher-made, not standardized, tests. The former are specific measures, the latter, general ones. When the purpose of the test is to compare the student with a large population in a broad content area, standardized tests may be in order.

Types of Standardized Tests

Standardized tests usually measure general intelligence, achievement, aptitude, or interest. A brief description of each follows.

Intelligence Tests   Intelligence is an ambiguous term often defined by phrases such as "mental abilities," "capacity to learn," and "the ability to cope successfully with new situations." Most intelligence tests require the person being tested to solve a series of previously unseen problems by manipulating factual information, perceiving relationships, making generalizations, and applying other cognitive skills.

Intelligence tests can be administered on either an individual or a group basis. Individual tests, such as the *Stanford–Binet Intelligence Scale* and the *Wechsler Intelligence Scales*, tend to be more reliable than the group tests, but because they require one test administrator for every person being tested, they also tend to be more expensive and more time consuming.[2] Group tests, such as the *Otis Quick-Scoring Mental Ability Test* and the *Lorge–Thorndike Intelligence Tests*, while somewhat less reliable than the individual tests, still have good predictive validity and are much more commonly used.

When looking at an individual's IQ score you should remember that (1) "intelligence" has no precise definition and therefore cannot be measured precisely, (2) most intelligence tests are verbally oriented and culturally biased, and (3) they cannot be interpreted without understanding a statistic called a "standard error" included in score interpretation data. The standard error is intended to be used to construct an interval into which the student's "true" score would be likely to fall. For example, if a student's IQ score is 100 and the standard error is 10, it is commonly interpreted to mean that there are about two chances in three that the student's IQ is between 90 and 110. This is considerably different from stating that the IQ is exactly 100.

---

[2]Further data on the instruments included in this section may be obtained by referring to Oscar Buros, ed., *Mental Measurement Yearbook, Seventh Edition* (Highland Park,, N.J.: Gryphon Press, 1972).

Achievement Tests   Achievement tests are focused more narrowly than are intelligence tests. Intelligence tests function by posing problems and giving individuals the freedom to integrate whatever skills and knowledge they have at their command to solve those problems. Little effort is made to test the individuals' abilities in any specific subject area. The intention of the achievement test is somewhat different. Achievement tests specify particular subject areas (such as mathematics, reading, and language) and then test students' abilities in each of those areas by providing appropriate subtests.

Test manufacturers intend their tests to evaluate content achievement, but they are faced with the complex problem of attaining reliability, discrimination, and good biserial correlations and consequently are in a peculiar position. The more precise and detailed the questions that are asked, the farther the test may get from a particular school's instructional objectives, the lower the content validity will become, and the less likely will be the purchase of the test by large numbers of schools. On the other hand, if the manufacturers use a minimum of detailed facts and depend upon those concepts that are common knowledge, they must depend more upon analytical skills to achieve statistical goals. With this dilemma in mind, it is not hard to understand why the results of achievement tests and IQ tests will often correlate highly. Both tend to emphasize general data widely accepted as "important."

Although achievement tests deal with more specific areas than do intelligence tests, their scores are *not* necessarily more precise. Both kinds of scores are best thought of as estimates, both can be affectd by variables such as student illness, tension, and distraction, and both need to be interpreted in light of specific students and objectives. Some educators have found that achievement test scores can be made more useful if they are compared with norms constructed for a specific school rather than with national norms. There is an inherent danger in using scores from any standardized test as the sole criterion for establishing expectations of individual students or for making decisions about them.

Some of the commonly used achievement tests include the *California Achievement Tests*, the *Metropolitan Achievement Tests*, and the *Iowa Tests of Educational Development*.

Aptitude Test   Whereas achievement tests focus on what students have already achieved, aptitude tests focus on their potential for future development. Aptitude tests function by grouping into occupationally oriented categories those items designed to measure specific abilities. For example, one of the most commonly used aptitude tests, the *Differential Aptitude Test Battery*, includes items involving verbal reasoning, numerical ability, abstract reasoning, space relationships, mechanical reasoning, clerical speed and accuracy, and language usage. Another commonly used aptitude test, the *General Aptitude Test Battery*, includes items involving vocabulary skills, numerical ability, spatial relations, form perception, clerical perception, motor coordination, manual dexterity, and finger dexterity. By evaluating the results of such tests, guidance personnel are able to suggest vocational fields in which students are most likely to experience success. Some fields, such as music and art, require unique kinds of abilities for success, and specific aptitude tests have been developed that focus very narrowly on those abilities.

It should be noted that few aptitude tests are known for their high predictive validity. It is not uncommon for a student who has shown a low aptitude in some area later to become interested in that area and go on to become highly successful in it. The importance of the student's own goals should never be minimized.

Interest Inventories   Most interest inventories are similar to aptitude tests in that they are oriented vocationally. However, whereas most aptitude tests function by sampling specific kinds of skills, most interest inventories function by sampling student attitudes toward particular kinds of activities. Since students' likes and dislikes are subject to more rapid changes than are their abilities, interest inventories are generally regarded as less valid predictors than are either achievement tests or aptitude tests.

The most commonly used interest inventories include the *Kuder Preference Records*, the *Strong Vocational Interest Blanks*, and and the *Thurstone Interest Schedule*.

General Utilization Factors

When using standardized tests, two points should be kept in mind. First, all test administration directions must be followed explicitly. The generally high reliability of standardized tests stems partly from the fact that all students who take the test do so under conditions as nearly alike as possible. Every student is provided with the same materials and environment and is given the same amount of time in which to complete various sections of the test. As a general rule, students' scores will become less reliable to the degree that testing conditions are allowed to vary.

And, second, although a good deal of time, money, and expert help were probably used to construct, refine, and norm any given standardized test, the score a student earns on that test still reflects only a sample of ability. To avoid making foolish, unfortunate, and even tragic decisions concerning any individual, it is imperative to obtain as much and as varied data as possible. Standardized tests provide just one input.

ALTERNATE EVALUATION PROCEDURES

Once you begin to use specific objectives and focus on the ultimate skills, students will be able to demonstrate, paper-and-pencil tests may receive less emphasis. There are few instances in which being able to pass a test is the ultimate reason for learning. Because the use of precise instructional objectives can increase the use of evaluation devices other than formal paper-and-pencil tests, and because these "alternative procedures" lend themselves so well to the evaluation of individual performance, the issue of how to make these alternative evaluation procedures valid and reliable needs examination. The following points can assist in building alternative evaluation procedures that will withstand critical scrutiny.

1. *Specify standards clearly.* Since spelling out standards clearly is so critical, it is reemphasized here. As an illustration, consider the following objectives. Each involves a student construction, but in each case the product is less important than the cognitive skills necessary for its construction. You will be able to:

A. Write a "mailable" one-page letter to a company or politician in which some problem is delineated, a desired course of action is outlined, and supporting rationales for that action are given. ("Mailable" is a business term used to denote a letter that is free from errors in spelling, grammar, punctuation, usage, etc., and ready for signature and mailing.)

B. Demonstrate your understanding of "power politics," in part, by assuming the role of leader of some small foreign government and describing, in less than three pages, (1) why some commodity under your control is critical, (2) why your current manipulation of that commodity (its price, availability, or use) is justified, and (3) how you plan to resist pressures to stop such manipulations.

C. Construct a 2' × 3' poster designed to sway people's opinion for or against some controversial issue and describe, in less than three pages, how each element (color, message, design, or figure placement) helps make the poster a powerful communicator.

The elements included as part of the minimum acceptable standards for these objectives partially spell out the criteria to be used in assessing achievement, and in each case the "product," by itself, is clearly insufficient. The objectives are designed to assess synthesis- and evaluation-level skills and unless students manifest those, they cannot meet all the criteria.

Suppose, however, the student wrote the following letter in response to the first objective.

Dear Sir:

I recently purchased a new Doohicky and it does not work right. Neither the store I purchased it from nor your factory representative accepted responsibility for the Doohicky's malfunction and now I'm tired of fooling with it and want a refund. Unless I get a refund within two weeks, I will turn the issue over to my attorney.

Sincerely yours.

This letter contains all the elements suggested in the objective, and the teacher may be pressed to give the student credit for achieving the objective. On the other hand, the letter leaves room for improvement. What can be done?

2. *Whenever possible, provide a model.* Models are helpful from a number of standpoints. Students will find them helpful because they will have an actual sample of the final product. Regardless of how explicitly written criteria are, actually seeing an acceptable product will help sharpen the student's mental picture of what is expected. The picture can be strengthened further if both good and bad models are provided and explanations of why they are good and bad are included.

Through the use of audio tapes, videotapes, and actual samples, as well as written models, you can provide models for virtually every kind of behavior or product students are to manifest. The possibilties are limited only by the teacher's imagination.

3. *Provide a checklist.* A checklist is really an elaboration of the stated minimum acceptable standards. It will be impossible, in most cases, to specify all important steps or criteria in every objective, but in the case of those objectives calling for the construction of some product, regardless of whether the product is a paper or a paperweight, a checklist can help students. In the case of the sample letter, for example, students could have been given a checklist for writing letters to companies that included items such as, "Did you specify where and when you brought the product and did you explain exactly what your problem was?"

Checklists can function as both instructional and evaluative aids. As instructional aids, checklists provide students with a logical sequence of steps of points that, if followed or included, lead to the development of an acceptable product. As evaluative aids, checklists provide students (and evaluators) with a list of the specific points being sought in the final product, and since checklists can be much more detailed than the standards included in instructional objectives, they can be particularly helpful to students.

Checklists, like models, can be constructed to guide students toward the achievement of virtually every kind of expected behavior. If the checklists are clear enough, there is no reason why they, together with models, cannot be an aid in attaining a reliable grading system that enables you to differentiate between quality levels of students' work. The more you rely on measures of student achievement other than formal paper-and-pencil tests, the more students will see a practical value in what they are learning. What is learned is seldom important in and of itself; its importance stems from how it can be used.

Individual "alternative" forms of evaluation can also be used in concert with one another and with "traditional" forms of evaluation in the formation of specific "contracts" with individual students. A student doing independent study might, for example, contract with you to pass a test for a grade of "C," pass the test and do a report that meets set criteria for a grade of "B," and pass the test, do the report, and make a presentation for a grade of "A." Contracts are useful when you individualize the learning process, and alternative forms of evaluation can provide many appropriate possibilities for the formulation of these contracts.

CALCULATING GRADES

Grade Calculation Schemes

Preset Levels   Most students at some time experience an evaluation system wherein grading standards are preset. In many cases students are given standards such as A = 90–100, B = 80–89, C = 70–79, D = 60–69, and F = anything less than 60. In most cases the standards were set arbitrarily at some "traditional" level. Why do educators use such an arbitrary grading system? For one thing, the determination of grade levels for any objective test is, in the final analysis, a subjective decision, and opinions differ as to which, if any, is *the* best. For another, this particular method is advocated by proponents for two reasons. First, many students and teachers are familiar with having grades calculated on the basis of preset levels and feel comfortable with this system. Grading "on a curve" or by some other method gives the appearance of being less consistent than the preset level method and is thus (in their minds) open to more suspicion. Second, once the grade levels are set, they can remain set. This means that, by constructing tests of varying difficulty, you can control grades. The preset level grading method does not contain any built-in mechanism to guarantee a somewhat normal distribution of scores, and therefore there is no necessity for some percentage of the students to fail. By constructing easy tests, you can guarantee success for every student.

The obvious disadvantage is that, since so many people are familiar with this grading scheme, they are prone to accept the grades at face value (e.g., an 85 as a "B") and never bother to question what the "B" represents. As has been pointed out, the designation of some number as an "A" or a "B" is arbitrary; it has no relationship except to itself. Yet when it is used as a measure of student achievement, great meaning is often attached to it. It seems to say more than it really does.

The "Curve"   Another way of calculating grades is known as grading "on a curve." The curve referred to is the "normal curve" or the curve that results if the frequency of some characteristic normally distributed among a very large population is plotted on a graph. Statisticans use procedures in which the resulting graph is divided into areas through the use of standard deviations (SDs). These SDs theoretically remain constant, with about

34 percent of the population falling between the mean (average) score and one SD above the mean, 34 percent falling between the mean and one SD below the mean, and most of the remaining scores divided between one SD and two SDs above and below the mean. See Figure 6.

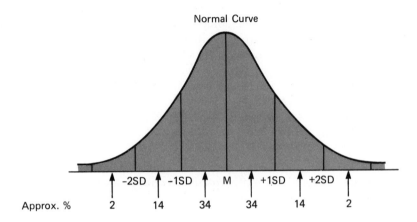

Normal Curve

	-2SD	-1SD	M	+1SD	+2SD	
Approx. %	2	14	34	34	14	2

FIGURE 6   Normal Curve

Standard deviations and the normal curve are useful because they are based on the mean score rather than on some arbitrarily fixed point. Thus, if you administer a particularly difficult test containing 100 items and the mean score happens to be 23, you can still assign "A" to "F" letter grades by calculating how far above or below the mean each score is and then applying the standard deviation cutoff points. If you had decided previously that an "A" was going to be any score one and one-half standard deviations above the mean, it would not matter whether the mean was 23 or 83. One and one-half standard deviations would be calculated from that point and the grade assigned.

There are a number of formulas by which approximations of the standard deviation can be calculated, but one often used because of its ease is that suggested by W. L. Jenkins.[3] The steps to this procedure are as follows.

(1) Arrange all the scores from high to low, (2) find the sums of the top one-sixth of the scores and the bottom one sixth, (3) subtract the sum of the bottom one-sixth from the sum of the top one-sixth, and (4) divide the difference by one-half the total number of scores. In equation form the formula is

[3]Paul B. Diederich, "Short-Cut Statistics for Teacher-Made Tests," *Evaluation and Advisory Series,* no. 5 (Princeton, N.J.: Educational Testing Service, 1960), p. 23.

$$\text{Approx. SD} \quad = \quad \frac{\text{sum of top sixth} - \text{sum of bottom sixth}}{\text{half the number of students}}$$

Suppose that you had a class of twelve students and gave them a twenty-item test worth 100 points. After deducting 5 points for each incorrect response, the scores were calculated to be 95, 90, 85, 75, 75, 75, 70, 70, 65, 65, 60, and 40. Suppose further that you had decided upon the following standard deviation cutoff points (where M = mean):

A $\geq$ M + 1.25 SDs
B = M + 0.25 to + 1.249 SDs
C = M − 1.00 to + 0.249 SDs
D = M − 2.00 to − .999
F > M − 2.00 SDs

Grades for the class of twelve based on a curve could be estimated by the following procedure using Jenkins' formula:

$$\text{Approx. SD} \quad = \quad \frac{\text{sum of top sixth} - \text{sum of bottom sixth}}{\text{half the number of students}}$$

$$= \quad \frac{(95 + 90) - (60 + 40)}{6}$$

$$= \quad \frac{185 - 100}{6}$$

$$= \quad \frac{85}{6} \approx 14$$

Next, calculate the point equivalents to the standard deviation cutoffs by adding the approximate SD to, and subtracting it from, the mean score.

$$\text{Mean} \quad = \quad \frac{\text{sum of scores}}{\text{number of scores}}$$

$$= \quad \frac{95 + 90 + 85 + 75 + 75 + 75 + 70 + 70 + 65 + 65 + 60 + 40}{12}$$

$$= \quad \frac{865}{12}$$

$$\approx \quad 72$$

Since an "A" is any score 1.25 SDs or greater above the mean, the point equivalent can be found by multiplying 1.25 by 14 (the approximate SD) and adding the product (17.5) to the mean (72). The minimum "A" grade is therefore 17.50 + 72, or 89.5. Since the "B" range is 0.25 to 1.249 SDs above, its point equivalent can be found by multiplying 0.25 by 14 and adding the product (3.5) to the mean (72). The "B" range thus extends from 72 + 3.5, or 75.5, to 89.49. Similarly, the "C" range would be found by multiplying − 1 by 14 and *adding* the product from the mean. The "C" range would extend from 72 − 14 or 58, to 75.49. The "D" range would extend from 72 − (2 × 14), or 44, to 57. The "F" range would be anything less than − 2 SDs, or anything less than 44. The actual test scores might then be determined by using the following scale.

A = 90 or better
B = 76 to 89
C = 58 to 75
D = 44 to 57
F = 43 or lower

The grade distribution for the scores given at the beginning of this problem would then be

95 = A	75 = C	65 = C
90 = A	75 = C	65 = C
85 = B	70 = C	60 = C
75 = C	70 = C	40 = F

Practice Problems for Assigning Marks Using a Curve Calculate the mean score and approximate standard deviation, to the nearest tenth, for the following 24 test scores using the Jenkins method and its equation as follows.

24, 22, 20, 19, 19, 18, 17, 17, 16, 16, 15, 15, 15, 14, 14, 13, 13, 13, 13, 12, 12, 12, 11, 11

First calculate the mean (average) of the scores (add all scores together and divide by the total number of scores). Compare your calculated mean to the work following:

13	15	17	24	
12	14	17	22	
12	14	16	20	71
12	13	16	19	82
11	13	15	19	96
11 +	13 +	15 +	18	+ 122
71	82	96	122 =	371

$$\begin{array}{r} 15.45 \\ 24\overline{)371.00} \\ \underline{24} \\ \cdot131 \\ \underline{120} \\ 110 \\ \underline{96} \\ 140 \end{array}$$ Mean = 15.45

Now calculate the approximate standard deviation. Compare your work with that shown next. Check any discrepancies. Determine the differences between your work and the answer provided.

$$\begin{array}{cccc} 13 & 15 & 17 & 24 \\ 12 & 14 & 17 & 22 \\ 12 & 14 & 16 & 20 \\ 12 & 13 & 16 & 19 \\ 11 & 13 & 15 & 19 \\ 11 & 13 & 15 & 18 \end{array}$$

Sum of top sixth scores   = 24 + 22 + 20 + 19 = 85
Sum of bottom sixth scores = 11 + 11 + 12 + 12 = 46

$$SD = \frac{85 - 46}{12}$$

$$= \frac{39}{12}$$

$$= 3.25$$

Assume that the school district wishes you to assign marks on the curve using the standard deviation scale given here:

MARK	SD ABOVE OR BELOW THE MEAN
A $\gtreqless$	+1.5 SD
B =	+0.5 to +1.49 SD
C =	−0.5 to +.49 SD
D =	−1.75 to −0.51 SD
F >	−1.76 SD

Assign the grades the students would receive using the scale given above to the scores provided. Compare your grade assignment with the answers given using mean = 15.45 and SD = 3.3.

Calculating "A" grades (scores 1.5 SD above mean and greater):

$$\begin{array}{r} 3.3 \text{ (SD)} \\ \times\, 1.5 \\ \hline 165 \\ 33 \\ \hline 4.95 \text{ scores above mean} \end{array} \qquad \begin{array}{r} 15.45 \text{ (mean)} \\ +\ 4.95 \\ \hline 20.40 \end{array}$$

Scores 20.4 and above get "A's." There are two scores above 20.4.

Calculating "B" grades (scores between 0.5 and 1.49 SD above mean):

$$\begin{array}{r} 3.3 \text{ (SD)} \\ \times\, 0.5 \\ \hline 1.65 \end{array} \qquad \begin{array}{r} 15.45 \text{ (mean)} \\ +\ 1.65 \\ \hline 17.10 \end{array}$$

Scores from 17.1 to 20.4 get "B's." This means that the students with scores of 18, 19, and 20 would get "B's." There are four scores in this range.

Calculating "C" grades (scores between 0.5 below the mean to 0.49 above the mean):

$$\begin{array}{r} 3.3 \text{ (SD)} \\ \times\, -0.5 \\ \hline -1.65 \end{array} \qquad \begin{array}{r} 15.45 \text{ (mean)} \\ -\ 1.65 \\ \hline 13.80 \end{array}$$

Scores from 13.8 to 17.1 get "C's." This means that the students with scores of 14, 15, 16, and 17 would get "C's." There are nine of these scores.

Calculating "D" grades (scores between 1.75 and 0.51 SD below the mean):

$$\begin{array}{r} 3.3 \text{ (SD)} \\ \times\, -1.75 \\ \hline 165 \\ 231 \\ 33 \\ \hline -5.775 \end{array} \qquad \begin{array}{r} 15.45 \text{ (mean)} \\ -\ 5.78 \\ \hline 9.67 \end{array}$$

Scores from 9.7 to 13.8 get "D's." This means the students with scores of 11, 12, and 13 would get "D's." There are nine of these scores.

Calculating "F" grades (scores more than 1.76 SD below the mean):

$$\begin{array}{r} 3.3 \text{ (SD)} \\ \times -1.76 \\ \hline 198 \\ 231 \\ 33 \\ \hline -5.808 \end{array} \qquad \begin{array}{r} 15.45 \text{ (mean)} \\ -5.81 \\ \hline 9.64 \end{array}$$

This means that students with scores below 9.6 get "F's." There are no scores this low.

The assignment of grades would look like this:

A	24	C	17		14	13
	22		16		14	12
B	20		16	D	13	12
	19		15		13	12
	19		15		13	12
	18		15		13	11

Although estimating standard deviations and grading "on a curve" enables you to assign grades on the basis of statistical procedures, the procedure has rather serious disadvantages. Standard deviations originate from large samples in which the normal curve of percentages apply; that is, 50 percent of all cases will always fall below the mean, approximately another 34 percent will fall between the mean and one SD above the mean, and approximately another 14 percent will fall between one and two SDs above the mean. With small samples, such as those found in classrooms, these percentages are much less exact. Once you decide upon a set of cutoff points, you are virtually guaranteeing that there will be inequities because of the sample size. For instance in the one example given, there are no "D" grades; in the other there are no "F" grades and only two "A's."

Another closely related point concerns the fact that standard deviations are calculated with respect to mean scores. This means that in an advanced class a student might have to get a 95 to get an "A," whereas in a slower class, a student might need only a 65. Since an "A" is an "A" in the final records, many educators have reservations about grading "on a curve." The reservations are particularly great when grades are calculated on a curve in advanced classes in which students compete with each other for a handful of high grades, when such grades would have been assured had they been in a regular class.

Eyeballing Another method of calculating grades consists simply of tallying the scores on a scale, looking for natural divisions in the distribution, and assigning letter grades to these divisions. Although this "method" seems haphazard, it is often used in practice even though decisions are completely arbitrary.

It can be seen from looking at a tally of the scores in our first example that there are three natural divisions. A decision must be made as to the cutoff point for "A's" and "B's," "B's" and "C's," and so on. There are no right or wrong answers here. Depending upon your assessment of how difficult the test was, how well you feel the teaching had gone, or the like, you may assign grades in a variety of patterns.

SCORES	FREQUENCY OF EACH SCORE
100	
95	1
90	1
85	
80	1
75	111
70	11
65	11
60	1
55	
50	
45	
40	1
35	
	0

Here are four possible eyeballing grading patterns for grade distribution:

Scores	Freq	Grade		Scores	Freq	Grade		Scores	Freq	Grade		Scores	Freq	Grade
100				100				100				100		A
95	1			95	1			95	1	A		95	1	
90	1	A		90	1	A		90	1			90	1	B
85				85				85		B		85		
80	1	B		80	1	B		80	1			80	1	
75	111			75	111			75	111			75	111	
70	11	C		70	11			70	11	C		70	11	C
65	11			65	11	C		65	11			65	11	
60	1	D		60	1			60	1			60	1	
55				55				55				55		
50				50		D		50		D		50		
45				45				45				45		D
40	1	F		40	1			40	1			40	1	
35				35		F		35		F		35		

Credit   When working with precise instructional objectives and the Logical Instructional Model, it soon becomes obvious that the key to success for students is to attain the minimum acceptable standard described in the objective or in supplemental checklists or descriptions. Many educators who are using such a model have gone to a "credit" system. It is, perhaps, the simplest of all methods available.

At the outset of instruction all the competencies are delineated. They may be modified by student input, but a final decision is reached. Each of them has a minimum acceptable standard or criterion level (see Chapter 3). As students demonstrate a competency, they are given credit and proceed to the next level. When all competencies are completed for the course, the student is finished. Under individualized instruction, the "normal curve" now reflects *time* rather than *scores*. Instead of the majority of students receiving an average grade, they will finish about the same time. Instead of receiving a high mark, a brighter student will achieve the competencies sooner.

Many schools have attempted to blend grading schemes with such programs. This is usually done by assigning an average grade for the basic competency and then encouraging "quest" or "enrichment" activities for high grades.

Grading and Subjectivity

All the grading methods examined have had one point in common. In each instance the method depended upon some subjective decision. The preset level method required a subjective judgment concerning the placement of the levels; the "curve" method required a subjective judgment concerning the standard deviation cutoff points; the "eyeballing" method depended entirely upon subjective decisions; and even the "credit" procedure required subjective judgments concerning the level of proficiency desired to receive credit.

Some educators argue that, since all grading methods ultimately depend upon subjective decisions, none is any better or worse than any other. The advantages and disadvantages balance out. Without intending to add to the argument, it can be said that any choice should be guided by at least two factors: (1) the circumstances in which you find yourself (for instance, a particular school may have a set policy concerning grading) and (2) the importance attached to the material included in the test (very definite standards may be kept in mind for crucial material and more flexibility allowed with other material).

REPORTING GRADES

Assuming one or another of the many available methods to arrive at grades has been adopted, the question of how most effectively to communicate information regarding student progress still remains.

Many school systems have adopted a policy, at least with respect to standardized tests, of not reporting the student's exact score at all. To minimize the misinterpretations associated with "exact" scores, many school systems convert these scores to *stanines*. Stanine is a term that stands for "standard nine," a structured distribution that consists of nine equal intervals. The nine intervals account for 100 percent of any given population with the intervals representing 4 percent, 7 percent, 12 percent, 17 percent, 20 percent, 17 percent, 12 percent, 7 percent, and 4 percent of that population, respectively. Most standardized tests provide tables by which individual scores can be converted to stanines and thus placed in an appropriate interval. Because the intervals created by the stanine distribution are so large, teachers can be fairly certain that any given student's "true" score falls into the stanine interval indicated by the test score.

Stanines, like scores you calculate, are best reported to parents and students in a conference. You can explain more fully the implications of particular grades as well as how the grades were calculated. Teachers find it important to be able to substantiate any grade given or comment made, and they can minimize parental uncertainty or anger by initiating explanations about grading procedures and providing reasons for using whatever grading scheme was selected. Having an understanding of the mathematics involved in a particular grading method means very little, however, if grades do not reflect achievement or nonachievement of specific instructional objectives. Parents are not normally interested in how sophisticated a grading system may be; they are interested in how well the grades reflect what their child has accomplished.

Teachers who are concerned with the need to report evaluations, rather than just grades, will find that parent-teacher (or parent-teacher-student) conferences or telephone conferences yield better results than do one-way mailing of grades or comments. Conferences enable you to relate factors such as effort and dependability to the student's actual achievement. Conferences are even more valid if the student is present and can provide additional input, provided that the conference does not degenerate into an accusation/defense session.

Because conferences are sometimes difficult to arrange, educators rely heavily on some other reporting device—usually a report card. Unfortunately, grades on a report card do not really reflect a student's specific abilities, even though a great deal of importance is frequently attached to report card grades. If the school depends solely upon report cards, you should explore the possibility of including with each report card a list of the instructional objectives for the class or course with indications of those that the student achieved. Such a list will provide parents with a much clearer picture of what their son or daughter has actually accomplished.

TEACHER EVALUATION

Any logical discussion of teacher evaluation must be based on the understanding that, when students, peers, administrators, and parents evaluate a teacher, each may use a different set of criteria and that, when the teacher engages in self-evaluation, still another set of criteria may be used. When your students evaluate you, for example (and they will whether you ask them to or not), they may include among their criteria your ability to explain things clearly, your fairness, and your ability to stimulate and maintain their interest. Your peers might evaluate you partially on your ability to come up with innovative instructional ideas and your willingness to share those ideas. School administrators might include criteria concerning your ability to get reports in on time, your contributions to good community relations, and your ability to maintain order in your classroom. Parents might have other criteria, and you, yourself, might have still others.

The point to keep in mind is that each individual who engages in teacher evaluation does so from a particular perspective, with particular expectations and with their own ideas of how the ideal teacher should look and operate. Their evaluation(s) of you will be influenced by these factors, and you will want to take these factors into account as you attempt to make sense of the evaluations. It is suggested that you try to acquire as much feedback as you can concerning your performance as a teacher and that you sift through this information looking for points (good or bad) that recur. It is likely that, if different people find the same aspect of your performance worthy of comment, you should look closely at that behavior with an eye toward capitalizing on it if it is a strength or remedying it if it is a weakness.

Regardless of how many other people evaluate you, you will likely be your own most persistent critic. Here are some specific techniques you can use to acquire feedback concerning your own teaching performance.

Teacher Performance Tests

A teacher performance test (TPT) is simply a lesson you plan specifically to evaluate a particular instructional procedure. In keeping with the Logical Instructional Model, you should first specify one or two precise instructional objectives that students can achieve within a single class period. This is important to protect the evaluation from biasing factors such as student study after class and similar variables.

The second step in using a TPT is to preassess. You must be sure that students are not already able to demonstrate the objective(s) or, conversely, that they do not lack the necessary prerequisite skill. If some students fall into either category, you will want to either find some other activities for them during this particular class or discount their evaluation results.

The third step is to specify the particular instructional procedure that you want to try. Keep in mind that any given procedure may work well one time and not so well another time. You are likely, therefore, to want to try the same procedure again under conditions as nearly alike as possible, so you will need an accurate description of what you planned to do and what you actually did.

The next step is to establish a minimum acceptable level of class performance. This standard is different from the minimum acceptable standard specified in the objective(s) in that here you are using your professional judgment to decide on a minimum percentage of students who must be able to demonstrate the objective(s) before you will consider the instructional procedure effective. There is no one "right" percentage.

The final step is to go ahead and teach the TPT. If the minimum number of students you established as a cutoff point are able to demonstrate the objective, you have empirical evidence that for those students, under the conditions that existed, the instructional procedure used was effective. You will, of course, want to verify your findings by repeating the TPT a number of times. If the TPT results indicate that the instructional procedure is not effective for you, with those students, under those conditions, you may want to look more closely at what actually took place during the lesson.

Audio and Video Recordings

So much takes place during a typical lesson that it is difficult to recall with accuracy after the lesson all that went on during the lesson. Fortunately, technology can assist you. Most schools have audio tape recorders and many have videotape recorders as well. If you can arrange to tape your TPT (or any other lesson) you will likely find the playback highly informative. You may find, for example, that you tend to cut off students' responses or that you do not often reinforce students for their contributions. Problems like these may be discerned by analyzing a taped lesson, and you can use this kind of information as a basis for self-improvement.

Interaction Analysis Techniques

In addition to simply listening to, or watching, a playback of your lesson, you can utilize any one of the various interaction analysis techniques. One of the most common of these, developed by Edmond J. Amidon and Ned A. Flanders, is known as *Flanders' Interaction Analysis.*[4] This technique is based on the delineation of nine categories of student and teacher verbal behaviors. The analyst uses the numbers assigned to each category of verbal behavior to encode, every three seconds, the kind of interaction (if any) that is taking place at that moment. The list of numbers can then be analyzed to determine if particular interaction patterns are used to the exclusion of other patterns and whether the interaction pattern recorded was what the teacher intended. The technique is useful for quantifying verbal interaction

[4]Edmond J. Amidon and Ned A. Flanders. *The Role of the Teacher in the Classroom* (Minneapolis, Minn: Association for Productive Teaching, 1967).

patterns, and it is not intended as a technique for determining whether those patterns are good or bad. Judgments of that sort should depend more on the kind of interaction intended and the extent to which the interaction pattern facilitates students' achievement of the specified objectives.

Another interaction analysis system was developed by Morine, Spaulding, and Greenberg.[5] Either system can help you ascertain what actually transpired during the lesson, and both help you to quantify that information.

Student Evaluations

As helpful as the techniques cited are, you will still want direct feedback from your students regarding their perceptions of your effectiveness. One way in which to acquire student feedback is periodically to ask for anonymous evaluations of what they like about your teaching and what they believe needs to be improved. This technique will likely generate many comments concerning your personality characteristics and interpersonal relations (as opposed to your pedagogical skills), but the input is still useful in identifying strengths and weaknesses.

Another technique is to formulate a list of factors you feel students can evaluate fairly and ask them to respond to those points on a periodic and anonymous basis. As long as students are sure their evaluations will have no negative effect on their grades or on their relationship with you, they will be truthful in most cases.

Peer Evaluations

The evaluations you get from students will provide you with some information about your teaching, but that information is likely to concern your teaching style more than your teaching effectiveness. For information about the latter point, you can turn to TPTs, pre- and posttest comparisons, and peer evaluations.

Peer evaluations are particularly useful if you select the peer who does the evaluating. This is so because if you do the selecting you are likely to choose a teacher you respect and whose opinion you will respect. That teacher can provide feedback concerning both process and product and, more important, can also suggest ways of improving.

Administrative Evaluations

Regardless of what other evaluation techniques you may use, you can rely on your school administrators to also evaluate you. If you are wise you will ask your principal for a copy of the teaher evaluation form or list of

[5]Greta Morine, Robert Spaulding, and Selma Greenberg, *Discovering New Dimensions in the Teaching Process* (Scranton, Pa.: International Testbook, 1971), p. vi.

criteria that will be used as the basis for your evaluation. A perusal of this form or list will alert you to the particular points the administration considers important. One factor that will unquestionably be viewed favorably will be the measures you take with respect to self-evaluation and self-improvement. If you can document that you are making consistent efforts to assess your own effectiveness, administrators cannot help but think better of you than if you make no efforts in this direction.

SUMMARY

The first part of this chapter surveyed important points concerning the evaluation of students' progress. It is suggested that evaluation be tied to specific instructional objectives, that those objectives be communicated to students prior to instruction, that students be evaluated in a variety of ways with an increasing emphasis on techniques other than formal paper-and-pencil tests, and that students be provided with frequent feedback concerning their learning progress either in the form of formal tests or informal comments and self-evaluation devices. Tests can be constructed either as criterion-referenced or norm-referenced instruments, and a chief difference between the two is that the goal of the latter is to achieve a spread in the scores whereas the former has as its goal discerning whether students can perform at a minimum proficiency level.

Objective tests are most useful for sampling the breadth of students' knowledge of some topic, whereas essay tests are most useful for sampling the depth of students' evaluating, creative, or synthesis skills. Even though the purposes are different, some similarities exist between objective and subjective tests. The items or problems on both types of tests need to be worded simply and precisely, and both types are most effective when they require students to apply, rather than simply to recall or repeat, information. Objective items and essay items should not be included on the same test, because they require different kinds of cognitive skills, and students waste time shifting from one cognitive orientation to the other.

Standardized tests are used mainly to measure general kinds of abilities such as intelligence, achievement, aptitude, and interest. Part of their reliability stems from their emphasis on general rather than on specific skills. The norms associated with standardized tests usually reflect the average performance of large numbers of students from a wide sample. The size of the sample contributes to the stability and utility of the norms.

You will be wise to emphasize tasks that require the integration of many subskills and information. Such tasks not only emphasize the practicality of what is being learned, but they also decrease the need for formal paper-and-pencil tests. Students can be helped to succeed at these alternative tasks if the standards are specified as precisely as possible in the instructional objectives, if both good and bad models are provided for students to examine, and if checklists of important steps or points are included.

All grading methods ultimately depend upon some subjective judgments, and any one of several methods might be most appropriate depending upon the situation. These procedures, when used in conjunction with a provision for two-way communication with parents and students, will provide those most concerned with the information necessary to make intelligent decisions.

Teacher evaluation is just as necessary as student evaluation. When discussing teacher evaluation it should be remembered that each evaluator, whether peer, student, parent, or administrator, brings to the task a unique set of expectations and a unique idea of how the ideal teacher should look and act.

A particularly useful basis for evaluating teachers is to assess the extent to which their students can achieve the specified instructional objectives. This can be determined by using a teacher performance test that is a lesson planned and taught specifically to evaluate instructional procedures.

Whether teachers use TPTs, pre- and post-test score comparisons, student evaluations, peer evaluations, or administrative evaluations, it is important to note that all feedback concerning teacher performance can be used as a basis for self-improvement, that no one piece of data is conclusive by itself, and that a good teacher will continually be trying to improve and, to this end, will use any and all feedback possible.

NINE
PUTTING THE PIECES TOGETHER—PLANNING A UNIT

Up to this point we have looked at parts of the instructional process (the construction and classification of objectives, the various ways of providing instruction, and evaluation) as separate entities. Now it is time to put those parts together in a sequence that will help students learn effectively.

One often-used method of "putting the parts together" is in the form of a unit plan, and in this chapter we are concerned with explaining the functions, construction, and utilization of unit plans. We will also look at ways of continually upgrading unit plans. This kind of information will aid you in gathering together and organizing information to make your instruction more interesting and effective and will help your students acquire skills and information more easily. Instruction that is well organized benefits all concerned.

OBJECTIVES

When you complete this chapter, you will be able to:

1. Explain, in writing, the functions of at least three unit plan components. (Comprehension)
2. Construct an outline of a unit plan and describe, in less than two pages, which instructional experiences will be included and why. (Analysis, Synthesis)
3. Construct a unit plan for a given length of time in your teaching field, including a rationale, precise instructional objectives, suitable content and instructional activities, optional activities, and an evaluation procedure. (Synthesis)

PLANNING UNITS

The task of generating a list of precise instructional objectives for an extended period and of deciding how to help students achieve those objectives seems, at first glance, to be extremely complex. If approached haphazardly, its conplexity is multiplied and made even more difficult. Few teachers, of course, wish to approach any task in a disoriented fashion, so they make an effort at organization. In the case of large blocks of time, the structure often takes the form of dividing the possible course content into broad categories to facilitate the achievement of specific objectives. These categories can be the basis of units of work.

What Is a Unit Plan?

A unit plan is a compilation of precise instructional objectives, content appropriate to the achievement of those objectives, instructional experiences appropriate to both the objectives and the content, optional experiences, and needed materials. The plan often begins with a rationale and ends with an evaluation instrument. A unit plan represents your most complete conceptualization of what students will accomplish in a given block of time (usually from three to six weeks), and how they will go about working to ensure success. A unit plan is your plan of action and your overall strategy.

Generating Appropriate Objectives

Many teachers begin the process of selecting precise instructional objectives used in unit plans by listing the major skills and information students should acquire. A home economics teacher, for example, may decide that students should demonstrate competencies such as the following.

1. Given the food intake (kind and quantity) of a "typical" undernourished individual, list in writing the specific nutrients missing and the probable effects (diseases or symptoms) of such a lack. (Analysis)
2. Plan menus for seven days for a family of four (one pregnant adult, one very active male adult, one typical ten-year-old, and one infant) that meet the minimal needs of each family member. (Synthesis)
3. Given four one-day menus, decide which is best for you, and in less than two pages defend that choice by citing specific facts and examples. (Evaluation)

Once these and other major objectives are written, many teachers find it useful to write subsidiary or enabling objectives for the major objectives that are particularly complex. Enabling objectives facilitate daily lesson planning by breaking the major objective into subskills that may be achieved within a single class period. Possible enabling objectives for the first of the preceding examples might include the following.

1. List, in writing, at least three foods in each of the basic four categories. (Knowledge)
2. List, in writing, the specific deficiencies known to cause pellagra, rickets, and beriberi. (Knowledge)
3. Given the specific geographic location of a described underdeveloped country, identify, in writing, particular diet deficiencies that might exist and explain why. (Analysis)

If you take the time to attach to each objective the proper taxonomic domain and level, it becomes relatively easy to scan the objectives to see if emphasis is being placed on too few levels. It often happens, for example, that too many low-level cognitive skills are emphasized at the expense of the higher-level skills. If such a disparity becomes obvious, steps should be taken to shift the emphasis. It is essential that the objectives focus on the skills and information that will be of greatest overall use to the students as they assume adult roles in society.

Writing a Rationale

Having decided upon objectives, there should be no question in your mind concerning the importance and utility of the skills and content to be learned. Nevertheless, it is not uncommon for students to ask, "Why do we have to learn this?" or for an entire class of students to sit with expressions on their faces that indicate they cannot see the relevance of the content to their own lives.

Unless you have given some serious thought to questions concerning the importance and utility for students of the information or skills to be learned, you may be forced to answer with responses that will be deemed superficial by students. Students do not usually accept rationales such as, "You need this for the college entrance exam," "Because I said so," or "Most people think this is important." The most effective rationales are those that indicate to the students how the new information or skills can be of immediate personal use.

Less effective rationales may include arguments that the acquisition of certain skills may improve academic performance in a number of related subject areas or contribute directly to specific vocational plans. Although teacher and student views are frequently parallel, rationales written with the students' point of view in mind are more effective.

Sample Rationales

1. *For a short unit on compiling reports ethically and legally.* Whenever factual reports such as term papers, theses, dissertations, and business reports are compiled, it is often necessary to refer to material written by

someone else. These references make it possible to capitalize on research and reports that bear on the report being written. However, because they were written by someone else, recognition must be given to the author(s) to give credit where it is due and to avoid charges of plagiarism (copying). This unit is designed to show you how to record various bibliographical materials in a logical and concise manner.

2. *The metric system.* Any modern industrial nation depends on its ability to measure a quantity accurately and to state that measurement in written form. This act of communication is found everywhere in our daily lives, and we all use units of measure to purchase, create, and relax. Who can avoid pounds, ounces, cups, inches, miles, gallons, and degrees Fahrenheit in food and clothing purchases, automobile use, or weather reports? The answer is: the approximately 90 percent of the world's population who use grams, centimeters, kilometers, liters, and degrees Celsius. They use the metric system of measuring rather than the "English" system.

The United States is the only major industrial country that does not use the metric system of measurement, and there is considerable effort being expended to assist us in converting, also. Our current system of measurement is confusing, redundant, and often difficult to use for scientific work. People who believe that they are on firm ground using "our" system are invited to test their acquaintance with the following questions:

How many cubic inches in a gallon?
How many feet in a fathom?
How many square feet in a square mile?
Which is larger, a dry quart or a liquid quart?
How many pounds in a "long" hundredweight?
How many feet longer is a nautical mile than a land mile?

This unit is intended to provide you with an understanding of the metric system and to provide you with practice in using metric units of measurement and in converting our current measurement units to metric units. The information is timely since many food products already carry both our current measurement units and the metric equivalents and many highway signs specify kilometers as well as miles. The switch has begun and this unit can help you prepare for it.

Specifying Content

Even before the unit is put into use, the precise instructional objectives begin to prove their value. The objectives suggest the specific content to which students will need to be exposed if they are to achieve the objectives. Since unit plans are generally made well in advance of the time they are used, you have sufficient time to sift through a great deal of material concerning, and related to, the chosen topic. As you select the most important and/or interesting content for inclusion in the unit, you frequently discover relationships among facts and concepts that previously eluded you.

Taking the time to acquire content from a number of different sources has advantages. A variety of sources act as an internal accuracy check assuring that information is correct, the examples appropriate, and the anecdotes relevant. This kind of preparation tends to increase your self-confidence. This self-confidence, in turn, tells students that you are well prepared, know what you are doing, and are convinced the material is worth learning.

There are many sources to which you can turn for supplemental content for unit plans. Among the obvious sources are your own college tests and notes, personal experiences, and the school library. Many of the sources in the library have low reading levels, and you can scan them relatively quickly and extract relevant information with a minimum of effort. The librarian may have suggestions for other possible aids.

One of the best sources of information for unit plans are compilations called *resource units*. Many public schools, state departments of education, and university instructional materials centers maintain resource units on a wide variety of topics. These compilations often contain such items as lists of possible instructional objectives, rationales, subject-matter outlines, suggested instructional experiences, optional experiences, instructional aids, bibliographies, and even sample tests. The wealth of material available in most resource units can tempt you to build your own units solely from this material, but resource unit material should be supplemented not only with the most current material available but also with whatever other material you feel is needed to meet the specific objectives and instructional needs of your particular students.

The subject-matter outline for the unit should cover all the information students will need to achieve the objectives. The outline should be complete enough to be used without the need for supplemental sources (which may not be available when needed) or "remembered" material (which may be forgotten when needed). A helpful rule to follow is that, if the content is important to students (or if it will help students learn or remember something), it should be written into the outline, including not only facts, figures, definitions, diagrams, and explanations but also supplemental information, such as examples and anecdotes.

The primary advantage to building a comprehensive subject-matter outline is the elimination of last-minute research or attempts to find appropriate examples. Everything perceived as needed should be built into the unit while you have the time and the resources to be selective and thorough. A second advantage is that you will become familiar with the "big picture." When you know the exact nature of the material to be presented in the future, you can refer to points yet to be made (thus cueing the students) and can more readily refer to points previously made (thus appropriately reinforcing prior learning.)

Selecting Instructional Experiences

Each instructional experience, like each portion of content and each use of mediated instruction, should be selected on the basis of how well it will help students achieve the precise instructional objectives. The objectives themselves will suggest appropriate instructional experiences. For example, a low-level cognitive objective such as, "You will list, in writing, at least two characteristics of carbohydrates and two characteristics of lipids," could easily be facilitated by a teacher presentation or a film. A higher-level cognitive objective such as, "Given a series of facts and fallacies concerning diet and nutrition, you will underline each of the facts," might be better achieved in a guided practice session accompanied by student discussion.

When selecting instructional experiences, effective teachers consider the types of analogous (practice of skills similar to, but not the same as, the final skill) and equivalent practice (practice of a skill virtually identical to the final skill called for) that students will need as preparation for the demonstration of the instructional objective. For the objective cited earlier concerning dietary facts and fallacies, a teacher may wish to plan one lesson that would provide analogous practice (such as listing fallacies on the board and briefly discussing why they are fallacies) and another lesson that would provide equivalent practice (such as examining articles containing both facts and fallacies about diet and nutrition and identifying the specific facts and fallacies).

Collecting Mediated Instructional Aids

When some part of a particular unit will be learned through the use of mediated instruction, unit planning allows for long-range planning. The long-range view made possible by good unit planning enables you to order films, books, videotapes, models, and other instructional aids early enough to assure delivery when needed. Early delivery will ensure sufficient time to preview material, test equipment, and still make alternate plans if either the material or the equipment is unavailable or unsuitable.

To get information about films and filmstrips, teachers often find it helpful to survey film and filmstrip catalogs available in the school library, the audiovisual department, or the film and filmstrip libraries maintained by nearby colleges and universities. Additional sources include the state department of education, many public utilities, the local telephone company, large corporations, and national organizations. (See Chapter 7 concerning mediated instruction for specific addresses).

The following types of information concerning films and filmstrips are helpful if included in the unit plan.

1. The exact title of the film or filmstrip.
2. The name of the company that produced the aid (sometimes needed in ordering).
3. The length of the aid in minutes or frames. (Make sure there is time in available time modules to use the aid effectively.)
4. Whether color or black and white.
5. The address from which the aid can be obtained.
6. The cost.
7. Rental or loan conditions. Of particular importance are the deadline for ordering to ensure delivery when needed (two weeks in advance, six months in advance, etc.), and the length of time the aid can be retained.

In addition to films and filmstrips, you should take advantage of other forms of mediated instruction. As a general rule, the more variety in instructional experiences, the more chance students will become genuinely involved in the material.

ORGANIZING THE PARTS OF A UNIT: AN ABBREVIATED MODEL

The preceding unit plan components can be arranged in many ways. A simple outline form is one way, as exemplified in the abbreviated model that follows. A full model is included as Appendix B.

I. Rationale
  The information in this unit will help students plan balanced diets, which, in turn, will help prevent serious illness and assist in minimizing other physical problems such as hidden malnutrition, obesity, and acne.
II. Objectives
  The students will:
  A. Write an explanation of the function of each of the following: amino acid, protein, basal metabolism, calorie, lipids, and hemoglobin. (Comprehension)
  B. Given a list of foods, correctly classify at least 80 percent of them into carbohydrate, protein, or fat categories. (Knowledge)
III. Subject Matter
  A. Functions of food
    1. Supplies energy for maintaining life and carrying out daily activities.
      a. Nutrients required for these functions:
        (1) Proteins
        (2) Fats
        (3) Carbohydrates

b. Energy demand must be satisfied before the body uses food for other functions such as growth.
2. Builds new cells and repairs those that are worn out every day.
   a. Nutrients required for these functions:
     (1) Proteins
     (2) Minerals
     (3) Vitamins
3. Regulates complex body processes.
   a. Nutrients required for these functions:
     (1) Proteins
     (2) Minerals
     (3) Water
     (4) Fats
   b. Examples of body processes:
     (1) Movement of fluids
     (2) Activation of enzymes (a protein secreted by living cells)
     (3) Coagulation of blood

IV. Materials and Experiences
  A. Functions of foods
    1. Materials:
      a. Overhead projector, grease pencil, and acetate
      b. Nutrition chart
      c. Mimeographed handout listing functions and sample foods
    2. Experiences:
      a. Present information via teacher presentation
      b. Use overhead to list functions and nutrients as they are presented
      c. Use mimeographed handout as basis for further discussion

Another procedure for organizing unit plans is to write out separate lesson plans for each of the objectives. Since the objectives, subject matter, instructional experiences, and materials have already been selected (or, in the case of instructional experiences, at least seriously considered), the writing of separate lesson plans is greatly facilitated. The advantage to such an organizational pattern is that extremely little preparation is needed once the unit is under way. The disadvantage is that the lesson plans may impose too rigid a structure on the progress of the class, thus discouraging deviations from the plans even when such deviations would be worthwhile.

Still another way of organizing unit plans is by subject matter and experiences that are to be used. You may decide, for example, to use certain subject matter or certain instructional experiences to stimulate interest in the unit. Other blocks of subject matter and other experiences may be designated for use in developing understanding and general instruction, while still others may be earmarked for concluding kinds of activities such as summarizations and reinforcement. If you organize unit plans according to introductory, developmental, and concluding categories, you can use that pattern in conjunction with either of the patterns described earlier.

DECIDING ON OPTIONAL ACTIVITIES

There are two major categories of optional activities you may consider for unit plan inclusion. The first includes any that students may be interested in. For example, activities such as constructing a bulletin board, model, or diorama, participating as a panel member in a panel discussion, or engaging in an independent study project have the potential appeal for a wide variety of students.

A second category includes those designed for exceptional students. Perhaps the most common experience found in this category is a carefully selected special reading opportunity. As you gather and select content for units, you will encounter numerous sources of information written at differing difficulty levels and representing various points of view. If you build a file of short, annotated bibliography cards on such sources, you will have a ready-made pool of sources to which students with varying abilities can be directed. In this way slower students can be given material written at a lower level so they do not fall behind, whereas brighter students can be directed to more challenging material, such as special readings, reports, interviewing. The key is to gear optional activities to the specific abilities of the students in the class.

The optional activities section is an excellent place for you to place experimental experiences. Since you are likely to generate some innovative and creative instructional possibilities while planning units, these untried experiences may be listed in the optional activities section and attempted on a voluntary basis by students. If the activities prove fruitful, they may become part of the regular instructional activities.

PLANNING FOR EVALUATION
AND FUTURE USE

The final step in planning a unit is to construct the instrument(s) needed to determine whether the objectives have been achieved. The objectives of the unit dictate the types of evaluation instruments needed. At the same time that the evaluations are constructed, you may wish to construct answer keys or appropriate models. If skill tests are to be used, appropriate checklists need to be constructed.

The experienced teacher will have written objectives that require students to synthesize a number of subsidiary skills in the process of demonstrating competence in the objective. Such objectives enable you to develop evaluation procedures that communicate to students the applicability of the content more clearly than traditional evaluation procedures. Objective and essay tests have important roles, but it is desirable to supplement them with other forms of evaluation whenever possible. (See Chapter 8 for other suggestions for evaluation.)

After the unit plan has been constructed and the components are in polished form and suitably organized, you may find it useful to make an expanded title page, which includes the title of the unit, the name of the course for which the unit was written (such as American History, Home Economics I, etc.), the type of student and grade level for which the unit was designed (such as general—freshmen; college preparatory—juniors; etc.), a brief overview of the unit (four or five lines describing the main points covered), a brief statement describing the unit preceding or following the unit (to help place the unit in a logical sequence), and a close estimation of the time frame needed for the unit.

This information wil save you time when instructional programs are being planned for future classes and the use of a previously written unit is being considered. Such concise data also facilitate the sharing of unit plans among teachers if such arrangements can be made.

SUMMARY

A unit plan is a compilation of precise instructional objectives, subject matter, instructional materials and experiences, optional experiences, and appropriate evaluation instruments all of which are concerned with a central theme or topic.

A major advantage to unit planning is that such planning usually takes place when you have the time and the energy to construct realistic and taxonomically balanced objectives, to sift through a large amount of subject matter and extract that which is most appropriate, to plan for varied instructional experiences, to preview films and filmstrips, to create innovative optional experiences, and to build appropriate evaluation instruments.

The following outline shows the components that may be included in a completed unit plan.

UNIT PLAN COMPONENTS

I. Title Page
   A. Title of unit
   B. Name of the course for which the unit was designed
   C. Academic and grade level of students for which the unit was designed
   D. Brief overview of the unit
   E. Statement describing preceding and/or following unit(s)
   F. A close time estimation

II. Objectives
   A. Should be stated in terms of observable and measurable outcomes
   B. Should be balanced so that there is not too much emphasis on any particular level (although there should be more higher-level cognitive objectives than any other kind)
III. Subject Matter
   A. Should contain *all* the information (facts, definitions, examples, explanations, anecdotes, etc.) students will need to achieve the objectives
   B. Should be gleaned from a variety of sources
IV. Materials and Activities
   A. Should include appropriate ordering information for mediated instructional aids
   B. May be organized as a general outline, separate lesson plans, or in broad categories such as introductory, developmental, and concluding
   C. Should contain an annotated bibliography of sources (both used and possible)
V. Optional Activities
   A. Should contain optional and enrichment activities open to all students, with another section designed for exceptional students
   B. Can serve as a proving ground for innovative ideas
VI. Evaluation Instrument(s)
   A. Must reflect objectives
   B. Must have answer keys, and/or models, and/or checklists
   C. Greater utilization of evaluation forms other than formal paper-and-pencil tests recommended

TEN

ORGANIZING FOR DAILY INSTRUCTION—LESSON PLANS

As you have seen, a unit plan is a powerful instructional tool because it enables you to plan instruction on a large scale and to incorporate in those plans a variety of learning experiences. Lesson plans are equally powerful tools because they enable you to take the overall instuctional strategy exemplified in a unit plan and divide it into segments that can be completed (conveniently and logically) in single class periods.

This chapter will examine some of the arguments for and against lesson plans (yes, there are honest disagreements among professionals here too), some of the components included in typical lesson plans, steps for writing lesson plans, and some lesson plan models.

OBJECTIVES

When you complete this chapter, you will be able to:

1. List, in writing, at least three components of a lesson plan. (Knowledge)
2. In a paper of no more than two pages, explain at least two possible advantages and two possible disadvantages associated with lesson plans. (Comprehension)
3. Given a precise instructional objective, describe, in writing, at least two possible teaching-learning activities that are logical outgrowths of the objective, and explain how these activities will help students achieve the stated objective. (Application)

4. Observe a peer-taught, fifteen-minute lesson and, using a copy of the plan for that lesson, write down all instances of differences between the lesson as planned and the lesson as taught. (Analysis)
5. Construct a one-page lesson plan so the instructional objective, the content, and the teaching-learning activities are directly related to one another in such a way that, if the plan were followed exactly, it would be logical to expect students to achieve the stated objective. (Synthesis)
6. Given a sample lesson plan for a hypothetical teaching situation, judge whether it is a good or bad lesson plan, writing at least five reasons for that judgment. (Evaluation)

PROS AND CONS OF LESSON PLANNING

Teachers have been debating the pros and cons of lesson planning for years. The main reason no agreement has been reached is that both sides are able to support their positions with convincing arguments. Those teachers who favor lesson plans, for example, include the following points among their arguments:

1. Lesson plans specify the instructional objective of the lesson and thus help keep the main purpose of the lesson clearly in focus.
2. By containing all the important content, lesson plans help assure that no crucial points will be inadvertently omitted.
3. Lesson plans include teaching-learning activities that were determined to be most likely to help students achieve the instructional objective(s), thus eliminating, or at least decreasing, the need for improvisation.
4. Lesson plans provide a basis for determining how effective particular teaching-learning activities were in helping students achieve particular objectives and thus provide a basis for modifying instructional methods.
5. Lesson plans facilitate long-range planning by providing a record of what was taught during each lesson, thus assisting in maintaining continuity.
6. Lesson plans are essential if a substitute teacher is to do more than conduct a supervised study period in the teacher's absence.

Opponents of lesson plans have an arsenal of arguments to support their position:

1. Lesson plans are largely unnecessary since most teachers already know what and how they are going to teach.
2. Once teachers go to the trouble to write a lesson plan, they may tend to follow that plan as closely as possible, rather than feel free to capitalize upon immediate student interests.
3. Planning lessons takes an inordinate amount of time, and this time could be better spent doing content-area research or gathering instructional material.

4. The presence of a lesson plan can cause complications when a teacher chooses to deviate from the plan and an administrator expects the plan to be followed.

5. Once a series of lesson plans is written, if any lesson goes much faster or slower than was anticipated, subsequent plans must be modified or scrapped, thus wasting time and effort.

Obviously, both sides have some sound arguments. There are, however, three other points that you should keep in mind. The first is that, since it is generally not possible to individualize all instruction, some group instruction will be necessary. Second, there is little doubt that lesson plans help beginning teachers to feel more at ease and confident in the classroom and therefore help them to be effective. Third, many school systems and individual principals require their teachers to prepare written lesson plans, and some go so far as to require that those plans be approved before they are implemented.

LESSON PLAN COMPONENTS

Objectives

Teachers write lesson plans primarily to increase their effectiveness in helping students to learn or, to be more precise, to increase their effectiveness in helping students to achieve specific instructional objectives. It follows, therefore, that a crucial component of a lesson plan is the instructional objective. It is the objective that states exactly what students will do at the end of the lesson.

The prime source of objectives for lesson plans is the master list of objectives that you generated for the course or unit. If, when these original objectives were written, you wrote them so they could be achieved within single class periods, no difficulty is encountered when transferring objectives from the master list to the lesson plans. Certainly low-level cognitive objectives such as, "You will be able to list, in writing, at least three components of a lesson plan," are amenable to such transfer since students can achieve them within a single class period; but unit and course objectives frequently reflect final behaviors and thus must be broken down into subobjectives before they can be used in daily lesson plans. It may be possible for you to use the complex objectives as they are and have the lessons carry over to another day, but it is more likely that you will divide the complex objectives into a number of less complex, enabling or en-route objectives, each of which becomes an objective for an individual lesson plan.

There are at least three reasons for trying to avoid carrying a lesson over to a second day. The first is that the longer the wait between the use of particular teaching-learning activities and the assessment of student performance resulting from those activities, the less sure you can be that your teaching resulted in student learning. Waiting even one day, for example, can enable numerous variables to affect student performance. Without accurate information concerning the effectiveness of instructional methods, you are less able to modify, and thus to improve, those methods.

The second reason is that stopping properly in midlesson is easier said than done. Under ideal circumstances, lesson closure includes summarization, review, student demonstrations of competence, and a report to students concerning their progress. This kind of closure provides students with a feeling of accomplishment and serves as an impetus to further learning. Some elements of the ideal closure will have to be omitted or at least modified if the lesson is carried over to a second day. The degree to which students achieve a feeling of accomplishment and are able to continue the lesson on the following day depends greatly upon what kind of closure you provide. If you anticipated the problem and built into the lesson plan a series of possible stopping points (which is tantamount to writing a series of mini-lesson plans), and if you kept track of the time, you could provide for summarization and review and lay the groundwork for the next day's lesson. If you do not plan for this contingency you may find yourself trying to make one last point after the class should be over and half the students are out the door. In this case the value of the time and effort committed to the lesson may be in jeopardy.

The third reason concerns effective time utilization. When a lesson is carried over to a second day, it is difficult to determine how much time will be needed to complete the old lesson and how much time will be available for new work. If you continually find yourself with awkward blocks of time left at the end of class periods and are unable to improvise or plan activities for those blocks (for example, by giving individual help to students), you will have to deal with growing student boredom and its attendant problems. (Interestingly, the problems of excess time and student boredom sometimes result from the use of instructional objectives that are too simple or too easily achieved.) It is best to avoid carrying lessons over to a second day and instead to break complex objectives into less complex enabling or en-route objectives. One example of such a subdivision is provided now.

Suppose you and your college instructor saw value in developing the ability to analyze lessons on the basis of what actually took place in comparison with what the teacher had *intended* to take place. An objective reflecting this ability might be, "You will observe a one-hour lesson and, using a copy of the plan for that lesson, write an in-class paper that cites each instance of difference between the lesson as taught and the lesson as planned."

While this objective may seem reasonable at first glance, a second look reveals that if you are to observe carefully what is going on in the class and compare that with the plan for that lesson, you will miss some differences while you write down your observations. The problem could be avoided by dividing the original objective into two subobjectives:

1. You will observe a lesson taught within a single class period and take sufficient notes to enable you to compare the observed lesson with the plan for that lesson with respect to objective, content, and teaching-learning activities.

2. You will, using your notes, write a paper of no more than four pages comparing the observed lesson with the plan for that lesson citing specific instances of differences between what was observed and what was planned with respect to objectives, content, and teaching-learning activities.

These two enabling objectives provide sufficient time for you to demonstrate the desired competencies and are therefore suitable (at least in that respect) for use on individual lesson plans.

One source for objectives for impromptu lesson plans is unexpected events. Although the vast majority of lessons will be planned before they are taught, events sometimes occur that should rightfully preempt planned lessons. When these events occur, it is your responsibility to devise and share instructional objectives so that the efforts of the class to capitalize upon the learning potential of the interrupting event are focused on some clearly understood goal. Your proficiency in this skill makes the difference between an unexpected event causing confusion in the classroom and the same event becoming the basis of an interesting and profitable learning experience.

Content

The content of a lesson plan is dictated by the objective and consists of the actual information (the facts, definitions, explanations, etc.) that students will need to achieve competency. You should not try to write into the content every single thing that will be covered, nor should you try to rely on the content portions of a lesson plan for information with which you are not familiar. The functions of the content component are to help assure that in the midst of a hectic or complex lesson you do not unintentionally omit crucial points and to provide a means of ensuring the relevancy of the content with respect to the objective.

The *form* of the plan will depend upon the teaching-learning activities selected. A lecture, for example, is facilitated best by a word or phrase outline of factual information. A discussion moves most smoothly if the plan consists of key statements, examples, and pivotal questions with possible answers. Activities such as demonstrations or experiments can progress according to plan with a content component consisting of procedural steps and descriptions, whereas art lessons might require limited verbal but extensive visual content, such as slides or pictures. Regardless of the form of the content, it should still contain the minimum data students will need to achieve the objective.

Some instructional objectives require that students demonstrate a skill that is not dependent upon specific content. Once the basic information concerning that skill has been conveyed, other lessons may provide students with practice in that skill, although the "content" for these lessons may have little or nothing to do with the original objective. For example, examine the following objective: "You will write a computer program that will use at least two nested do-loops, will run in less than two minutes, and will result in an accurate printout." Aside from the technical information necessary, the content on the program could consist of anything from information about a company's payroll requirements to an airline's flight schedule. Trying to concoct hypothetical content on the moment as a vehicle to develop a skill can be a nerve-wracking experience, and because this procedure is prone to error, it can seriously weaken an otherwise strong lesson. Depending upon the objective, basic factual information and/or practice data may be needed.

Teaching-Learning Activities

The teaching-learning activities are those in which you and students will engage during a particular lesson to facilitate achievement of the lesson plan's objective. Often teaching-learning activities will be implied by the instructional objective. In most instances you will want to select activities that will provide students with either analogous practice or equivalent practice, or both.

For example, if an instructional objective was, "You will describe, in one paragraph each, at least four ways information can be fed into a computer," appropriate activities might include a short demonstration or filmstrip concerning input modes (to provide basic information), a discussion during which students could suggest examples, a review period to allow students to review main points orally (analogous practice), a time during which students would actually write short explanations of input modes (demonstration of the stated competence), and a short session in which students receive feedback through a discussion of selected student responses.

Five separate teaching-learning activities were included in this single lesson. By selecting a variety of activities, you provide for a "change of pace," thereby reducing the possibility of students becoming bored. Of course, in the hands of the proficient teacher one activity may be used consistently without boredom and in the hands of an inexperienced teacher all the activities described may become deadly. It is a good idea, however, to look back periodically through lesson plans to see if there has been too much reliance on just one or two types of activities.

Materials

Occasionally you will wish to use instructional materials that are not readily available in classrooms. A delineation of these items (such as films, projectors, models, collections, etc.) in the lesson plan serves to remind you to make sure the required materials are available when they are needed. Since not all lessons will require special materials or equipment, it is not necessary to include this component in every lesson.

Evaluation

In the description of teaching-learning activities, one activity listed was student demonstration of the stated competence. Since the point of the lesson plan is to help students achieve a particular competence, it is obvious that it is essential to have planned the demonstration of that competence as the basis for evaluating the lesson. Ideally, this demonstration should be a part of the lesson on that day, but it may take place at a later time.

The evaluation component may contain space for you to write comments relative to student achievement of the objective, the reaction of the class to particular teaching-learning activities, and possible ways in which the lesson could have been improved.

Time

Since you will be operating within certain time limitations, you may want to assign approximate lengths of time to each of the planned activities. This procedure is particularly helpful for beginning teachers since they often have a great many details requiring their attention and sometimes lose track of time. It can be a shock to hear the dismissal bell ring or to be informed by a student that the time is gone and realize that the lesson is only partially completed.

Miscellaneous Components

Since lesson plans reflect the needs of the particular teachers who write them, not all plans have the same components. Most lesson plans provide for an instructional objective, content, and teaching-learning activities, and many contain sections for materials, evaluation, and time estimations. Other components are often included, however, that are not as common. Because they are largely self-explanatory, they are listed here with no discussion: homework assignments, date, title of course and/or subject, grade level, title of the unit, special announcements, preassessments, and preliminary tasks. Additional components may be added at your discretion.

WRITING A LESSON PLAN

As an example of beginning to write a lesson plan, it will be assumed that you have a master list of objectives for an elementary computer science course and have decided to write a plan for an objective that states, "You will describe, in one paragraph each, at least four ways information can be fed into a computer."

Having selected the objective, you next survey a variety of sources, both to make sure that what is remembered about the topic is accurate and to find out if any new data concerning the topic have been added since your last academic contact. The research indicates that there are at least ten ways to feed information to a computer, and you decide to condense the findings in a short outline. For example,

INPUT DEVICES AND MODES

1. *Punched cards.* Either a beam of light activating a photoelectric cell or a metal brush is used to detect the presence or absence of a hole at each predetermined spot on a card. These data are then converted to an electrical impulse and "read."

2. *Punched paper tape.* Analogous to a continuous punched card; however, the metal brush cannot be used for reading because of the inherent weakness of the material.

3. *Magnetic tape.* Spaces on a strip of magnetic tape are magnetized or demagnetized. These spaces are then "read" by a device sensitive to magnetic fields.

4. *Light pens.* A light-sensitive penlike device is held against a cathode ray tube and used to indicate certain areas to the computer. Light pens are often used in conjunction with more conventional terminals.

5. *Terminals.* Typewriterlike devices that can be used to code data directly into a computer via either direct electrical hook-ups or indirect hook-ups such as acoustic-couplers.

6. *Consoles.* Analogous to terminals but usually connected directly to the central processing unit.

7. *Electron pens.* Analogous to light pens, but utilizing a stream of electrons on either a CRT display or an electric table. Specific spots are activated by the electron stream.

8. *Magnetic ink.* A magnetically sensitive device compares configurations of characters printed in ink containing a ferromagnetic substance with a series of precoded configurations. When a match occurs, the computer "recognizes" the character and converts its value into a series of electrical impulses. Magnetic ink is used extensively on checks.

9. *Optical scanners.* Marks made in pencil at small but specific spots on a sheet of paper are "read" via reflected light and converted to a series of electrical impulses. Optical scanners are used extensively to machine score tests.

10. *Profile scanners.* Still in the experimental stage, but will use a TV-like device to convey images to a computer for comparison against a series of precoded images. When matches occur the data are acted upon. Has been used to enable robots to move about freely and for crude personnel identification.

To select appropriate teaching-learning activities, the next step is to preassess the students' knowledge concerning input devices. To accomplish this, you might decide to make the first teaching-learning activity an exploratory discussion during which students would be asked to list and, if possible, explain input devices with which they are familiar. Student responses could be listed on the board by a student or on an overhead projector, which would enable you to maintain eye contact with the students. Of course, you may have predetermined that this content will be new to the students and may therefore be able to eliminate preassessment procedures.

Assuming the students would provide relatively little of the information, you might decide to make the next teaching-learning activity the presentation of material to provide the remaining data. The form of this presentation could be any that you deem effective using whatever means are available. It would be logical to follow the presentation with any of the possibilities for student-centered analogous practice and to follow this practice with a period during which students could attempt the objective. By selecting at random two or three student responses, and going over them orally, a final review could be provided and students could also receive evaluations of their progress.

Having done all the thinking, gathering, organizing, and condensing, you can now write out the lesson plan in its final form. Generally speaking, you will find that the plan will be most useful if it is on a minimum number of sheets of paper. The final form of this lesson might very well look like the plan in Figure 7 (c) on page 190. There are, however, a great number of possible formats from which you can choose. A small sampling is included in Figure 7 (a–d). Rather than adapting any of these formats exactly, you may find it easier simply to arrange the components to reflect your personal preference. Once this is done, you can duplicate a number of blank lesson plan forms.

For practice, you may wish to write a one-page lesson plan to help students achieve the following objective: "The student will be able to list, in writing, at least three components of a lesson plan and at least one example of each." These efforts can be compared with those shown in Figure 7 (a–d).

SUMMARY

There is varying agreement among educators concerning the need for experienced teachers to write lesson plans. Advocates of lesson plans claim that plans are needed to focus attention on the lesson's objective, as a basis for improvement of instructional methods, as a record of what was taught and what students accomplished, and for utilization by substitute teachers. Opponents of lesson plans claim that written plans are superfluous for experienced teachers, inhibit teacher freedom, and are rendered useless if a preceding lesson does not go according to plan. Even in the midst of this disagreement, however, there are few educators who argue that beginning teachers do not benefit from written lesson plans, and none who can deny that many school systems require their teachers to write such plans.

Success in learning depends to a large degree upon the skill of a teacher in bringing together objectives, content, and teaching-learning activities, all of which are appropriate for a given group of students. The compilation of these elements into a lesson plan enables a teacher to ascertain the legitimacy and logic of their interrelationships and to add, delete, or modify elements to achieve greater coherency.

The most common components of a lesson plan include the following:

1. *Instructional objective.* States what students will be able to do at the end of the lesson.
2. *Content.* Consists of the basic information the student will need to achieve the objective or serves as a vehicle for the accomplishment of the objective. Often takes the form of a word or phrase outline.
3. *Teaching-learning activities.* Briefly describes the specific activities in which the teacher and students will engage during a particular lesson. Sometimes divided into student activities and teacher activities.
4. *Materials.* A listing of those aids needed for a lesson but not usually found in the classroom.
5. *Evaluation.* A space for comments concerning procedures for assessing student achievement of the stated objective and informal assessments of the effectiveness of particular teaching-learning activities, particularly with an eye toward future improvement.
6. *Time.* Approximate lengths of time allocated for each activity.
7. *Assignments.* Descriptions of out-of-class learning activities.
8. *Preassessment.* Determination of whether students need the planned instruction. (Usually takes the form of a pretest, an informal assessment of student standing, or a student attempt at the final objective.)
9. *Special announcements.* Usually administrative.
10. *Preliminary or routine tasks.* Taking attendance, distributing announcements, and so on.

Other components might include the date, the title of the course, subject and unit, and grade level.

Experience has shown that some or all of these components can be combined in one- or two-page lesson plans and that such plans can increase the probability of one's success as a teacher by increasing the probability that students will learn.

After deciding which components best fit particular needs and deciding upon a convenient lesson plan format, you would be wise to duplicate a number of blank lesson plan forms. Their use will make writing lesson plans easier and will help assure that important components are not omitted. All these preparations will help you do a better job in the classroom and help make the teaching-learning process more enjoyable and valuable.

CLASS: Secondary Education   GRADE LEVEL: Junior

DATE: 10/3

UNIT: Instructional Planning

PRELIMINARIES: Take attendance, make announcements.

ANNOUNCEMENTS: Evaluation of records for graduation begins next Monday.

OBJECTIVE: The student will list, in writing, at least three components of a lesson plan and at least one example of each. (Comprehension)

PREASSESSMENT: Ask students to demonstrate objective. If they can do so, go on to next lesson.

CONTENT: Lesson Plan Components

  1. A precise instructional objective (what students will be able to do).
  2. Content (the information to be covered).
  3. Teaching-learning activities (how the lesson will be taught).
  4. Materials (instructional aids needed).
  5. Evaluation (assessment of success).
  6. Time allotments (duration of each activity).
  7. Preassessment (are students already competent?).
  8. Date, course, grade level, unit, announcements, assignments.

Examples of Components: Use this plan as a source of examples.

Component Priorities

  1. What would be the minimum components you would need for a viable lesson plan? (Probably an objective, content, and activities.)
  2. When would other components be useful? (For use by substitute teacher or principal.)

ACTIVITIES AND TIME: Present components via tape-slide sequence (10 min.); short discussion concerning priorities and examples (10 min.); review components via recitation and write components on chalk board as students list them (5 min.); have students write components and examples (10 min.); discuss points made in randomly selected papers (10 min.).

ASSIGNMENTS: Have students construct a one-page lesson plan for a lesson of their choice for tomorrow's class.

EVALUATION: (Have students turn in lists of components. Check to see how many students achieved the objective. Evaluation of lesson procedures.) Students were able to accomplish the objective, but the use of an overhead projector to record student suggestions for components would have helped.

FIGURE 7(a)   Model for Lesson on Lesson Plans Utilizing All Components

DATE: 10/3

OBJECTIVE: The student will list, in writing, at least three components of a lesson plan and at least one example of each. (Comprehension)

CONTENT: Lesson Plan Components

1. A precise instructional objective (what students will be able to do).
2. Content (information to be covered).
3. Teaching-learning activities (how the lesson will be taught).
4. Materials (instructional aids).
5. Evaluation (assessment of success).
6. Time allocations (duration of each activity).
7. Preassessment (are students already competent?).
8. Date, course, grade level, unit, announcements, assignments.

ACTIVITIES:

1. Begin by asking students what would be the very least they would need to know, as substitute teachers, to teach a lesson.
2. List responses using an overhead.
3. Order the responses given from most important to least important and add from the component list any that were missed.
4. Agree upon at least three basic components (probably objectives, content, and activities).
5. Have students demonstrate objective.
6. Discuss points made in randomly selected papers.

FIGURE 7(b)   Model for Lesson on Lesson Plans Utilizing a Minimum Number of Components

CLASS: Elementary Computer Science   UNIT: I/O Devices

DATE: 10/3

OBJECTIVE: The student will describe, in one paragraph each, the ways in which at least four devices can be used to feed information into a computer. (Comprehension)

CONTENT: Input devices and modes include at least the following:

1. *Punched cards.* Metal brushes or photoelectric cells detect holes.
2. *Paper tape.* Analogous to punch cards.
3. *Magnetic tape.* Spots are magnetized or demagnetized on a strip of plastic tape coated with a ferromagnetic substance, and their state is "read" by the computer.
4. *Terminals.* Typewriterlike devices used to code data directly or indirectly into a computer.
5. *Consoles.* Analogous to terminals but usually linked directly to the CPU.
6. *Electron pens.* Penlike devices that "write" with a stream of electrons. Used with CRT displays and electric tables.
7. *Magnetic ink.* Character configurations written in magnetic ink are matched against precoded configurations. Used on most checks.
8. *Optical scanners.* Uses light reflected from pencil marks made at specific locations on a sheet of paper to "read" data.
9. *Profile scanners.* Still experimental but will use a TV-like device to convey images to a CPU for comparison with precoded images.

TEACHING-LEARNING ACTIVITIES:

1. Begin by engaging students in a discussion of how information can be fed into a computer. List points on the overhead projector (5 min.). Possible questions:
   a. What are those strange figures at the bottom of most checks? (Numbers written in magnetic ink.)
   b. What happens to machine scored tests after you finish coding in your answers? (They are run through a device that senses— via a beam of reflected light—exactly where your marks are, and these data are then fed into a computer via electrical impulses.)
2. Presentation over the remaining points using the overhead projector (15 min.).
3. Turn off the projector and review the main points via questions and answers (10 min.).
4. Hand out paper and have students attempt the objective (10 min.).
5. Collect the papers and go over two or three (at random) to provide feedback to students (5 min.).

   MATERIALS: Overhead projector.

   EVALUATION: The papers will be checked by the teacher. (The teacher adds comments about the effectiveness of the lesson.)

FIGURE 7(c)   Model for Lesson on Computer Input Methods Utilizing Suggested Components

DATE: 10/3

OBJECTIVE: Each student will explain, in writing, at least six characteristics of Romanticism. (Comprehension)

CONTENT:

1. Definition: Romanticism is a way of looking at life and at oneself with a state of mind centered around emotions.
2. Major characteristics of Romanticism
   a. A return to "nature"
   b. Sympathy for the rural life and its activities
   c. Sentimental contemplation
   d. Predominance of imagination over reason
   e. Idealization of the past
   f. Concern for all that is aesthetically beautiful in the ideal sense
   g. Praising of childhood
   h. Idealization of women
   i. A wish to explore the personal inner world of dreams and desires (soul searching)

LEARNING ACTIVITIES:

1. Show students pictures of a jackhammer and a sunset and ask what thoughts each brings to mind.
2. Explain and discuss briefly the term "Romanticism."
3. Divide the class in groups of four or five and have half the groups act out a three-minute skit portraying people as they normally are, and the other half act out three-minute skits portraying machinelike, unemotional people (after the fashion of *Star Trek's* Dr. Spock).
4. Lead discussion of students' skits emphasizing the value of emotions. Introduce the various points listed in the content section if they are not introduced by students. List the points on the overhead as they are made.
5. When all points have been discussed, erase board and, via direct questions, review main characteristics of Romanticism.
6. Have students demonstrate objective, then use overhead to allow students to check their responses against the previously constructed list of characteristics.

MATERIALS:

1. Pictures of a jackhammer and a beautiful sunset.
2. Overhead projector, transparencies, and grease pencil.

EVALUATION: At the end of the period pass out lined paper and ask students to explain at least six characteristics of Romanticism. Provide immediate feedback concerning achievement of the objective by allowing students to grade their own papers. Use overhead to project complete list of characteristics.

FIGURE 7 (d)   Model for Lesson on Characteristics of Romanticism Utilizing Suggested Components

ELEVEN
INDIVIDUALIZING
INSTRUCTION

Among the ideals continually advocated by educational theorists has been the notion of individualized instruction. Educational psychologists point out that, because every student is unique and has different readiness levels, ideally, teaching should be *individualized*. The term "individualization of instruction" has, however, come to stand for a variety of ideas such as (1) special individual lesson plans, (2) self-paced instruction, (3) self-selected curriculum, and (4) large-group instruction with individual help. This chapter explores possibilities for self-pacing via the use of self-instructional materials. It also presents, in the form of a self-instructional package, the fundamental steps necessary for building self-instructional materials.

OBJECTIVES

When you complete this chapter, you will be able to:

1. Explain at least two advantages and two disadvantages of the use of self-instructional materials in your own teaching field in no more than two pages. (Analysis)
2. Construct a self-instructional package that meets the criteria set forth in this chapter and is suitable for use in your teaching field. (Synthesis)

THE SYSTEMS APPROACH
TO INDIVIDUALIZING

There are a variety of ways a self-instructional package approach can achieve self-pacing. One is to operate separate classrooms as self-contained units wherein each teacher decides how to achieve the objectives. Another is to combine several classrooms, departments, or the entire school under one larger system for instruction. Whatever the administrative procedure adopted, all approaches are based on the construction of sets of self-paced instructional packages that have objectives encompassing a variety of domains and levels. Following is a description of a typical middle school system's concept for self-instruction. It is not a description of any particular school but has elements of many that are in operation. Included are some of the processes necessary to engage in a changeover from a traditional school, although a more complete analysis is the province of texts on supervision or curricular development.

After achieving staff agreement (no easy chore in itself) that a thrust toward a self-paced systems program is desirable, the hypothetical school can initiate a first phase toward a gradual changeover. The recommended first step is an agreement among staff members of each department upon the objectives of that department. These objectives will undergo the critical examination described in Chapters 3 and 4, including an analysis of terminal and en-route objectives, and identification of the necessary prerequisite skills for each objective identified.

After the identification of objectives, a procedure for building self-paced instructional packages and pilot testing is organized using small numbers of students. No attempt is made at this point to convert classrooms to a systems approach. The packages are offered as supplements to, or temporary replacements for, the regular instructional program. Built-in evaluation procedures for the constituent parts of the packages to be used by the student are included (for example, questions such as "What learning activity was helpful?" and "Did you understand the objective?"). In this way, the packages are polished and improved.

As a department increases its stock of proven self-instructional packages to the point at which all objectives of a particular course are covered, that course may be put on a systems basis. Assume that there are three teachers of eighth-grade English during the third period each day. When self-instructional packages have been built for the entire course, the decision can be made to try the packages as a system that includes all three classes.

At this point the role of the teacher changes dramatically. Instead of fulfilling the traditional role, the teacher's new responsibilities will focus on four basic activities. First, a teacher will have a responsibility to the system that replaces responsibility to a single class. For instance, instead of keeping track of grades for each student in the one class, a teacher may keep track of the packages completed by students in all three classes. In return, another teacher who previously kept track of materials for his or her own class may now keep track of material for all three classes.

Second, the teacher will be expected to write new packages and to review old and new materials. Continual additions and improvements are necessary to keep a system viable. If there is a problem with a particular package, immediate alteration is required. The teacher most concerned with that particular package must be willing to modify it quickly to ensure success of the system. This package building implies a growing need for proficiency in the production and selection of media. Most packages need a variety of learning modes to be successful. As new information and ideas appear in the content areas, the teachers should be alert to the possibilities of including good new ideas in the packages. Microcomputers are proliferating very rapidly and are ideally suited to use on a self-instructional basis.

Third, the teacher should expect to serve on content-area committees that will continue to examine the selection and evaluation of objectives in terms of overall school goals and community changes. A perfectly good set of terminal objectives for last year's student population may become obsolete because of the influx of a new type of student population during the course of the year. The committees may also consider many other issues connected with the operation of the system, such as new package adoption or revision of old packages.

Finally, the teacher becomes an advisor and counselor in addition to a content-area specialist. The student-teacher contacts become more one-to-one as the teacher assists each student with particular concepts or procedural details.

The role of the students also changes as they work through a course using self-paced materials. Assuming that the required objectives of the course have become the objectives of learning packages, the student may consult the teacher about which package should be worked on next. A plan and appropriate materials may already have been prepared individually for the student, and he or she may only need to consult that plan; or the student may consult a routing sheet that all students are following. After determining which is the next learning package, the student may select that package from his or her personal set of materials or may go to a central location and check out an individual package. Once the package is in the student's hands, work can begin.

Packages take a wide variety of forms, but most contain a preliminary statement of the skills that will be demonstrated upon completion of the package. If the student does not fully understand the precise instructional objective as stated, he or she will need the assistance of one of the teachers. At this point (depending upon the sophistication of the package), the student may take a preassessment test that will enable him or her to determine

(1) which learning activities need to be engaged in, (2) which learning activities may be omitted because of prior knowledge, or (3) whether he or she already has the competency and can go immediately to the final evaluation instrument. In some cases a preassessment may be set up under test conditions, and the student may demonstrate the competency directly after or during preassessment.

After determining the specific learning activities necessary to build the skill needed to demonstrate the competency, the student begins to work at these activities. It is at this point that many programs succeed or fail. The learning activities must be interesting. They need to include a variety of learning modes and should be based on sound learning principles. Films, filmstrips, guest speakers, records, multimedia kits, lab work, and field trips are just some of the learning modes that students can use to acquire skills and information. Reading is not the only option available in the self-instruction packages.

After completion of the learning activities, the student is ready for evaluation. Evaluation can take many forms. If it is to be a test, the student may acquire a copy of the examination from the teacher and go to a special area to take it, or the student may be tested at a central station in the school that has its own support staff. Results from this test should include feedback if the necessary minimum competency is not attained so that the student can determine which learning activities need reemphasis or whether an alternate learning activity is more appropriate to specific needs.

The system for informing students of their progress and for keeping accurate records can range from individual record keeping by teachers to a computer-oriented surveillance of an entire school. The information is vital for continuous process adjustment.

By blending a combination of "required" packages with a variety of "self-choice" packages, students can begin to have some control over curriculum content. While it is obvious that eighth-grade students need to continue to write to improve competency in written communication skills, the choice of content between science fiction and sports short stories for instance, can be left to the students if both types of literature will help them to attain the same skill competency.

THE EFFECT OF SELF-INSTRUCTIONAL
PACKAGES ON THE CURRICULUM

The Purpose of Package Programs

The most persuasive reason for the increased popularity of self-instruction package programs is their potential for individualizing instruction. Although educators' implementation of this long-advocated position on individualization is, unfortunately, far from complete, self-instructional packages provide an effective start in the right direction.

A second reason for the implementation of self-instructional package programs is the opportunity they afford for rigorous curricular examination. When the question is asked, "What is the student going to be able to do after completing the self-instructional package," the reply necessitates examination of a behavioral objective, and the result may be a clean-up of outdated curricular inclusions.

A third reason for self-instructional package programs is that they eliminate duplication of material and ensure inclusion of important material. It is well known that, when course guides are displayed for classes in the secondary school, they often do not reflect the actual teaching. Teachers may neglect certain content areas and overemphasize or reteach other areas. Self-instructional package programs eliminate this problem since, once a student can demonstrate a competency, he or she need not rehash the old material again.

A fourth reason for considering the use of self-instructional materials is they can be of great use in meeting the needs of mainstreamed students. Since these students may need an individualized instructional program in some parts of your course, the use of self-instructional materials might help you meet the needs of those students in an educationally sound and expeditious manner.

The Teacher as Advisor

When a self-instructional package program is underway, the teacher assumes a new set of responsibilities. Without describing in detail the extent of this change, it is worthwhile here to point out a new phenomenon in the relationship between student and teacher generated by a self-instructional package systems approach.

Under a traditional education system, the student's perception of the teacher-student role often approaches that of an adversary. The instructor assigns the work, teaches the class, administers tests, and hands out grades. The student competes with other students for attention and grades and learns that the teacher is the most powerful element in the process. Oftentimes learning is inhibited by the threat of competition with peers, the possibility of alienation of the teacher, fear of the subject content, or previous unsuccessful experiences.

In a self-instructional package program the student is not competing with peers but is striving to achieve a predetermined competency level. The teacher in this situation has the opportunity to work *with* the student to reach this mutual goal. The student's success becomes the teacher's success, and together they can take mutual pride as competency in each area is proven.

Teachers taking full advantage of this role possibility will find a more relaxed interchange building up between themselves and the students, leading to more profitable personal relationships.

Packages as Enrichment Activities

One problem faced by all teachers handling large classrooms is how to accommodate the bright student who has conquered the current material. One common technique utilized by textbooks and teachers is to provide a set of topics and encourage the students to generate a project of their own . There are several disadvantages to this approach if a complete independent study program is not in effect. The first is that independent study projects can be a time-consuming enterprise for the teacher. Four or five active "independent scholars" in addition to a room filled wih other students can increase the work load beyond feasibility. A second disadvantage is that, without structure, the topic limits and approach of the projects can easily get out of hand. A third problem is that at just about the time the bright student gets rolling on the project, the class has caught up and is starting work in a new area. The bright student must stop the project (generated from an interest in the last topic) and shift gears into the new area. Students may lose interest when they have time to return to the old project.

Having a series of supplemental self-instructional packages for each topic can offer relief for several of these problems. The student may pick among them according to interest and, because of their calculated length, complete as many as time permits before the next unit.

Things do not always go in practice exactly as in theory, so there will be occasions when there will not be enough packages and more will have to be built and other occasions when the student will assert that none of the possible packages is interesting. But a self-instructional package program can certainly assist you in providing enrichment for many bright youngsters.

Remedial Use of Packages

When it has been discerned that there is no point in having a student continue in a classroom topic because he or she has fallen too far behind in the regular classroom pace, it is possible to shift to a self-instructional package program on an individual basis. This technique is applicable in those instances where the course is broken down into discrete topics. In these instances, the student need not continue in frustration in that unit, but can move to a series of slightly less difficult objectives in a self-instructional package program where he or she can experience success. When a new topic is started, the student can be shifted back to the classroom with a "fresh start" in that topic.

When the class content builds throughout the year and each new piece of information depends upon mastery of the previous information, the student may be shifted to a self-instructional package program at the point at which learning from class presentations is no longer profitable. That is, enough new terminology and concepts are being used in the course of instruction that the student does not benefit from the presentations. The student may or may not be on a package program for the rest of the course. In some instances, the self-instructional package program may allow him or her to catch up with the class. Even then, however, the student often prefers to stay in the package program because of the success experienced.

Extended Absence

In some instances when self-instructional package programs are available as a counterpart to the traditional classroom situation, the student who is absent because of illness or other circumstances can keep pace with the class by undertaking self-instructional package programs at home. One drawback, of course, is that packages are often not self-contained and refer the student to other material, which must be obtained from the school, or the public library, or other sources. In addition, when the packages have several possible learning modes, students may be faced with the problem that the best learning modes for them are available only at school. In spite of these obstacles, many students have been able to keep up with their schoolwork while physically away from school through the use of self-instructional packages.

Partial Package Programs

In some classrooms teachers are blending packages with regular classroom instruction. In one popular approach to partial programs, the students are involved in topics related to the content of the regular class during time opened specifically for self-instructional packages. Students might be doing traditional classwork on Monday, Wednesday, and Friday; on Tuesday and Thursday, however, they work on any of the several available self-instructional packages. During this time they operate independently and are given credit for competencies gained.

A second approach has the self-instructional packages built more closely into the curricular content of the traditional class. There may be less of a variety of self-instructional packages, sometimes as few as three or four, and they are reproduced in enough quantity so that the class may be broken into groups by interest areas or ability.

Each group area works on the related self-instructional packages for a portion of the time. In some cases students can start the self-instructional packages with some group work and then branch out to individual work. In other instances a subgroup of students with the same self-instructional package can be brought together during the work period for a particular learning activity and then returned to individual work.

Modified Systems Programs

Some programs combine aspects of a traditional classroom with a total systems approach. Various procedures are used but only one is examined here.

Students are broken into three groups and each individual starts on the self-instructional package assigned to that group.. The time allotted for completion of the package is enough so that about two-thirds of each group will have demonstrated the competency by a specified date. During work periods occasional compulsory traditional classes are held as part of the learning activities described in this package. At the end of the allotted period, the two-thirds who demonstrated the competency move to the next set of self-instructional packages. The one-third who did not demonstrate the competency may be recycled through the classroom activities along with the students who are moving into the same package from one of the completed self-instructional package groups. In this fashion a student will have three "cycles" to complete a self-instructional package in which some of the learning activity is based on traditional classroom-type instruction. After a particular package is repeated three times, other forms of instruction are substituted for the classroom part of the learning activities.

BUILDING A SELF-INSTRUCTIONAL PACKAGE—MODEL PACKAGE

Part 1: Objective for Model Package 1

Following a model and a set of instructions, you will be able to construct a self-instructional package in your content area suitable for use by pupils and containing a minimum of five prescribed elements listed in this package. These elements must exhibit the minimum qualitative criteria described in the evaluation section of this package. (Synthesis)

Part 2: Self-preassessment

If you have already built one or more self-instructional packages, you may compare them with the criteria in the evaluation sections to see if they meet the criteria. If so, they may be submitted to your instructor for evaluation. Since you were not working with the instructor on the project, be prepared to answer technical questions about it to demonstrate clearly that it is your own work. Even if you have already built an instructional package, you may wish to build another to satisfy this competence, because (1) the more times you work at this skill the better you will become, and (2) no teacher ever has enough self-instructional packages to satisfy all the needs of students.

Part 3. Learning Activities

You will:

1. Study the section "Constructing Self-instructional Packages" found in this package.
2. After this preparation, you are ready to begin construction of your package. Follow the steps described in the section "Constructing Self-instructional Packages" and in the evaluation section of this package.
3. Use the "Checklist for Constructing Self-instructional Packages" to check each component of your package.
4. Schedule a help session with your instructor if you feel it is necessary.

LEARNING ACTIVITY 2:
CONSTRUCTING SELF-INSTRUCTIONAL PACKAGES
(THIS SECTION IS THE READING FOR LEARNING ACTIVITY 2)

This self-instructional package on self-instructional packages will serve as our model to guide you step by step in the construction of your own self-instructional package. You will want to prepare your own with care so that you can use it in your work.

We shall build each of the four basic divisions in the self-instructional package separately, always being careful that each step focuses exactly on the objective. Before we are done, your self-instructional package should at least include

1. A clear, precise instructional *objective*.
2. A procedure for students to *preassess* their ability in the subject area and guide themselves to appropriate activities.
3. An interesting set of *learning activities* that will build the student's ability as described in the behavioral objective.
4. An *evaluation process* that will assess whether or not the student has acquired the competency described in the behavioral objective.

In addition to these four basic sections, your self-instructional package may include other elements, such as

1. A list of materials that the student will need to complete the package.
2. An enrichment section to guide the student to additional activities in the same content area.
3. A discussion of the approximate time needed to complete the entire package or parts of the package.

4. A rationale explaining why it is important for the student to acquire the skills or information described in the objective.
5. Optional learning activities to help students attain the objective, not necessary if the student engages adequately in the required learning activities.
6. Self-evaluation prior to the final evaluation, to provide feedback of competency before actual attempts are made at final evaluation.
7. A section early in the package alerting the student to schedule certain items in advance, for instance when any learning experiences involve scheduling a room, special material, or group session.
8. Any other sections that may seem appropriate because of the unique nature of the content of a particular package.

EVOLVING THE PACKAGE

In theory, a package could evolve from mutual student and staff recognition of curricular need. For instance, it could become apparent in a home economics class that students lacked ability in personal money management. If enough students felt frustrated because of personal money mismanagement, a self-instructional package on that topic would evolve.

Since you may not yet have had enough practical experience to be able to identify areas of student frustration in your own teaching field, simply select some topic in which you are interested (or which may have caused you some difficulty) and use that topic as the basis for your self-instructional package.

Step 1 From a school library, obtain a typical text in your content area that might be used in a high school. Locate in that text a topic you find interesting.. If you choose, you may utilize sources of content material other than a textbook.

Step 2 Translate this content into precise instructional objectives. At this point you may need to review Chapters 3 and 4 to write good instructional objectives. You should include more than just lower-level cognitive objectives. In the objectives for this model package, there are both knowledge-comprehension objectives and higher-level objectives. You may particularly wish to review the part of Chapter 4 dealing with the taxonomic levels in the cognitive domain before proceeding.

Suppose you are an industrial arts teacher and you have chosen to develop your self-instructional package somewhere in the area of metalwork. The text you have chosen is *Metalwork, Technology and Practice,* by Oswald A. Ludwig and Willard J. McCarthy.[1]

[1]Oswald Ludwig and Willard McCarthy, *Metalwork, Technology and Practice* (Bloomington, Ill.: McKnight and McKnight, 1969). p.53

In looking through Chapter 6 on "Layout Tools," you decide that a self-instructional package could be built on the use of inside calipers. There seems logically to be two levels to a self-instructional package on this topic: first, we wish the student to comprehend information *about* calipers; and second, we wish him or her to be able to *use* calipers. After some thought, objectives such as the following are generated:

1. After studying specific material on the care and use of inside calipers, the student will be able to demonstrate comprehension of that material by answering correctly nine out of ten written completion-type questions.
2. When presented with a set of inside calipers, a steel rule, and a piece of iron with five holes drilled in it, the student will be able to use the calipers to measure the inside diameter of four of the five holes to within one-sixty-fourth of an inch.

The first objective is at a skill level lower in the cognitive domain than that required in the second objective. The second objective is a combination of the cognitive skill *application* (level 3) and psychomotor skills.

This procedure of delineating what you wish your student to be able to do after the instruction should cause you some real thought and introspection. Do not be satisfied with an objective because it was easy to build. Try to analyze what it is that you really wish the student to be able to do and translate that into words that communicate powerfully. The student should be able to understand immediately from the objective what competency will have to be demonstrated. If some of the words used in the objective are complicated and are only later defined in the material in the learning activities, it is absurd to assume the objective will perform its intended function.

Step 3   Although the order of the self-instructional package as used by the student has the preassessment section next, you are generally better off arranging the rest of your self-instructional package first and then returning to build the preassessment. This enables you to set the link-ups to the corresponding learning activities from each part of the preassessment activity.

Let us return to our example. We ask ourselves, "How can I transmit the necessary background information about the use and care of inside calipers most easily to the student?" and "What alternative learning procedures for this objective can be made?" Some of the possible ways to transmit this information are by having the student

1. Read material from a text.
2. Read articles on the subject from trade magazines.
3. Read specially produced material prepared by the teacher (usually the material most precisely tuned to your objectives).

4. Listen to commercially produced audio tapes on the subject.
5. Listen to audio tapes produced by the teacher.
6. Modify items 4 and 5 of this list by listening to the tape while viewing accompanying handouts.
7. View a filmstrip made either commercially or locally.
8. View and listen to a tape-slide presentation—either commercially or teacher produced.
9. Refer the learner to a student who already has the competency. The "tutor" uses a special guide to make sure all the points required are covered and receives some credit for successful demonstration of the competency by the "pupil."
10. Arrange small help sessions during lulls in the class for the students who have signed up on a special sheet.
11. View and listen to a filmstrip on the subject while filling out an accompanying worksheet that emphasizes the important points in the filmstrip.
12. Engage in a single linear "programmed learning" sequence covering the material.
13. Engage in a more complex, branched program using a computer terminal.
14. Engage in any other learning activity deemed appropriate.

After you decide upon instructional modes for the learning activity, the material that will make the learning activities "come alive" must be built. For the first objective, in which the student is learning about the care and use of calipers, let us assume that the learning activity chosen is a teacher-prepared sound filmstrip. All the content material is gathered and arranged into a script. The script is then recorded on a tape cassette. It is found that the entire taped content runs twelve minutes. Simple photographs are then taken of the main points emphasized in the script, and the student is told in the script when to move to the next slide. A good way to focus on the important points would be to have an accompanying worksheet, which students could fill out as the tape-slide sequence is viewed and from which they could later study.

Some teachers are concerned about making the quality of their work look professional. It certainly does not hurt for the slides to look as though they came out of a magazine and for the voice on the script to sound like Richard Burton, but it is not *necessary* to have perfection in order to have a high degree of learning take place. In fact, students identify with everyday photos of other students used in the slides and respond to the voice on the tape when it is someone they know. Using a tape cassette, a set of slides clearly numbered from 1 to 30, and a simple hand-held slide viewer can be as effective as a slick professional treatment. If alternate learning activities are desired, the script may become reading material generously illustrated with the prints and made available as checkouts from the materials center.

For purposes of learning to *use* the inside calipers, it is obvious that the student should engage in the equivalent practice necessary to gain the proficiency. For this, the second objective points clearly to the self-instructional learning activity required. A series of various-sized holes are drilled into pieces of metal and identified with a key. Students simply engage in the necessary amount of practice until they are measuring the inside diameter of the holes correctly. (Our example objective's criterion level is probably too low, since after one gets the "feel" and some practice with inside calipers and micrometers, measurements accurate to within 0.005 inches should be possible.)

This objective happens to align itself well with the equivalent practice providing immediate feedback to students as they practice. Other learning activities, like this self-instructional package on building self-instructional packages, may not be so easy to design. For instance, if you are using this book independently, the only way you can check the objectives you design for your package is to compare them with the objectives in this package, the objectives at the beginning of many of the other chapters, and the samples in Chapters 3 and 4. If you are using this book in conjunction with a class, your instructor should also be able to give you advice as to the appropriateness of your objectives and the rest of your self-instructional package as you build it.

You should now try your hand at building your instructional learning activities. It may be that your objective leads you to a particular activity. You may want to ask yourself the following questions to guide your choice and work:

1. Are the materials necessary for building the activity available?
2. Is the importance of the objective large enough to warrant multimodal activities?
3. Is the target population of students who will use the package confined to a particular level, thereby restricting the range of the possible learning activities?
4. What restrictions does the content of the objective place upon learning activity development?
5. What do I know about learning activities that have been used for this content area in the classroom that will be effective for a self-instructional package?

After building the learning activities, it may be possible, even though the entire package is not complete, to explain the objectives to a small sample population and obtain suggestions improving the learning activities. A "trial run" can often save a lot of headaches. It can be especially helpful to ensure the alignment of the objective with the learning activities. You may also be able to get ideas from your peers or your instructor at this point to help polish these activities.

Step 4   Without forgetting that we will return to build our preassessment section, the next step is to design the evaluation for our self-instructional packages.

Whatever the skills we described in our objective, they will be checked to ensure that the student can now demonstrate the described competency at the minimum criterion level. The first objective in our example leaves little doubt about our check. We wanted the student to show comprehension of facts about the care and use of inside calipers, and we were willing to accept as a demonstration of that competency "correctly answering nine out of ten written completion-type questions." We have left out of the objective other conditions surrounding the demonstration of the competency, so the first thing our evaluation section should do is communicate any and all conditions. Let us assume that there is a test center in this school, so the instruction may be something like, "When you have completed the learning activities and filled out your worksheet, and feel that you understand the material, report to the test center for the short completion exam on this material. If it is the first time that you have taken the exam, ask for Test #0034 on *Calipers*—Form I. If you have taken the test before, ask for Form II. You will be expected to complete nine out of ten completion questions correctly on this test."

If we had decided to include a trial test, then the preceding instruction would be modified to encourage the student to take this self-administered trial test and check his or her work against provided model answers. In this circumstance the trial-test answers would direct the student to the approximate part of the worksheet for review in case of missed answers.

A sample item of the form described in the objective might be, "An inside caliper is a two-legged, steel instrument with its _____ bent outward." (See Learning Activity 2, slide 4, or Learning Activity 3, page 5 for review.) Answer: Legs.

The second objective also leads us to an obvious evaluation. It implies the use of inside calipers, a rule, and a piece of metal with holes drilled in it. The operation of the typical test center may or may not preclude the student from using these materials there. Let us assume that we cannot use the test center. Then our instructions might read: "When you have completed the learning activities in this self-instructional package, and you feel that you can successfully use inside calipers to measure the inside diameter of holes drilled in metal, ask your instructor for the steel bar for testing and the test answer sheet for this objective. Bring a 6-inch steel rule and an inside caliper with you at this time. You will need to measure four out of five holes to within one-sixty-fourth of an inch to demonstrate this competency."

If you know that you will be involved in a self-instructional package program with certain restrictions, build them into your instructions. For instance, you may know that you will be evaluating only on Tuesdays and Fridays. Then say so in your evaluation section.

A much less satisfactory procedure for this objective would be to describe and illustrate a series of inside caliper measures on a straight written test administered in the test center. In this instance the student would answer questions about the descriptions and pictures. We could assume that, if the student could honestly answer such questions, he or she could find the inside diameter of drilled holes. Such assumptions are risky and should be avoided, although analogous situations can be found throughout school systems.

You should now build your evaluations for your self-instructional package. The trial test is a sound procedure and should be used if possible. Make sure test items are straightforward and clear. At this point you may wish to refer to the section in Chapter 8 on evaluation (page 133) for guidance in the construction of criterion-referenced test items.

It is often hard to determine initially how well the student must perform on a new test instrument on untried learning activities. Fortunately as your skill as a package writer increases, your intuitive notions about the proper criterion level will increase rapidly. A flat 80 percent proficiency level for all tests in a system is unrealistic. It is obvious that for this purpose alone conducting trial runs is worth the effort.

Step 5   We are now ready to return to the preassessment section. We have postponed it until now because, even though the behavioral objectives in your package tell you exactly what the students are going to be able to do at the end of instruction that they could not do before, they do not consider the instructional approach to be used. Building the learning activities and the evaluation section has structured an approach to help the student achieve the objectives, and this approach can now provide a basis for sequencing and referencing preassessment questions.

There are many facets to the problem of preassessment. Chapter 5 covers several approaches to rapid assessment of the readiness of individuals for learning. For our purpose we are interested in giving students a procedure to judge their own knowledge and skills in relations to the knowledge and skills presented in the package. Two procedures are often used. One is to ask a series of questions about the content. Students go through the questions carefully and attempt to answer them. Whenever they encounter a question they cannot answer, they can refer to a designated section in the accompanying articles. If students find that they cannot answer very many questions, then it is definitely best simply to start with the learning activities and go through them. If students know that they learn best from an alternative mode to reading, the slide filmstrips and audio tapes that accompany those learning activities can be used. If students know most of the answers and choose to use the preassessment to figure out which portions of the material they need to cover, the slide filmstrip and the audio tapes are more difficult to survey to find various parts. Therefore, it probably would be best to begin at the beginning, review all the material, and *emphasize* the parts that the questions have referred them to.

A second type of preassessment is described for this self instructional package. In this case, the evaluation will be of a product—a self-instructional package. Either the student has completed a self-instructional package in the past or has not. If he or she has, and it meets the qualitative criteria listed in the evaluation section, the student may immediately submit it to the instructor for demonstration of the competency.

Various procedures are acceptable for preassessment purposes. In some packages concerned primarily with a very specific set of facts, the preassessment, trial test, and final test may be virtually the same instrument. For instance, in the case of a set of precise safety rules for the chemistry lab, when the rules are specific enough and 100 percent competency is mandated, the three test instruments may be changed only enough to ensure comprehension and to avoid the rote memorization of a list of correct answers.

Going back to our example of the inside calipers, let us describe a third alternative. For purposes of illustration, assume that the shop teacher has a senior student who has majored in metalwork and is now a student assistant. For our preassessment we ask the students who believe they can use inside calipers to see the student assistant to demonstrate their ability. The assistant has a short checklist, and the pupils who feel that they already have the proficiency simply demonstrate each skill on the list. If they reach a certain level on the checklist, they need not engage in the package.

If this package is one of many covering the use of hand tool skills, the preassessment process could be the same for all of the packages. If that is clearly understood by all students, then there need not be any mention of preassessment in each of the separate packages. Instead, the condition can be announced generally and posted. On the other hand, it is always a good idea to repeat any uniform instruction in each package, so that nothing is left to chance and the instructor is protected.

At this point you should build your preassessment procedure and any instruments for the procedure. You will then have the four basic parts to your package completed and again, a trial run to check the complete flow is encouraged.

STEP 6   From the trial runs and self-analysis you may now have the feeling that other embellishments are needed to make the package complete. You may want to go back to the introduction of this article on "Constructing a Self-instructional Package" and review some of the additions that are often helpful to self-instructional packages. For instance, this model package has a checklist to use when constructing your own package.

In our running example of the inside calipers, the student may be alerted in a separate early section of the self-instructional package to schedule his or her final evaluation to demonstrate the ability to use the inside calipers a day in advance of the day the demonstration is to take place. This will enable the evaluator to schedule a mutually convenient time and to be sure all needed materials are on hand.

STEP 7   Before turning in your self-instructional package for final evaluation, use the Learning Activity 5 checklist to make sure you have included all the minimum requirements for a successful package, and that they make good sense in light of this discussion.

LEARNING ACTIVITY 5: CHECKLIST FOR BUILDING A SELF-INSTRUCTIONAL PACKAGE

1. Does your self-instructional package contain the minimum requirements of (a) a precise instructional objective, (b) preassessment, (c) learning activities, and (d) evaluation?
2. Do the objectives contain
   a. An observable terminal behavior that tells students what they should be able to do after completing the package?
   b. A minimum acceptable standard that explains how well they must be able to accomplish the objective?
   c. The conditions that describe the circumstances under which they will demonstrate the competence described in the objective?
3. Is the objective a valid one for the field?
4. Can the objective be evaluated in precise terms?
5. Does the preassessment section describe a procedure that will give the student the necessary information to determine their background in relation to the anticipated outcomes?
6. Is the procedure described in the preassessment section workable and not cumbersome?
7. Are there a variety of learning activities available in the learning activities section?
8. Can the student locate the cited material easily?
9. Do the learning activities concentrate on preparing the student to be able to accomplish the objective with a minimum of digression?
10. Are the learning activities designed at a level the student can understand?
11. Are the learning activities lively and interesting?
12. Does the evaluation truly check the competency described in the objective?

13. Will the evaluation tell the student and the teacher where the breakdown in learning occurred when the competency described in the objective is not demonstrated?

14. Are the instructions for the evaluation stated clearly so that there is no question in the mind of the student as to how to proceed?

15. Are all the additional sections you have included necessary?

16. Would additional sections be helpful?

Part 4: Evaluation

The evaluation of this objective is a judgment as to whether or not a package constructed by you meets the following minimum qualitative criteria:

1. One or more objectives that contain an observable behavior, conditions under which the behavior will be exhibited, and the criteria upon which it will be judged.

2. A preassessment of the competence already possessed by the student in the area described in the objectives. The preassessment should guide the student to the appropriate learning activities.

3. Precise learning activities (at least two), explained so that students clearly know what they are to do to acquire the competency. These learning activities will preferably have more than one instructional mode so that the students may select instructional procedures they like or learn from best.

4. An evaluation description, with precise directions as to exactly how the student will be evaluated, including where to go, who to see, and to whom to submit products.

5. Evaluation instruments. If the evaluation is to be a test, then that test must be prepared. If the evaluation is to be the assessment of a skill, then a checklist to guide assessment should be prepared. If the evaluation is to be the construction of a product, then a model and qualitative criteria need to be provided.

6. Internal consistency. The objectives, preassessment, learning activities, and evaluation should all zero in on the same competency. Material extraneous to that goal, and subtle differences in the thrust from one section to another, must be eliminated.

7. Any or all of the supplemental parts of packages that are mentioned in the article "Constructing Self-instructional Packages," such as worksheets, checklists, and self-tests, may be included.

8. Compliance with the "Checklist for Building a Self-instructional Package" found in this package.

When you are done with your package, make sure that you have covered items 1 through 8 of this list of qualitative criteria and see that you have complied with all of them. If appropriate, turn in your completed package to your instructor for final evaluation.

SUMMARY

The phrase *individualizing instruction* has come to refer to a variety of educational procedures generally aimed at providing instruction geared to the needs of individual students. In this chapter we have applied the term to the idea of self-pacing via the use of self-instructional packages.

Self-instructional packages are useful for presenting new information, but they are used more frequently to provide remedial or enrichment material. The basic parts of a self-instructional package are (1) precise instructional objective(s), (2) a preassessment section, (3) a learning activities section, and (4) an evaluation section.

It is important to keep in mind that, while self-instructional packages can be highly effective instructional and motivational tools, students still profit from your attention. In the final analysis, people learn best from people.

TWELVE
DISCIPLINE

One of the greatest concerns of beginning teachers is whether they will be able to establish and maintain a classroom atmosphere conducive to effective teaching and learning. In short, they are worried about discipline. In this chapter some of the basic causes of discipline problems are explored, first from the standpoint of basic human needs and then from the standpoint of specific teacher actions that will lead to fewer and less severe problems. Also described are various behavioral change procedures including operant conditioning, reality therapy, and chemotherapy, as well as a number of often-discussed classroom control measures. In addition, a discipline procedure involving the school disciplinarian is explained.

OBJECTIVES

When you complete this chapter, you will be able to:

1. Describe, in writing, at least one example of how each of the basic human needs might be manifested in a classroom. (Comprehension)
2. Describe, in writing, at least eight guidelines that can be used to help prevent discipline problems. (Comprehension)
3. Write a defense (substantiated by specific facts and examples) of your decision to use operant conditioning, reality therapy, or neither, in the classroom. (Evaluation)
4. Describe, in writing, a situation in which a teacher disregarded student needs and thus initiated an inappropriate disciplinary action, and then identify the need that was ignored and describe more appropriate actions. (Analysis, Synthesis)

5. When giving a series of hypothetical disciplinary incidents, select a remedial procedure of your choice and defend that choice with logical or empirical rationales. (Evaluation)

FOUR POSITIONS CONCERNING DISCIPLINE

Whenever educators discuss discipline problems, it is generally possible to delineate at least four philosophical positions. One is that discipline problems per se simply do not exist. Advocates of this position maintain that student behaviors usually labeled "discipline problems" are really nothing more than insignificant differences in normal human behavior. They claim these relatively minor differences would pass by quickly if teachers did not seize upon them, blow them out of proportion, and thus make them into bona fide problems.

A second, and somewhat related position, is that the teacher is the source of virtually all discipline problems. Advocates of this position maintain that it is only when teachers fail to make adequate plans, fail to keep students well occupied, or fail to act with sensitivity and humaneness that problems arise. They claim that, if teachers made, and carried out, adequate plans and were sufficiently perceptive of students' needs, discipline problems would not exist.

A third position is that students are the obvious source of virtually all discipline problems. Advocates of this position maintain that students are, in fact, young people who must learn to live in an adult world and should therefore learn to follow established rules and be made to bear the consequences of infractions of those rules. They claim that the way to reduce discipline problems is to punish each and every rule violation quickly, fairly, and surely.

The fourth position is that all people, students included, tend to do those things that bring the greatest pleasure. Advocates of this position maintain that students rarely cause trouble deliberately since to do so would generally result in unpleasant consequences. They point out, however, that sometimes the pleasure gained from an act outweighs the consequences suffered. A student might engage in "inappropriate" behavior, for example, to retaliate for a perceived injustice; the pleasure of "getting even" might outweigh the probable consequence. They also point out that some "inappropriate" acts (such as falling asleep in class) may be beyond the student's control. In both cases the act would seem "inappropriate" only in the eyes of the teacher.

Advocates of this position, assuming that people do not intentionally seek out conflict and trouble, claim that most discipline problems are the direct result of specific causes and are susceptible to logical solutions. They do not claim that any specific problem always has the same cause or that a solution that works in one instance will work in all similar instances, but they do claim that solutions to discipline problems can be found by looking for the causes of the problems and that students are both willing and able to help find appropriate solutions. This position rejects the premise that human nature is basically perverse and accepts the premise that people are basically good.

The authors of this text believe the last position is most defensible, and that the single most important goal of any discipline policy should be to develop self-disciplined adults.

MASLOW'S HIERARCHY

In 1943, A.H. Maslow described a theoretical hierarchy of human needs beginning with physiological needs and extending through needs for safety, love, esteem, and self-actualization.[1] It was Maslow's theory that people would devote their attention to the satisfaction of their most basic needs before they would divert their efforts to the satisfaction of less basic needs. He pointed out that full satisfaction of all needs is generally impossible and therefore most people are willing to accept a partial fulfillment of their most basic needs to achieve at least minimal fulfillment of their remaining needs. Thus a starving woman may share some highly desired food in order to satisfy needs for both food and esteem. Maslow qualified the priorities within the hierarchy by suggesting that some shifting might occur if the hierarchy were used to account for the behavior of specific individuals in specific situations. Martyrs, for example, place more importance on love, esteem, and self-actualization than on life itself.

Physiological Needs

According to Maslow's theory, the most basic needs are physiological needs such as air, water, food, elimination, sleep, and sexual release. Although there are other physiological needs, each of these six as it relates to classroom behavior is examined in the paragraphs that follow. In fact, you might want to consider each of the following discipline policy criteria for possible use as a yardstick against which more precise procedures might be measured.

Discipline Policy Criteria

OBJECTIVE: The development of self-disciplined people.

[1]A. H. Maslow, "A Theory of Human Motivation," *Psychological Review*, 50 (1943), 370–396.

PRACTICES:

1. *Truth*—Instructional objectives should reflect social, legal, and individual needs (in that order); learning activities should reflect the objectives; and statements should be factual and understandable.
2. *Fairness*—Interpersonal relationships and practices should be based on public and understandable expectations.
3. *Natural Consequences*—Individuals should bear the naturally occurring consequences of their actions whenever possible. Man-made consequences should be substituted only as a last resort and only when accompanied by an explanation of their relationship to natural consequences.
4. *Compassion*—Help a fellow creature along the path but remember that you cannot help someone learn to walk by carrying them.
5. *Legal and Ethical Obligations*—Know what you must do, what you can do, and what you should do to provide educationally sound learning and growing experiences.
6. *Professional Obligations*—Practice what you preach. Be a model.

Let us now look at a series of approaches to preventing and solving discipline problems.

Air   Few people like to be in a room that is hot, stuffy, or malodorous. If a classroom is overheated, lacks adequate air circulation, or smells bad, students (and eventually you) will, depending on the severity of the problem, begin paying more attention to the problem than to the work at hand. The resulting inattention to academic concerns can hardly be considered a discipline problem per se, but if you attempt to force students to be attentive instead of trying to eliminate the problem by opening a window or notifying the maintenance staff, real discipline problems can arise. Although it seems exceptionally elementary, simply assuring fresh air in the classroom can eliminate one potential source of discipline problems.

Water   The need for water does not generally constitute a major problem in most schools, particularly when it is remembered that Maslow was referring to such a need with respect to actual survival. Nevertheless, if students claim they are thirsty, not to allow them to drink will only focus more attention on such requests and make you appear unreasonable. Of course, unusually frequent requests for water should alert you to the probable abuse of the drink request or a possible medical problem.

Food   Unlike thirst, hunger is a major problem in some schools. Since the passage of the National School Lunch Act in 1946, the federal government has been providing free or inexpensive lunches to indigent students. In 1954 a school milk program providing inexpensive milk was instituted, and in the early 1970s some breakfast programs were begun as part of some early-childhood programs.

If you suspect that a student is irritable or inattentive because of hunger, you should first discuss the problem with the student. It may happen that the problem is one the student can solve with just minimal guidance. If the problem is beyond the student's control, or if it persists, the school administrators should be alerted. They may be able to provide food for the student via one or another school program, or they may arrange to have a social worker visit the home and try to solve the problem by working directly with the parents.

As a general rule you should expect students to be somewhat less attentive toward the end of the period immediately preceding lunch. Being aware of the fact that hungry students would rather contemplate hamburgers than algebraic equations may help increase your tolerance of student inattention.

Elimination   The need to eliminate bodily wastes, like the needs for air, water, and food, is not open to negotiation or discussion, and a student who really has to go to the bathroom is going to go with or without your permission. This need, like the need for water, can be used merely as an excuse to leave the room. While it is unwise for you to deny a student permission to go to the bathroom, if a particular student has the same need at the same time every day, you should suggest a visit to the school nurse and, if the problem persists, make an appointment with the nurse for the student.

Sleep   If a student falls asleep in class, you should follow a similar procedure. First, discuss the problem with the student. If the problem is beyond the student's control, or if it persists, alert the school administration or counseling department. If the sleepiness is due to some form of ill health, the school nurse may be able to provide some help; if the problem is caused because the student must work nights to supplement family income, the administration may be able to arrange alternative employment hours.

As with any of the preceding problems, it is best to talk with the students involved out of class rather than during class. This is particularly true with a student who has fallen asleep. It would be foolish to awaken the student simply to make a public issue of sleeping in class. It is usually possible for you to indicate, through nonverbal cues, that a nearby student should quietly awaken a sleeping student. If it is done discreetly, and if the sleepy student is then drawn into the class activities by being asked to answer not-too-specific questions or to offer an opinion during a discussion, the student may be saved the embarrassment of total class attention being drawn to the problem.

Sexual Release   Given the trend toward increased premarital sexual relations, it is obvious that teenagers are neither immune to the need for sexual release nor ignorant of ways of satisfying that need. While the problem is not generally one that manifests itself overtly, you should be aware that teenagers are sometimes preoccupied with sex and that the preoccupation can easily become a major problem if it is made a public issue. Private discussions with the student(s) concerned can help them understand the need to separate their physical concerns from academic concerns, and since the issue is usually a sensitive one for most students, one conference will usually be enough. If the preoccupation seems particularly deep-seated, or if it persists, referrals to appropriate school staff may be in order. Since teenage students have just undergone pubescence, they are naturally curious about their body, its functions, and its attractiveness to the opposite sex. Some concern about physical development and some flirtatious behavior is to be expected.

Safety Needs

Maslow theorized that after the basic physiological needs had been fulfilled or at least partially satisfied, the need for physical safety and well-being would begin to make itself felt.

At first glance it might seem as though modern-day students have little to fear concerning their physical safety, yet such is not the case. Today's schools can be, and too frequently are, violent places. In 1979, "110,000 teachers, 5% of the U.S. total, reported they were attacked by students, an increase of 57% over 1977–78."[2] This figure is shockingly high, but it is, nonetheless, just a fraction of the total number of violent incidents that occur in schools because it reflects only the *reported* assaults on teachers. There are undeniably many more assaults among students themselves in restrooms, hallways, and even in classrooms. With statistics such as these, there is no doubt that students have just cause to fear for their physical safety, and there is also no doubt that such fears interfere substantially with the teaching-learning process.

The practice of corporal punishment can constitute another threat to the physical safety of students. Despite years of controversy, corporal punishment is still practiced in many schools. In one survey, 64 percent of the teachers and 61 percent of the administrators contacted agreed that "corporal punishment, properly used, is an effective way to make students behave in school."[3] In the same survey it was revealed that 55 percent of the teachers and 80 percent of the administrators contacted agreed that "regardless of other available options, the option of using corporal punishment should be granted."[4]

[2]"Help: Teacher Can't Teach!" *Time*, 115, no. 24, June 16, 1980, p. 59.
[3]Jerry L. Patterson, "How Popular Is the Paddle?" *Phi Delta Kappan*, 55, no. 10 (June 1974), 707.
[4]Ibid.

In the face of these statistics there are other educators who claim that corporal punishment is not only barbaric but that its very nature, a dependence on force as opposed to reason, contradicts the intent of the educational process. They claim that, while corporal punishment may be expedient and may provide some satisfaction to the teacher, it actually teaches the student very little other than not to get caught. It appears reasonable to assume that, if educators are unable to explain the rationale for or against a particular act with sufficient clarity to convince a student, a session with a paddle will not do the job either. Further, if students are paddled they may come to view educators as bullies and will eventually dislike learning since it will be associated with threats, pain, and humiliation.

Still another source of concern over physical safety is posed by classes in which students are expected to engage in activities they feel might cause them harm. Prime examples include physical education classes in which students are expected to climb to the top of a high rope or to dive off a high diving board, home economics classes in which students are expected to work at hot stoves and ovens, and shop classes where students are expected to work with power and welding equipment. While the refusal of students to engage in such activities may be perceived by you as a discipline problem, such may not be the case. If the issue is not forced and the student is given more background information and more analogous practice, the problem will have a chance to work itself out.

Maslow's comment that young children prefer routines to unplanned activities may have some bearing on reducing students' anxiety over safety in high school classrooms.[5] If you consistently conduct well-planned lessons that minimize or eliminate unplanned time during the class period, students will be more likely to understand that time is valuable in that class and it is not to be wasted in extraneous activities or concerns. This business-like environment is more likely to foster a sense of security than is one in which there is unplanned time.

Love Needs

Maslow's description of love needs centers primarily on the love that usually exists between sweethearts, spouses, and parents and children. The need for this love has only an indirect relationship to classroom discipline because it is not your role either to provide or to withhold such love.

You can, however, be aware that students who are deprived of love at home may be less stable and more easily depressed than their more typical peers. Such awareness should prompt you to be more tolerant of the moods of such students and to make special efforts not to amplify the problem.

[5]Maslow, "Theory of Human Motivation," p. 337.

A second aspect of the need for love is the need to be accepted as one is. By moving to satisfy this human need you can help all students including those who are deprived of love at home. You should make it clear, by words and actions, that your first and greatest concern is for each student as a fellow human being. Teachers who convey this feeling to students tend to have fewer discipline problems because their students do not feel that they are being regarded as inferior. If a student misbehaves he or she knows the teacher will not regard him or her as inherently "bad," but simply as a person who has made a mistake. Such feelings help to increase amicable relations and help minimize the student-teacher adversary relationship that often springs up to interfere with the teaching-learning process.

Esteem Needs

The need for esteem is the need for a sense of worthiness both in the eyes of oneself and in the eyes of others. Although this need is less basic than the preceding needs, it is related more directly to classroom discipline and is more amenable to teacher manipulation.

A person's self-esteem is, at least partially, an outgrowth of his or her perceptions of personal abilities and of how others view those abilities. This being the case, you can help students build self-esteem by helping them succeed. For example, if students are having difficulty learning, you can help them help themselves rather than simply supplying answers or expressing disapproval. If the problem facing students is broken into smaller components and students are encouraged to work independently on each component with minimal assistance from you, they will eventually be able to overcome the larger problem. This procedure requires careful monitoring of each student's progress and helps students perceive their true abilities and to increase their sense of worthiness as they see their abilities increase via personal effort. Because this process helps students satisfy their need for self-esteem, it fosters favorable attitudes toward you and the school. Students are unlikely to jeopardize such a source of need fulfillment by causing discipline problems.

Peer esteem is often acquired by those students who excel at something deemed important by their peers or by those students who exercise their independence by defying "the establishment." Successful teachers capitalize on the first situation by identifying the most highly esteemed students and enlisting their cooperation in providing positive models of both behavior and work. If the enlisting is done tactfully (via appropriate praise and rewards), the teacher can acquire a powerful ally. If the enlisting is done crudely (via unearned praise, brides, or threats), the student may hold the teacher in contempt and can become an opponent rather than an ally.

The second process for student acquisition of peer esteem presents a more challenging problem. If you build a rigid classroom environment complete with a multitude of rules and regulations, and assume the role of dictator-in-residence, you may become the target of continual challenges. Many students will seek confrontations with you simply to gain the peer esteem that may result from "winning." From the student's standpoint, winning is measured by the degree to which one can get away with some rule infraction, publicly prove some rule is outdated or inconsistent, cause the teacher to lose patience, or use up class time that would otherwise be spent on activities perceived as meaningless. Regardless of how powerful your arguments are or how dire your threats, you will find yourself losing more and more confrontations. In turn, more students will seek confrontations to acquire peer esteem and your life will become a cycle of discipline problems.

One obvious way to minimize such situations is to cut down the numbers of rules and regulations students can violate. Since students generally do not violate rules directly affecting their own safety or rules they make themselves, other rules and regulations should be examined with a critical eye. Outdated rules and rules that are inconsistent with accepted practice should, of course, be eliminated, and rules made purely for administrative convenience (and many are) should have their worth balanced against the probability of their being used as a point of challenge by students. Fewer rules and regulations will help reduce the probability of student-teacher or student-administration confrontations and thus help reduce one source of discipline problems.

Another way to minimize confrontations is to deal on a one-to-one basis with students engaging in such actions. Rather than "having it out" with a student during a class, it should be possible to arrange to see the student out of class. This procedure will deprive the student of the chance to win a confrontation publicly, thus minimizing any expected peer esteem, but more important, it will provide a cooling-off period and increase the possibility that both you and the student will be able to discuss the problem calmly and rationally.

You also need to be careful not to attack, consciously or unconsciously, students' esteem by using sarcasm, ridicule, or humiliation as control devices. Belittling students will cause them to lose esteem in the eyes of their peers, and will cause you to be viewed as cruel and unfair. Such approaches will prompt students to retaliate in kind. You need to make it a point to protect students' sense of esteem whenever possible by treating students as you yourself would like to be treated.

Looking at the need for esteem from a positive standpoint, you can provide partial fulfillment of the need by publicly acknowledging students' successes, communicating to parents and administrators things that students do well, and providing public, positive reinforcement whenever appropriate. However, while it is true that earned praise and recognition can contribute to students' fulfillment of esteem needs, unearned praise can do just the opposite. If you praise students indiscriminately (as in efforts to win their friendship, support, or good behavior), the value of the praise as a source of need fulfillment will decline. Furthermore, users of unearned praise will appear to be patronizing, insincere, or untrustworthy. This, in turn, will cause students to be suspicious and unaccepting of praise even when it has been justly earned.

Self-actualization Needs

The last explicit need described by Maslow is the need for self-actualization, or the need to develop as fully as possible. As Maslow put it, "What a man *can* be, he *must* be."[6]

The need for self-actualization is related directly to classroom discipline. As students move through the education process, they are continually exposed to new and different avenues of physical, social, and intellectual development. If students believe that you are keeping them from continuing the kind of development they consider most important, or if they believe they are wasting their time and efforts in meaningless and irrelevant activities, discipline problems can increase.

You can help students to meet their need for self-actualization in a number of ways. First and foremost, you can involve students in the planning of instructional objectives and activities. Student participation will help to assure that objectives and activities are relevant to student goals and are perceived as such by students. You can also take the time to build and communicate convincing rationales for the planned content and activities. Even if students participate in the initial planning, it is helpful for you to remind them frequently of the relationship(s) between the ongoing instruction and their continued development. The more immediate the applicability of the new information and skills, the more easily students will see the relationship between the instruction and their development.

In some cases individual students may not see a relationship between their personal goals and the work the class is doing. In such cases the potential for discipline problems increases, since few students are willing to sit quietly and "waste" their time. You may need to make a special effort to discover and explain any possible relationships that do exist but that may have been overlooked by such students. If, in fact, no relationships do exist, you have a limited number of options. Keeping in mind that students have a need for self-actualization, you can allow them to plan and carry out independent student projects that are mutually agreed upon and that have some relationship to the ongoing work of the class. For some students another option is to explain how achievement of the minimal course objectives can contribute to the student's eventual acquisition of a high school diploma, which, in turn, can open many doors to further development. On

[6]Maslow, "Theory of Human Motivation," p. 382.

occasion you can discuss with the student whether taking a different course might be of more immediate use or whether retaking the course at a later time would be of benefit.

It is important for you to communicate to all students (not just the ones that are particularly troublesome) that you are aware of their need for self-actualization and are working specifically toward its fulfillment. Students who feel you are helping them grow physically, socially, or intellectually are less likely to jeopardize that growth by causing discipline problems.

In review, it has been pointed out how you can minimize discipline problems by being cognizant of the relationship of many such problems to some very basic human needs. By consciously helping students satisfy their needs, you will also be eliminating the causes of many discipline problems.

GUIDELINES FOR PRECLUDING
DISCIPLINE PROBLEMS

Using the background information on human needs, along with other psychological principles and common sense, the following set of ten guidelines can be helpful in organizing to preclude discipline problems.

Eliminate Physical Distractions   As has been pointed out, students who are concerned about their physical well-being are likely to pay less attention to classwork at hand. Simple steps, such as assuring a continual flow of fresh air through the room, maintaining a comfortable temperature, eliminating glare on the chalkboard, and establishing a reasonable policy concerning leaving the room for drinks or trips to the restroom, can help eliminate the causes of many "discipline problems."

Treat Students with Respect   Remember that students are fellow human beings and deserve to be treated with the same degree of respect and courtesy that adults extend to any of their peers. Students are likely to treat you the same way you treat them.

Elicit Student Help in Planning   A most frequently cited cause of student discontent is the feeling that the material they are asked to learn or the activities in which they are asked to engage are irrelevant. If students are allowed to participate in the planning and modification of instructional objectives and activities, and if you take the time to communicate sound rationales for those objectives, the problem of irrelevancy will decrease. Further, if students are involved in planning the instructional objectives and activities, they will be more likely to accept part of the responsibility for the achievement of those objectives and the success of those activities. Teachers who insist on doing all the planning themselves implicitly accept full responsibility for the success of those plans.

Maintain Reasonable Expectations   It usually does not take long for teachers to discover that mild student frustrations can be used to increase learning. The mildly uncomfortable feeling on the part of students, which continues until they achieve a goal, assists in speeding up the learning process. If you expect too little from students, this sense of frustration will be lacking, the work will be viewed as busywork, and the final sense of achievement students could otherwise have experienced will be minimized. At the same time, unattainable goals or artificial barriers to goal achievement must be eliminated or students will become overly frustrated, and this frustration can be manifested in the form of discipline problems.

Use a Variety of Instructional Experiences   An admitted cause of discipline problems is student boredom. You can combat this by building into your lessons a variety of different learning experiences. Not every student will be equally interested in each experience, but by having a number of different experiences in each lesson, you increase the probability of gaining and holding the interest of students more of the time. Interested students are less likely to cause discipline problems.

Provide Prompt Feedback   Students are generally extremely interested in finding out "how they did" on any given task. If a report is not forthcoming soon after the task is completed, students are apt to think that you did not regard the task as very important and therefore feel they wasted their efforts. This feeling will continue to grow as such instances multiply, with the eventual result that students will feel that whatever they do in that particular class is of little value. Such an environment is open to the generation of discipline problems.

Provide Positive Reinforcement   When evaluating students' work, many teachers concentrate upon the identification and correction of errors. If you continually emphasize what students do incorrectly without recognizing those things they have done well, students will become discouraged and resentful. Their needs for esteem and self-actualization will go unsatisfied and they may seek other, undesirable sources of satisfaction. You should point out sections of students' work that are well done and should encourage students to use those sections as models for the less well-done portions. Sincere, positive reinforcement can go a long way toward making corrections more palatable and toward satisfying student needs.

Be Consistent   If students perceive inconsistencies in your reactions to problems, or if they believe you are being unfair, their respect for you will decrease. Once you lose the respect of your students, discipline problems will begin to increase.

Foster Peer Approval   As was pointed out earlier, peer approval or disapproval is an important element in the life of most adolescents. At times this force may motivate students more than any other single element. Teachers who gain the respect and approval of the majority of their students can tap this force and use it to help maintain an environment conducive to learning. Students who are "with" a teacher can assist, in many subtle ways, in controlling their peers.

It must be pointed out that, although you can accept most forms of student support and can allow most forms of peer pressure to bear on students causing discipline problems, the tool cannot be used indiscriminately. Manifestations of peer pressure such as physical reprisals, ridicule, sarcasm, and humiliation cannot be tolerated. If you condone the use of such measures, the very student respect that generated the support in the first place will be lost.

Avoid Punitive Action   This principle is one of the most difficult for beginning teachers to follow. Many people have become accustomed to an eye-for-an-eye philosophy, and when you are inconvenienced by a student, your first inclination is often to inconvenience that student at least as much. There is little evidence, however, to support the idea that punitive action will have any lasting effect on deviant student behavior.

The selection of appropriate punitive action is not easy, nor is the prediction of consequent student reaction certain. An examination of common punitive actions follows:

1. *Detention.* This option punishes teachers as much as students since someone must supervise the detention. Often the student is bused to and from school or has an after-school job, and the hardship caused makes the punishment excessive. In other cases students may be involved in sports or some after-school club and the detention may therefore deprive them of one of the few school experiences that is keeping them from dropping out.

2. *Extra schoolwork.* There seems to be no evidence to support the idea that assigning extra schoolwork is helpful in eliminating discipline problems. In fact, it is likely that the assignment of such work will cause students to associate all schoolwork with unpleasant experiences and thus cause more harm than good.

3. *Repetitive sentences and the like.* The use of repetitive sentences and similar busywork assignments has found widespread and long-term use among teachers for years. There must be teachers somewhere who have found this device effective in maintaining good discipline, but locating such a teacher proves to be difficult. Such tasks are likely to cause students to equate schoolwork with busywork and to dislike both.

4. *Special seating assignments.* Special seating assignments usually take one of two forms. In the first form a seat is isolated from the rest of the class and students are assigned to it essentially as objects of ridicule. Ridicule is not effective as a discipline device.

Another form of special seating is to attempt to separate friends or arrange seats in a way that will minimize student interaction. This procedure is less satisfactory than using friendships in a positive way to foster intrinsic motivation. Further, separated students will still find ways to communicate despite your efforts.

5. *Physical labor or exercise.* The use of physical work or exercise is fraught with danger. A student who is asked by a teacher to do as little as move a desk and who is hurt in the process is in a position to bring suit against the teacher. In some states physical labor assigned to students is specifically forbidden.

Exercises, such as running the track, push-ups, and so on, are often used in physical education classes as punitive action. The same reservations apply here that applied in the assignment of schoolwork as punishment. How are students going to build an intrinsic desire for more exercise if it is deemed so distasteful by the teacher that it is used as punishment?

Occasionally a teacher in a classroom will use push-ups or some other physical action as punishment. Unlike the physical education teacher, who at least knows whether the student is physically able to do the assigned exercise, the classroom teacher may make an unjustified assumption about a student's physical abilities. It is possible that a student would rather injure himself or herself attempting the assigned exercise than lose face with peers, and it is unlikely that parents would lose the legal battle that could follow.

6. *Lowering of Grades.* In some school districts there are policies that condone the lowering of an academic grade for disciplinary reasons. This practice is analogous to withholding a diploma as punitive action when all necessary requirements have been met. In this case the courts have ruled that the diploma must be awarded.[7] In the case of grades, however, teachers can cloud the criteria for grading to the point where a grade could be lowered consciously or unconsciously because of discipline problems. This

---

[7]Anne Flowers and Edward C. Bolmeier, *Law and Pupil Control* (Cincinnati, Ohio: W. H. Anderson, 1964).

cannot be defended logically, since once a student has achieved an objective and demonstrated a competence it is senseless to deny the accomplishment. Teachers who engage in this practice will be deemed unfair by their students and will quickly lose a large measure of student respect.

7. *Banishment from the classroom.* Along with lowering grades are the procedures that can cause students to earn lower grades, for instance, actions that deny the student access to ongoing instruction. Insisting that the student stand outside the classroom may solve a problem for the moment, but you will eventually need to spend extra time teaching the material to the student if academic achievement is considered important. Further, you are legally responsible for your students while class is in session. By banishing a student from the room, you remove that student from direct supervision and can therefore be held liable if the student is injured or gets into additional trouble.

BEHAVIOR MODIFICATION: OPERANT CONDITIONING

Operant conditioning is the formal name given to the process of encouraging people to behave in particular ways by systematically rewarding desired behaviors. Obvious examples of operant conditioning techniques include the planned use of praise to encourage the completion of homework and the use of prizes to motivate students to do well in school.

As a process, operant conditioning is not concerned with root causes of undesired behaviors. Instead, attention is focused on discovering and capitalizing on particular rewards that will help individuals to modify their behavior. This emphasis on rewards rather than causes seems superficial to many educators and has caused many to express reservations about using operant conditioning techniques.

Among the arguments used by opponents of operant conditioning techniques is the opinion that they may cause as many problems as they solve. When teachers use operant conditioning techniques, the basic process is to identify the specific behaviors they wish to increase and reward the student when the desired behavior is demonstrated. Some educators maintain that it is not long until other students observe that one way to get extra attention or rewards from the teacher is to misbehave and then behave properly on cue. These educators also insist that operant conditioning techniques can be unfair to those students who behave properly.

Still another concern of many educators is that operant conditioning techniques imply that appropriate behavior should be demonstrated only because such behavior will generate an extrinsic reward such as praise, candy, money, or free time. They maintain that the use of rewards for appropriate behavior obscures the fact that such behavior has its own intrinsic rewards and will not, in fact, bring extrinsic rewards in the "real" world. They claim, therefore, that operant conditioning techniques mislead students by giving them a false impression of reality.

A further criticism leveled at operant conditioning practitioners questions the right of the behavior manipulator to make judgments as to what other people's behaviors should be. Operant conditioning practitioners must decide which behaviors are "good" and which are "bad" and use rewards to cause students to modify their behavior without necessarily making the students aware of the process. Such decisions, however, must be made daily by teachers to maintain an atmosphere conducive to the teaching-learning process. It is interesting to note that, in one survey concerning behavior modification of the 406 educators questioned, 85 percent agreed that it was ethical to "manage behavior regardless of the techniques employed."[8] If nothing else, the finding speaks eloquently of the importance educators attach to "good" behavior on the part of students.

Many of the attacks on operant conditioning have been prompted by aversion to its abuses by individual teachers who use it indiscriminately and without regard for its ramifications. When used properly, the rewards often pertain to student fulfillment of basic needs, such as the needs for esteem and self-actualization. Further, when teachers fully understand the ramifications of the technique, they are quick to point out to students the intrinsic rewards of the desired behavior and thus lead students away from continued extrinsic rewards.

Proper utilization of operant conditioning can minimize many of the problems associated with the technique and can thus provide teachers with an effective classroom control tool. Proper utilization of operant conditioning requires a careful and systematic series of steps designed to isolate and modify the undesirable behavior being manifested by a particular student.

Let us suppose, for example, that Tom periodically disturbs the class and that you have decided to try to modify his behavior via operant conditioning. Steps that would be appropriate follow.

Identify the Specific Behavior to Be Changed   What is it *exactly* that Tom is doing to disturb the class? There is a tendency to generalize about a student's misbehavior and to label a series of different actions as general misbehavior. If operant conditioning is to be effective however, it must focus on one specific behavior. In this case, the undesirable behavior is identified as a tendency to whisper to neighbors.

---

[8]Sherman H. Frey, "Teachers and Behavior Modification," *Phi Delta Kappan,* 55, no. 9 (May 1974), 635.

Determine What Generally Triggers the Student's Misbehavior   Does Tom begin whispering when a particular stimulus is presented (e.g., when discussion of assigned homework is initiated) or when a stimulus is withdrawn (e.g., when you shift attention away from him)? Although it may seem as though the student is question is always misbehaving, a careful analysis (after observation) will usually reveal the triggering stimulus. In this case it is determined that Tom begins whispering when the class starts to discuss the previous night's homework assignment.

Determine What Generally Happens Each Time the Student Misbehaves   When Tom begins whispering, what is your reaction? What is the reaction of the other students? This analysis of what happens immediately after the student misbehaves is important and it can be highly revealing. In this circumstance the analysis shows that, as soon as Tom begins whispering, you stop whatever you are doing and forcefully tell him to stop. Further, immediately following the chastisement, other students giggle and snicker, and Tom usually responds with some wisecrack.

Devise and Try Countermeasures   At this point the analysis has begun to point the way toward the solution of the problem. You know, for example that Tom's disruption of the class usually begins with whispering to neighbors, which, in turn, is triggered by your announcement that the class will begin discussing the homework assignment. Further, the disruption intensifies after a chastisement for whispering.

A number of countermeasures are available. One option is to ignore Tom's whispering, thus depriving him of reinforcement from the attention focused on him. While this option may work, it may be undesirable because other students may misinterpret the lack of action, particularly if Tom is a leader. A second option would·be to move Tom to a different seat where neighbors would be unlikely to whisper back. This option might work, but it may be less desirable than other possibilities because it is unlikely to bring about a lasting modification in Tom's behavior. A third option could emerge. For example, it may be that there is a cause-effect relationship between Tom's whispering and impending discussions of homework. It might be determined that Tom rarely does his homework and that his whispering is an attempt to acquire survival data prior to the discussion.

An operant conditioning could be initiated by waiting for a time when Tom is able to participate in a discussion of homework and then praising him for his good work and valuable contributions. If the praise (or other reward) were forthcoming each time he contributed to the discussion without whispering beforehand, the whispering might soon cease, because he would recognize that it was no longer necessary. This procedure, while effective, depends upon waiting until Tom does his homework and could turn out to be a long-term approach.

A fourth option to speed up the reinforcement process could be initiated. Keeping in mind that the class disruption is caused in part by Tom's whispering and in part by your reaction to that whispering, you might find the following steps effective:

1. Make specific homework assignments for each student.
2. Privately encourage Tom to do the assignment.
3. Call on some students to discuss their homework, but call on Tom the first day only if he has done his homework and ignore whispering if it occurs.
4. Again make specific assignments and privately encourage Tom to do his.
5. As soon as Tom has made an effort to do the assignment, even if it came only as the result of heavy prompting, call on him during the discussion and praise his contribution. Again ignore his whispering if it occurs.
6. Repeat steps 4 and 5 each day, praising Tom's contributions and ignoring his whispering. The whispering should decrease and disappear within a few days. If it does not, the analysis must be reexamined for alternative explanations for the behavior.

The point of the operant conditioning process is to focus attention on desired behavior and to provide an incentive for the student to engage in that behavior. The incentive may be praise, points, or any other reward valued by the student, and the expectation is that the desired behavior will soon become self-reinforcing and will replace the undesirable behavior which is never reinforced.

Keep in mind that sometimes the removal or withholding of a stimulus (for example, the denying of an opportunity to receive attention and reinforcement from peers) is as effective as the presentation of a stimulus (for example, the giving of praise or rewards). Once the right stimulus is found for any individual, a procedure is established to help bring about lasting behavioral changes via operant conditioning.

BEHAVIOR MODIFICATION: REALITY THERAPY

Reality therapy is another behavior modification tool that utilizes student needs, but its philosophical orientation is significantly different from that of operant conditioning. In operant conditioning, individuals undergoing the conditioning are generally unaware that their behavior is being manipulated. No attempt is made to treat individuals as responsible people to make them partners in a joint effort to modify behavior, or to help them see the cause-effect relationships between their behavior and its short-term and long-term consequences.

Reality therapy, on the other hand, makes individuals the prime movers in the modification of their own behavior. Reality therapy is predicated on the idea that people engage in those behaviors they believe will bring them relatedness and respect (i.e., which will satisfy one or more perceived or unperceived needs) but that some individuals have either a distorted idea of what their goals are or a distorted idea of how to achieve them. Reality therapists see their role as a "perception sharpener"—one who attempts to help the individual perceive the reality of the situation.

Reality therapy begins with the current situation. Although reality therapists are well aware that many problems have roots in past events, they are not willing to allow those past events to become excuses for present actions. The individual's attention is focused on the behavior to be modified, not on the root causes of that behavior, and the individual is helped to see the consequences of continuing the undesirable behavior as well as the consequences of modified behavior. The following step-by-step procedure is illustrative of how you might use reality therapy to deal with Tom's whispering.

Help the Student Identify the Undesirable Behavior   In this case you would arrange to see Tom privately. In the process of discussing the "problem," you elicit the identification of the problem from Tom. It is important that Tom identify it, because then he is taking the first step toward its solution. If you make the identification, Tom is likely to look to you for the solution to the problem rather than to seek that solution for himself.

Care is exercised not to ask Tom *why* he is engaging in the undesired behavior (whispering). To do so would provide him with an opportunity to offer an excuse for his actions and to focus attention on the excuse rather than the action. Again, the reality therapist does not deny that there may be legitimate reasons for inappropriate behavior—he or she simply insists on beginning with the inappropriate behavior rather than with a series of antecedent events. After discussion Tom should identify whispering as an inappropriate behavior.

Help the Student Identify the Consequences of Undesirable Behavior   It is important that the consequences identified be real and logical. If the environment is manipulated so the consequences of a particular action are unreasonably harsh or virtually meaningless, the situation becomes contrived and unreal. In such a situation reality therapy is less effective. In this case, for example, telling Tom that he will be suspended from school if whispering continues is unreasonable. Similarly, it would be unreasonable to tell him that inappropriate behavior will have no consequences. It is appropriate, however, to point out that consequences are often cumulative and tend to get more and more severe.

Through discussion it is determined that Tom's whispering disturbs other students and that part of your responsibility is to maintain an atmosphere that is quiet and conducive to concentration. In keeping with that responsibility, Tom should conclude that continued whispering will logically result in some form of exclusion from the group, which, in turn, will adversely affect progress.

Help the Student Make a Value Judgment About the Inappropriate Behavior and Its Consequences   The purpose of this step is to help the student see that the inappropriate behavior is contributing more to eventual unhappiness than to immediate or long-range happiness. The student is likely to have inaccurate perceptions about the effects of the behavior and may need help in making a value judgment about its desirability or undesirability. If the student does have difficulty making a value judgment about the behavior itself, then the focus is directed at making a judgment about the consequences of that behavior. In any event, the student is helped to conclude that the inappropriate behavior is undesirable or that it will bring more unhappiness than happiness. In the example, Tom admits that whispering can bother other students and that one student should not interfere with the right of other students to learn.

Have the Student Formulate a Plan for Changing the Behavior   Once Tom has concluded that the behavior is not, in fact, in his own best interests, the next step is for him to suggest alternatives to that behavior. If possible, he should be encouraged to propose an alternative behavior, for example he will:

1. Simply stop whispering.
2. Admit to not knowing an answer or not doing his homework rather than try to acquire last-minute information via whispering.
3. Tell you before class when he is not prepared and then will not be called upon to answer questions.

Of these three alternatives, the last is the least acceptable, and you should reject it if Tom does not see its inappropriateness, because it forces you to share responsibility for his action when, in fact, that responsibility belongs to him. It is important that Tom recognize that (1) the current situation is a result of his own behavior and (2) he can be extracted from the situation by engaging in behaviors that are both socially acceptable and conducive to achievement of personal and other people's success and happiness.

Have the Student Select, and Implement, a Specific Alternative   After Tom (perhaps with your help) has generated alternatives, he should decide which alternative to utilize. At this point your role is to monitor carefully to determine how well Tom is following the plan and to offer supportive praise.

As was pointed out earlier, the differences between the operant conditioning approach to behavior modification and the reality therapy approach are many and significant. It is unlikely that both approaches will appeal to all teachers or that all teachers will be able to use both with equal effectiveness. It is suggested, therefore, that before either approach is decided upon, you assess your own philosophical position concerning classroom control and behavior modification. Haphazard or indiscriminate use of either or both of these procedures cannot only be frustrating and futile, but it can also harm your rapport with students. Used properly, however, these procedures can enable you to bring about lasting behavioral changes.

A DISCIPLINE PROCEDURE INVOLVING THE SCHOOL DISCIPLINARIAN

Regardless of how carefully you plan and how skillfully you conduct your lessons, there will still be numerous minor disruptions of the ongoing classwork that can develop into major discipline problems. In the mind of every teacher is a conceptual model of an "ideal" teaching-learning environment. Each teacher's model varies from those of most other teachers, and some teachers are willing to tolerate a much broader range of deviant student behaviors than are others. All teachers will find, however, that their typical classes will deviate, in one degree or another, from the ideal model and that there will be some points at which the degree of deviation approaches unacceptable levels.

When you feel that some overt action on your part is necessary to maintain a reasonable teaching-learning environment, you must decide whether that action will cause a greater disruption than will the continuation of the deviant behavior. Jacob S. Kounin reports that teacher-initiated disciplinary acts (which he and his associates labeled "desists") can have significant effects on the other students in the class who are not the target of discipline. These effects have been called "ripple effects." In one study it was found that teachers who use angry or punitive desists often cause other students in the room to refocus their attention from the work at hand to the disturbance and the teacher's reaction to it. Simple reprimands, on the other hand, tend to have a lesser negative ripple effect.[9] Kounin also

[9]Jacob S. Kounin, *Discipline and Group Management in Classrooms* (New York: Holt, Rinehart and Winston, 1970), p. 49.

reported that interviews with high school students indicate that, if a teacher is viewed as fair and is generally liked by the students, his or her desist actions are less likely to cause ripple effects destructive to the teaching-learning environment.[10] One could conclude, therefore, that to deal successfully with most discipline problems, you should establish good rapport with your students and should use simple reprimands to deal with occasional deviant behavior. Mild desists can include actions such as moving toward disruptive students, standing by them, glancing at them, and directing questions at them, as well as direct reprimands. Further, reprimands should be in the form of direct statements rather than questions. "Would you please stop talking?" is less desirable than "Please stop talking," because it does not invite a verbal student response.

If the mild desists you use are not effective and the previously discussed preventive measures are being used, or if reality therapy or operant conditioning techniques have failed, you must have a plan of action. In some schools, teachers are told exactly what disciplinary procedure to use. If such a policy exists, it should be followed precisely. If no complete policy exists, you should develop your own based on whatever policies do exist. The following procedure is predicated on the possibility that the student may need to be referred to the school disciplinarian.

The Six Steps in a Model Discipline Procedure Involving the School Disciplinarian

1. *Each time a violation of proper classroom decorum is observed, tell the offender to desist.* As pointed out, if the teacher is respected and utilizes a mild reprimand, the danger of negative ripple effects will be minimal.

2. *Initiate, if it is deemed appropriate, a reality therapy or operant conditioning approach.* Note such efforts on an anecdotal record card.

3. *If the deviant behavior persists, tell the student to remain in the room after the class is dismissed.* If the class precedes a lunch break or the end of the school day, the subsequent conference can be more leisurely. If the student is scheduled for another class immediately, you should keep the conference as brief as possible and should write a note to the teacher of the student's next class explaining the tardiness. In either case the purpose of the conference should be to explain to the student that violations of proper classroom behavior have occurred and to attempt to obtain a commitment from the student that such misbehavior will not reoccur. (Note the difference between this tactic and its counterpart in reality therapy.) The conference should be brief, businesslike, and to the point. It should be recorded on

[10]Ibid., p. 142.

an anecdotal record card with a specific explanation of the offense and date. The student should sign the card and you should retain it. This will help convince the student that you are serious and that you intend to follow through.

4. *If the offending student continues the disruptive behavior, schedule a mutually convenient time for a longer conference with the student.* The reason for assuring that the time for the meeting is mutually agreeable is that students will find reasons why they cannot meet at teacher-decided times. You should be willing to meet before, after, or at an appropriate time during the school day. Make sure that the student understands the commitment to meet. If there is any doubt about the student's showing up, make two copies of the time and place and mutually initial each copy.

It should be made clear to the student that such a conference is not synonymous with detention. The purpose of this conference is to review the student's offenses and to outline the consequences of future offenses. You should explain why the offenses cannot be tolerated (because they disrupt the teaching-learning process and keep other students from learning). The focus of the conference should be on identifying and eliminating the misbehavior, not on the student personally. A record of the conference, offense, date, and so forth should be added to the anecdotal record card and the student should again sign the card.

At this point the student may feel that the procedure and conferences are a bother (or even a little painful) but will also realize that the teacher means business. Notice that no punitive action has been taken. The emphasis is on changing the behavior of the student, not on punishing him or her. The student should be told at this point that further misbehavior will result in his or her parents' being contacted.

5. *If the misbehavior persists, enlist the aid of the student's parents.* Since the student was apprised, as part of step 4, of the consequences of continued misbehavior, he or she should not be surprised at the initiation of this step if the misbehavior persists. At the next offense, remind the student as he or she leaves the room that the parents will be contacted and their support enlisted. Once this step is announced it is important that the contact with parents be made as soon as possible, preferably before the end of the school day. If this is not done, the student may arrive home before you call and set a stage that is difficult or impossible to cope with. Once the contact is made, you should go through the anecdotal record explaining the actions taken and enlisting support. A record of the home contact should be made on the anecdotal record card.

6. *If the problem persists, the student is referred to the school disciplinarian.* Before making this referral, contact the disciplinarian and discuss with him or her the anecdotal record with the list of offenses and corrective efforts.

This is important because the disciplinarian must understand that you have had a minimum of two conferences with the student and have contacted the parents. Once the disciplinarian understands that the problem is not superficial, he or she can try working with the student. If the disciplinarian decides upon some punitive action, the choice will be his or hers, not yours.

7. *Steps 4, 5, and 6 are repeated.* Before referring the student to the office again, another conference should be held and another contact with parents made. This cycle should continue until (a) the student's behavior changes as home, class, and office pressures mount, (b) the disciplinarian removes the student from the class, (c) the school term ends, or (d) the student removes himself or herself from the class.

Obviously you will be most satisfied if the student modifies the behavior voluntarily, but your primary responsibility is the education of the entire class, and if one student is thwarting that education and refuses to modify his or her behavior, you are obligated to take all reasonable measures to fulfill the educational commitment to the rest of the class.

POTENTIALLY DANGEROUS PROBLEMS

It is probable that most teachers will eventually encounter what can be labeled a "potentially dangerous problem," for instance, fighting, verbal or physical abuse of staff members, drinking, drugs, overt defiance, sexual assault, or malicious destruction of property. In such a situation it is almost always too late to attempt remedial action. Because of the legal ramifications, such problems are handled best by experienced administrators. Unfortunately, it is not easy to decide the best course of action in these volatile situations. In some cases the student will be rational enough to proceed directly to the office alone. In other cases you may need to accompany the student to the office. If you must leave a class to escort a student to office, you should ask a nearby teacher to monitor the class. In many schools, classroom-office communication is possible and the teacher is able to summon help without leaving the room. The immediate goal is to keep students from causing harm to themselves or to others.

HYPERACTIVITY AND CHEMOTHERAPY

Sometimes when teachers see a student who is continually restless, given to sudden outbursts, or unable to concentrate on the work at hand, they attribute it to hyperactivity. Hyperactivity is generally thought to be caused by the inability of an individual to assign priorities to the many sensory inputs constantly bombarding the brain. Most teachers are simply not qualified to diagnose such problems, but many try to do so anyway. What occasionally happens is that a teacher mistakes lapses of attention, restlessness, or even the normal exuberance of youth, for hyperactivity. Having "diagnosed" the problem, the uninformed teacher may call the student's parents (or have the school nurse call them) and suggest that they take the student to a physician and "have the doctor give him something to control hyperactivity."

Unfortunately, some physicians will, after only a cursory examination, accept the teacher's "diagnosis" and prescribe a treatment on that basis. The typical treatment for hyperactivity is the prescription of amphetamines such as Ritalin and Dexedrine. Although these drugs act as stimulants for adults, they act as depressants for children. It is difficult to predict accurately the exact effect of any specific drug on any specific child, and a growing number of children are being adversely affected by such chemotherapy. Even worse, because of the increasing instances in which drugs are prescribed for students on the basis of inadequate diagnoses, many students are exposed to drugs who do not need to be. In the spring of 1974 one researcher, Dr. Herbert E. Rie, reported to the American Medical Association that "about twice as many children are being given drugs for hyperactivity as should be."[11] Teachers must accept at least part of the blame.

If you suspect that a student may be hyperactive, your initial step should be to double-check the basis for the suspicion. The procedures include keeping a written record of the frequency of each "hyperactive" act, checking with teachers to see if the student is demonstrating similar behavior in other classes, and engaging in discussions with the school nurse and guidance personnel to see if they have been told of any specific problems the student may be having.

If the suspected behaviors are persistent and not just isolated examples, the collected data should be discussed with the guidance department and nurse. If the results of this conference indicate that an examination by a physician is in order, then the parents should be involved in a separate conference in which such an examination is recommended. At this conference the parents are provided the list of incidents without suggestions that the student is hyperactive or that he or she needs drugs. The *doctor alone* should diagnose the problem and prescribe any treatment.

Assuming that you are informed of treatment, it is then your responsibility to continue to monitor the student's behavior. In this way the effectiveness of the treatment can be determined and its eventual elimination hastened. The ultimate goal, of course, is to help the student to control his or her own behavior without the use of chemicals.

---

[11]Herbert E. Rie, address to the American Medical Association at its annual meeting in Chicago on June 25, 1974. Reported in *The Daily Pantagraph*, Bloomington-Normal, Ill., June 26, 1974, p. C-10.

SUMMARY

In attempting to prevent discipline problems it should be kept in mind that students are human beings with all the needs common to human beings. A. H. Maslow has described five of those needs (physiological, safety, love, esteem, and self-actualization), and each has ramifications for the prevention of discipline problems. Most important, if students' basic needs are not satisfied, or if students believe that school is standing in the way of need gratification, discipline problems are likely to develop.

In light of student needs and psychological principles, ten guidelines are suggested to assist teachers in precluding discipline problems. If discipline problems emerge, two techniques that can be used to modify student's behavior by capitalizing on their needs are operant conditioning and reality therapy. Operant conditioning is a technique whereby the conditioner brings about modifications in an individual's behavior by presenting stimuli valued by that individual. The technique is usually employed without the knowledge of the person whose behavior is being manipulated and for this reason, along with the fact that the individual may become dependent on the stumuli, many educators are reluctant to use it as a classroom control measure.

Reality therapy is another behavior modification technique, but it differs significantly from operant conditioning in that it helps the individual become the prime mover in the modification of his or her own behavior. Previous events are not accepted as excuses for current behavior, and attention is focused on the real consequences of continued inappropriate behavior as opposed to the consequences of behavior modified to become socially acceptable.

Unfortunately, these measures are not always effective with all students and at times the teacher must rely on a set plan of action to deal with persistent behavior problems. One such plan is described and discussed in the chapter, and at its foundation is the philosophy that the ideal way to handle discipline problems is to help the offending students change their behavior by helping them to realize the intrinsic benefit of conforming to acceptable standards of behavior, rather than to force them to adjust through the use of punitive measures.

Another technique seeing more use in controlling some discipline problems is chemotherapy. This technique is usually restricted to students labeled "hyperactive," but because the term is interpreted loosely and the real problem is diagnosed poorly, many students are compelled to take drugs who should not be doing so. Chemotherapy is intended to solve medical problems, not discipline problems.

THIRTEEN

THE MANAGEMENT
OF CO-CURRICULAR
ACTIVITIES

A secondary school principal once asked the staff of his school to rank each subject-matter area and various student co-curricular activities according to how well they helped students reach the goals described in the seven cardinal principals: health, command of the fundamental processes, worthy home membership, vocation, citizenship, proper use of leisure time, and ethical character.

After their responses, it became obvious that the co-curricular activities program was a crucial factor in the school's attempts to meet those goals. Even the teachers most adamant about the sanctity of their classrooms and the importance of their subject admitted that, overall, the co-curricular activities program was meeting more needs than any one subject area.

OBJECTIVES

When you complete this chapter, you will be able to:

1. Describe in your own words at least three common arrangements for student government structure in a typical secondary school. (Knowledge, Comprehension)
2. Given an application for student body cash boxes for a club sale, fill out the application and describe procedures for obtaining the cash box. (Comprehension, Application)
3. Given a hypothetical assembly theme, organize a program that will be entertaining to a group of high school students and involve all members of the hypothetical club you are sponsoring. (Synthesis)

4. Given a hypothetical club situation in which a club is deciding upon which of several objectives to pursue, judge which of several suggested objectives would be of most benefit to the students to adopt and defend that choice by submitting at least four logical rationales. (Evaluation)

5. After selecting a hypothetical sponsorship role, write a series of at least six precise instructional objectives appropriate to the club or activity being sponsored. (Synthesis)

EXTRA PAY

One of the problems that must be faced in regard to teacher participation in co-curricular activities is the continuing controversy over extra pay. For many years, it was assumed that all teachers should participate in a minimum amount of co-curricular activities sponsorships and that this responsibility would be divided approximately equally among the staff. As certain activities took more and more time, the notion of extra pay evolved. Usually the athletic staff was the first to receive extra money. Then the band director was awarded a few extra dollars. This was soon followed by the drama teacher (three plays a year), the sponsor of the yearbook, and so on.

It is obvious that there is no easy solution to the problem of extra pay, because it is so difficult to make extra pay equitable. As an example, about the time an extra-pay schedule is closely reflective of the actual work put in by staff members, one of the staff may retire. Perhaps he is the choir director and received $150 extra pay for directing the choir at two PTA meetings, one music concert in conjunction with the school band, and the Christmas assembly. He is replaced by a young, energetic teacher who attracts many students into the choir, adds an a capella choir after school on a volunteer basis, raises funds from the community, and organizes a series of assembly presentations at neighboring schools. Everyone is happy at the new publicity the school is receiving. The parents are pleased at the attention given their children, and the new teacher organizes an "awards banquet" at the end of the year, giving small trophies to the "most outstanding choir member," "most inspirational . . .," and so on.

The next year the board of education wants to raise the extra pay for choir directors to reward this teacher for all his hard work, but in the other high school in the district, the choir director is continuing with just the usual two PTA meetings, one musical concert in conjunction with the school band, and the Christmas assembly.

An exaggerated case? Not at all. Besides, even if the board could raise the salary of the choir director at one school and not the other, at about that time the teacher may very well have been recognized as outstanding and have been offered a job at the local community college as choir director at an increased salary.

What happens when extra pay is in the pay schedule? There is usually a specific range of money that the school district has to pay salaries. In some instances, without realizing it, teachers who want extra pay are taking dollars from all teachers and are giving those dollars to a few. On the other hand, if everyone is given extra pay, schools may as well be back on a salary schedule without extra-pay considerations included.

In some schools no extra pay is given, but teachers who involve themselves heavily in co-curricular activities are given fewer classes to teach. That is, if the normal daily load is six forty-five-minute classes, the varsity football coach may only teach three physical education classes and then start coaching at the beginning of the last period of the day. Often, the band and choir are scheduled classes. With modular scheduling, more of this type of time compensation for teachers is possible.

TYPES OF SPONSORSHIP

As a teacher in a secondary school, you will likely find yourself involved in various kinds of co-curricular activities programs. Some patterns of organization key all activities around the school to clubs. It is the clubs that sponsor dances, sales, and the like. In other schools, the student government seems to be the driving force behind activities. In large schools often a teacher has emerged in a subtle or recognized administrative capacity as activity director, and all activities seem to emerge from his or her office. Regardless of the organization, however, the following descriptions are typical of the possible involvement in which you may find yourself.

Clubs

The quality and quantity of clubs on a high school campus vary tremendously. Few campuses have no clubs. Some seem to have many clubs, but they function in name only, holding few meetings and conducting no real activities. Others have a number of very active clubs. Clubs function best, and will involve sponsors and students most, when they are an outgrowth of a subject-matter field. It is probably difficult not to find at least a remote link between any special-interest club and some aspect of the curriculum, but the more remote the link, the more tenuous the position of the club. In addition, the strength of the club and its members is almost always related to the sponsor: weak sponsor, weak club. In some instances it is the special interest of a sponsor that makes a club successful, and when the sponsor leaves the school, the club disbands.

A comprehensive list of clubs is impossible, but a few here deserve comment.

CLUB	COMMENT
Girls' league	Often an important club on a campus with several subdivisions.
Boys' league	Hard to form; girls seem to be willing to join "girls' league" just because they are girls, whereas boys require special-interest subsections.
Foreign language clubs	In larger schools there is often a French club, a Spanish club, etc. In small schools one club seems to work. Events held might include the Roman banquet and assisting in the foreign exchange student program.
Science clubs	Sometimes broken into more specific areas (e.g., physics club), these are usually active in getting students involved in science fairs and field trips.
Girls' athletic associations	Most girls' physical education departments organize an active club that not only sponsors on-campus activities but also engages in intra- and/or intermural sports. With current reemphasis on girls' participation in sports, some blending of girls' and boys' athletic clubs is taking place.
Lettermen clubs	The athletic program in a school may sponsor several clubs. Sometimes a big football school will have a separate club for football players only. This fragmentation is unnecessary, with the athletic club logically being involved in the annual sports awards banquets.
Pep club	On some campuses pep club membership is a prerequisite to being a drill team member or yell or song leader. This group often arranges for buses to away games and involves itself in rallies.
Forensics	Many schools have debate as a part of their regular curriculum and as co-curricular activities. Involvement of members (as with athletics) can become intense.
Thespians	A drama club usually emerges if the drama classes result in well-received productions. As with the forensics, national affiliations are possible.

Industrial arts	Often broken down into subclubs such as "car clubs," these clubs provide more opportunity for students to use shop equipment on their own time with school supervision.
Creative writing club; library club	Except for forensics, the English department of most schools generally has trouble generating a real special-interest group. Membership is usually small. When success is generated with such a club, much publicity can be a positive force for the club and school.
Math club	The math clubs on some campuses have become very active. Interschool competitions have emerged in some areas.
Glee club; pep band	Sometimes much of the music program on a campus is in the form of co-curricular activities. Members of clubs of this nature can receive important reinforcement from their public appearances.
Foreign exchange student clubs, world friendship club, field services	Clubs with a singular purpose in mind, to bring a foreign exchange student to the school and to send students to other lands, often are very successful. Their objectives are defined.
Other-interest clubs Ski club Chess club Scuba diving club Sailing club Riding club Surfing club, etc.	These clubs have more trouble linking themselves directly to a specific content area of most school curriculum. They live and die in terms of their sponsors. Many of these needs can be filled through sponsorship by an outside organization or agency other than the school.

Student Government

The second type of sponsorship in which you may become involved is in one of the forms of student government. The structure of student government varies considerably from school to school, but the most common organization is one that roughly approximates that of the U.S. government. That is, there is an "executive" branch, which is composed of the student body president, vice president, secretary, treasurer, and so on. There is a "legislative" branch made up of a representative from each homeroom, a particular academic area such as social science class, or a representative from each class operating at a specified time of day. Often there is a "judiciary" branch that is supposed to interpret the associated student body constitution and make parliamentary rulings and run elections. In a very few schools there is a student court system, but success with peers' standing in judgment of peers has usually been fraught with problems. As a counterpart to the state governments, each grade level usually has a set of elected officers that meet and generally have one or two functions each year. For instance, a junior class may conduct the junior-senior prom as its big annual event.

There is usually a "student council" or "cabinet" composed of various representatives that meets regularly. A typical structure might be composed of the student body officers, representatives from the pep squads, and the presidents of the classes. Sponsors may be assigned to any of these subsections of student government. Generally, one or the other of them emerges with the real control over student affairs, often the student council or cabinet. Sometimes this group meets daily as a class in "leadership" or "government" and because of this consistency can play and execute a wide variety of events more thoroughly than can other government segments limited to after-class meeting times.

Pep Groups

A third type of sponsorship includes the band, pep band, drill team, song leaders, yell leaders, flag twirlers, baton units, and the like. Sometimes all these meet during a period of the day under the direction of the band leader. In other schools the band and drill team may meet regularly after school and teachers are advisors to subsections. You are not likely to inherit the sponsorship of one of these groups unless you were involved in one of these activities as a student yourself, but sometimes circumstances will make you, without any experience, a sponsor of such groups. When this happens, you will need to burn the midnight oil to expand your background in a hurry.

Service Organizations

Another type of sponsorship that may occur is advisor to a service organization. The Key Club, "societies," or whatever, are groups that view themselves primarily as units that will tackle service tasks such as ushering at evening assemblies, acquiring support for needy students, serving at banquets, and so on. Almost every school has one or more of these groups, and, when sponsored well, students will want to be a part of them and will gain in self-concept, poise, and confidence.

Classroom-Associated Organizations

The final type of sponsorship mentioned here is the job that is usually handled partially in a teaching period. These are organizations formed to handle such things as the annual, school newspapers, glee clubs and other singing groups, drama, debate, and coaching assignments. All these are usually stipulated at the time of employment, and the teacher has had a specific background that qualifies him or her for that job. In all cases, however, a large part of the activity is taken care of outside of regular school hours and is considered co-curricular.

Events

Various types of events are usually a part of any co-curricular program. As a sponsor, any or all of these may be the big event of the year for a particular group. If so, you should be prepared to support, encourage, and guide the students as they work to make such an event a success.

Trips

For some schools a trip of some kind is a tradition for one of the classes or for a group. For instance, the honor society may go annually to the nearest large city for a play. Some districts have strict regulations about such trips, and it is wise for you, as a sponsor, to know these regulations precisely before making any commitments to a group. Some clubs seem to be organized with a trip in mind: for instance, the ski club's annual trip to a ski resort over Christmas vacation or the geology club's field trip to collect mineral specimens.

On occasion, a group such as the debate club may have a championship team that qualifies for a national championship tournament. The financing for such trips has often not been planned, and special fund raising has to be set up. In this event, you can find yourself spending a lot more time on the activity than you bargained for.

Even when there is not a trip per se there are times when clubs may hold an event either on or off campus. Again, there are usually specific school regulations governing this, and you need to become aware early on as to what these rules are. By and large, there is no purpose served by holding events off campus when they can be held on campus, but you can become involved in disputes with students who for some reason feel that an off-campus location somehow enhances the event. One of the main reasons for keeping events on campus is the issue of legal liabilities. The law is well established that teachers are not liable for student injuries incurred on the way to and from school. But students while on their way to and from other locations for school-sponsored events (involved in accidents) have a different legal ground on which to sue. There are, of course, some things that you simply should not do, for instance, loaning a senior student your personal car to pick up some decorations for an event. If involved in an accident, you may be held liable. When events are held off campus, it is more likely that supplies will not be there, and there is a greater chance that students will have to be sent on more errands.

Dances

Another commonly sponsored event is the dance. Dances take a variety of forms. There are, for example, after-the-game dances, informal record hops, dances with small guitar groups, and formal dances with big bands. Each of these involves more planning than the students (and often the sponsor) realize.

SALES AND MONEY MANAGEMENT

Every club seems to get involved at some point in the task of raising money. The obvious way to raise money is to buy somehing at wholesale in large lots, divide it up among the members, and sell it at a profit. Simple? It seems to be, but without good organization, sales can emerge as a major problem.

There are several types of sales. First, there are food sales. Some schools and states have regulations against certain types of open food sales. For instance, for years—and still today in some locations—a group of students will bring cookies to school and sell them at noon. The club has no outlay and all cash collected is profit. The problem, of course, is the question of cleanliness and cookie ingredients. Let a group of students turn up with food poisoning, and the sponsor is confronted with a lawsuit.

Students sometimes behave in unlikely ways. On one campus, for example, on each Tuesday for a month students purchased, and ate, enough dill pickles to fill a barrel, thus making a tidy profit for a club attempting to sponsor a Korean orphan. When the idea of a pickle sale was introduced, the sponsor had visions of a club stuck with a barrel of dill pickles and no student purchasers. But in fact, pickles sold like hot cakes. Other open food sales, such as pancake breakfasts, snow cones, and popcorn, can also be used if school regulations permit.

The other type of food sale is the closed container sale, mostly candy. In many large schools, a class or group is able to raise several thousand dollars within a week by selling candy to the community. Many candy selling programs exist, and the club's sponsor should insist that students talk with several salesmen before embarking on a project. There are programs with various prices at various volumes, prizes for students who sell the most, 40:60 dollar splits, 50:50 dollar splits, poor quality candy and good-quality candy with special school labels. It pays to deal with a firm that has been established for some time.

Other sales involve nonfood items. Key chains, good luck charms, school emblems, pep stickers, football programs, and sports cushions are all offered for sale at various times by schools. Again, sometimes unusual things go over well. A well-organized campaign once sold over 2,000 toothbrushes in four days. It should be noted that food is generally easier to sell than are unusual items. Sponsors should engage dealers who will accept the return of unused merchandise.

When involved in any sale, certain procedures must be followed. No matter how honest the students are, tight controls on checking out goods must be established, if for no other reason than to serve as an example of sound money management practices. A checklist must be kept of each student in the organization showing how much merchandise was checked out and when. Deadlines for returning the money and unsold goods must be set up and kept. If there is a sale of tickets, each should be numbered and the numbers recorded. Without such procedures, money and goods will inevitably be lost.

Most schools have an organized procedure for the collection of cash. A common practice is for the treasurer of the club to fill out a requisition for an appropriate number of cash boxes and change. Usually a secretary in the school has the responsibility for handling routine matters concerned with student body funds in the school, and the request reaches her desk. A typical cash box requisition is shown in Figure 8.

Cash Box Requisition
(Fill out in duplicate)

Organization   *Pep Club*

Event   *Button Sale*

Number of cash boxes requested _2_

_$34_   Cash   Composition:

_10_	$1 bills	$10.00
_4_	$5 bills	20.00
_0_	pennies 2 1¢	.00
_20_	nickels	1.00
_10_	dimes	1.00
_10_	quarters	2.50
		$34.00

Date and time of pickup   *11/25/83   3 p.m.*
Date and time of return   *11/26/83   8 a.m.*

Organization's Treasurer   _____
                                            Signature

Organization's Sponsor   _____
                                            Signature

FIGURE 8

After the sale has been completed, the student treasurer and sponsor will deposit the money with the secretary or staff member in charge of student body funds. Usually each organization has its own "trust" account that makes up a portion of the larger total student body funds. A typical deposit slip for funds is shown in Figure 9.

School Organization Slip
(Fill out in Duplicate)

Organization's name _____ *Girl's League* _____

Account number _____ 22 _____

Sponsor's signature _____

Treasurer's signature _____

Date _____ 3/24/84 _____

Composition of deposit:

25	pennies	$	.25
32	nickels		1.60
44	dimes		4.40
14	quarters		3.50
2	halves		1.00
22	$1 bills		22.00
12	$5 bills		60.00
14	$10 bills		140.00
1	$20 bill		20.00
14.05	Total in checks		14.05
		Total deposit	266.80
		Less cashbox change	34.50
		Net deposit	232.30

FIGURE 9

When events are held at night, depositing funds with the secretary or school official will not be possible until the day after. In the case of a large event, many schools have provisions for night deposit at the bank that is used by the student body. In the case of a championship football game, gate receipts can total several thousand dollars. In this case, not only are night deposits necessary, but a paid police escort is needed.

Purchase Order Requisition

For Office Use Only

Organization _____ Purchase order no. _____

Account no. _____ Date _____ Appropriation _____

Date needed _____ Date _____

Sponsor _____

Treasurer _____

Approved _____
                Administrator

Complete Description of Articles or Services	Quantity	Unit	Unit Price	Amount
			TOTAL	

Complete Name & Address of Suggested Vendors:

FIGURE 10

Unfortunately, in a few schools the entire organization for handling student body funds is slipshod. Some organizations and clubs prefer to operate independently of regular school channels. Such things as candy sales will be organized by a club, candy sold, and profits made and spent without reporting to the central student body accounting procedure. You must guard against being involved in this practice. Many teachers have found that coins collected in coffee cans and hidden in the bottom drawers of locked desks have a way of disappearing. A basic principle of any co-curricular activity program is to function as an example of good business practices.

If a club or group decides to sell a particular product, these products must be purchased.. Usually the school requires the club to requisition such items through proper channels.. A typical requisition form is shown in Figure 10. What the sponsor and club treasurer may get in return is a completed purchase order, ready to send, or the office may send the purchase order directly. On occasion, the sponsor and club committee may hand carry the purchase order to a local vendor and pick up the product themselves. In a third alternative, the sponsor may request a check and pay for the item at the time of pickup instead of giving the vendor a purchase order.

In some schools, all checks are requested from a central office. In others, the principal signs all checks. In still others, an activities director may sign the checks and the student body treasurer may countersign. Whatever the procedure, the club sponsor will need to request checks before a particular event takes place and anticipate who needs to receive checks. In a very few schools each club has its own checking account at the bank. This practice is less efficient and makes central reporting of student body funds difficult. In addition, certain states have sales tax reporting on items sold, and widely dispersed accounts make collection of data difficult.

ELECTIONS AND APPOINTMENTS

One area of sponsorship that is fraught with potential problems is that of elections and appointments. By appointments we mean the choosing of students to perform any student body role by a process other than election. The following is a list of roles that may be filled by a variety of procedures:

1. Student body government officers
2. Drill team membership
3. Varsity band
4. Pep band
5. Dance band
6. Cheerleaders
7. Baton twirlers
8. Flag twirlers
9. Song leaders
10. Class officers
11. Senate, homeroom representatives
12. Student court
13. Queens, princesses (homecoming, junior and senior prom, etc.)
14. Club officers
15. Special committees
16. Membership in honorary groups
17. Participants in talent shows
18. The casts of plays
19. Sports squads

Election for student body officers may take place in the spring or fall or both. Some schools elect for a semester, some for a school year. Some school elections are high powered, with voter registration, intense campaigning, primaries, and inaugural addresses. Other schools have little fuss. As a sponsor of an aspect of student government, it is important that you get to know election procedures early and well. For instance, if there is a regulation on the quantity and size of publicity posters, you may be called upon to make judgments of possible rule violations.

The big warning here is that, as a faculty member involved in student elections, you must make sure that election procedures are delineated and are carried out to the letter. This is not just to make the election an example of the larger public elections but to ensure that there are no repercussions throwing the election in a bad light because of a procedural question. Rumors spread like fire across a high school campus. If there is a technical slip, the school can be thrown into a temporary turmoil.

Probably the most important aspect of the election procedure is the counting of ballots and the subsequent announcement of victories. This counting must be organized and overseen by sponsors. Scrupulous attention to detail is mandated.

An even more ticklish area is that of appointments. If an election can be questioned, what of the appointment of the drill team or other pep squads? If an area has the potential for controversy, heartache, and ill will, this is it. Yet there seems to be no alternative. What *must* happen is that whatever procedures are to be used must be as fair as possible—and followed to the letter.

An often-used system for selecting pep squads is to have a preliminary tryout during which time a committee will cut the number of candidates to a reasonable size, perhaps twice the final group. As an example, suppose thirty-three girls are trying out for six song leader positions. A committee composed of the pep group sponsor, one academic faculty member, a visiting pep sponsor from another school, a visiting song leader from another school, and two senior song leaders use a rating sheet to assess each girl. Using these ratings, the group can be cut from thirty-three to twelve. These twelve are then placed on the student body election ballot and the six song leaders are elected from them.

It sounds like a fair process, yet, sooner or later, an irate parent and daughter will be crying "favoritism," and the subsequent agony of procedural review will have to be made. When this happens, you must have your procedures smooth and your records straight.

CONTRACTS

The school with which you are associated may or may not use many contracts. It is a good idea for you to make up written contracts, even if informal, with each merchant dealt with outside the school. The need for a contract with any bands or orchestras has already been mentioned. Any hiring of halls or other outside facilities should be negotiated formally. All sports events with other schools, along with the split of income from ticket sales, should be contracted. Ring sales, pictures, and the like are all contract negotiations.

The reason for the contract is to make clear *before* the actual sale or event exactly who will be responsible for what, and who pays for what. Without this arrangement, the sponsor may well be left holding the bag. Even with a contract, it is hard to foresee unexpected events. For instance, donkey basketball and donkey baseball games have been big money-makers in various parts of the country over the past years. Many promoters of these types of programs will ask for a flat fee, but upon negotiation, a contract may be signed that puts much less risk on the school and sponsor through a procedure using a percentage of the gate as the basic fee. Arrangements such as these are often available for a variety of shows and entertainers.

WORKING WITH OFF-CAMPUS ORGANIZATIONS

In addition to the multitude of possible salesmen who may be available for services and goods, you may also become involved with various off-campus organizations. Sometimes service clubs, business leaders involved in junior achievement, little league coaches, and the like get ideas that can mean the involvement of a particular sponsor and club. For instance, suppose that a local club decides that because of a rash of car accidents they want to make a batch of posters about safe driving to post in local merchant shop windows. They may run a poster contest, or they may come to the sponsor of the art club and offer to throw a poster party for all the club members at which all students in the club can get free goodies (cookies and punch), listen to records, and make lots of posters.

This type of project seems innocent enough, but the sponsor must make sure of several things. Where will the poster party be held? Perhaps in the artroom? If so, how will the teacher make sure that the supplies used are not furnished by the school?

You may find that as the sponsor of a club you will be expected to furnish the place, materials, food, and records in exchange for a check from the service club that covers materials. Even this is not bad if the art club is enthusiastic about the project and is willing to set up the committees and do the necessary work to make it go. If, on the other hand, the club members feel that this is just a job that has been forced upon them, then you will end up doing most of the work. You should find a way to let the service club know that the objectives and goals of the club do not mesh with the poster party idea without alienating the service club. At times this can be difficult.

When working with a community organization, you must maintain congenial relations by explaining the purposes of the club being sponsored so members of the community organization can see what activities of the club are appropriate for mutual benefit. Keep the school administration informed of what is taking place. Certainly organizing all club members to sell a product for the profit of a community organization that does not help to sponsor the high school club directly is not an acceptable activity.

ASSEMBLIES

Many schools have a regular procedure for scheduling assemblies. In some, there is an attempt to have only assemblies that involve students from their own and adjacent high schools. In others, outside speakers are used. In a few, no assemblies are scheduled, often because of a lack of a facility to gather the students together. Often assemblies are held on a shift basis, where part of the students will attend one period and part the next period. The problem of organizing an assembly-day schedule is up to the administration, so it will not be dealt with here. But you, and other faculty sponsors, may well be in charge of a particular assembly.

Some of the common student assemblies are the Christmas assembly, talent assembly, awards assembly, and assemblies sponsored by various clubs. For instance, as the science club sponsor, it may be traditional that every other year the science club sponsors an assembly. This means gathering together ideas, organizing them into a sequence of displays, skits, and so on, and going through various procedures until you are convinced that things will go smoothly.

If the science club so decides, it could raise money and pay a science speaker for the assembly or it may be able to line up one of the many speakers that work for the electric, telephone, or other companies who speak at such assemblies for free. Whatever the ideas and result, you need to guide the students as they make all the necessary arrangements, and you must have the answers when questions arise.

DISRUPTION OF CLASSES

One problem that seems to always be with the sponsors of clubs is that of class disruption. There seem to be certain unavoidable times when classes are disrupted by students involved in activities. For instance, all candidates for student government offices need to report a few minutes before an assembly to take their places and get set. As long as this assembly can be scheduled immediately after a longer break, there is no problem. But if that is not possible, then the candidates must leave their rooms early, which can disrupt the teaching flow. With the advent of modular scheduling, disruption problems of this sort seem to have been minimized.

Sponsors should do everything in their power to arrange club activity schedules so as not to disrupt classes or keep students out of classes. When this is not possible, sponsors need to make sure they work through the procedures set up by the school and keep the administration informed of what is happening. Sponsors of clubs may be doing a bang-up job with their club participants but inadvertently be alienating some of the staff by seemingly instigating a series of classroom disruptions.

OBJECTIVES AND CO-CURRICULAR ACTIVITIES

Existing clubs should have procedures set up by the school for the recognition of their existence. Usually these procedures involve the prerequisites of a minimum number of students interested in the club, a staff sponsor, and a constitution that has been approved by the administration, student council, and sometimes the board of education.

The constitutions of most clubs have a section delineating the purposes and goals of the organization. These sections suffer from the same problems of ambiguity with which objectives traditionally have been guilty. As a sponsor, you may have the opportunity to help club members add bylaws and amendments to their constitution that will spell out the objectives of their club more precisely.

A second use of the principles of precise objectives comes as the sponsor works with the students. Students and sponsors must realize that clubs function and stay healthy by committing themselves to a series of worthwhile projects. Often clubs will get involved in fund-raising projects, or will have an annual fund-raising project, without a purpose for the disbursement of those funds. Fund raising is a means to an end, not an end in itself. The more worthwhile the end, the easier it is to rationalize the enterprise. As a resident of an area, would a homeowner be more willing to buy a box of candy to raise money to help bring a foreign exchange student to the local high school or to help the freshman class throw a party? Both are common fund-raising objectives, but one obviously has a more worthy goal.

The sponsor should see that as many objectives as possible are verbalized in behavioral terms. Many times these may be in the affective domain. Of these, many will not be shared with the students as a cognitive objective would in the classroom, although there may be instances where the learning is cognitive and direct. For instance, if club meetings are disorganized and disorderly, the club sponsor may teach and involve the students in the use of Roberts' *Rules of Order*.

More often, however, the sponsor will notice a club member who could be helped to develop a social skill or attitude change and, by arranging his or her committee assignments and relations with the group, be able to assist the student in self-improvement. Again, the objective may be verbalized only in the mind of the teacher, but it helps guide decisions.

Objectives will initially have a less formal place in the operation of co-curricular activities than in the operation of classrooms because the goals of the club or organization are usually stated less precisely. As activities and purposes evolve during the course of the school year, meaningful objectives are formulated by the club members and sponsor that can be used to defend any activity in which they engage.

As an illustration, consider the sponsor of a girls' service organization. One of the goals in the constitution of the club is to help students with special problems. During the year a student is burned badly in a fire and is undergoing skin transplant operations. The students in the club find out that the family needs a thousand dollars to complete the operation and they vote to try to raise the money.

The goal of helping others has now been translated into the precise objectives of raising a thousand dollars for a worthy cause. During the implementation of the raising of the money, the sponsor can identify various roles that can be handled by club members that will assist them in various forms of growth. At the conclusion of a successful project, the sponsor can point out in meetings how each girl fulfilled her commitments and reinforce the growth that has taken place. On occasion, individual talks and encouragement for specific girls may be necessary during the course of the project. If the goal is not reached, then a real learning experience can result as the problems are analyzed and possible alternatives discussed that would have resulted in success.

A main problem to avoid as a sponsor is a general fragmentation of activities without a commitment to some clear goal. In such circumstances, students spin wheels and jump from project to project without completing anything.

THE SCHOOL CALENDAR

Almost all schools have an activities calendar that contains the entries of all club meetings, events, and use of facilities. In some cases this calendar is developed a year in advance so that a minimum of conflict of events will take place. Sponsors must ensure that all club events have been cleared with the administrator in charge of the school calendar, so that it is not discovered too late that one event is competing with another.

In some cases, conflict is impossible. For instance, the fall play may be scheduled right after football season. However, if the school has a championship team, the team may enter some sort of playoff. If so, conflict with the play is inevitable.

If a calendar is available, judicious planning on the part of a club may allow them to find a time slot during a lull period that can help to ensure an event's success.

SUMMARY

As a club sponsor, you may find that your involvement in activities encompasses unfamiliar areas. School rules and regulations governing clubs and organizations must be kept in mind as you learn to deal with the students in settings other than the classroom.

Elections, money handling, and appointment procedures can be painful unless organized and documented carefully. Scrupulous attention to detail is essential, lest a student or parent level accusations of unfairness.

The use of contracts will help you protect yourself and the school and expedite the accomplishment of a club's objectives. Other areas of concern are (1) maintaining good relations with off-campus organizations that involve themselves in student activities and (2) minimizing classroom disruptions because of activities.

Sponsors need to keep the organization's objectives in mind. It is easy to become involved in activities that lead the students away from the goals set up in the organization's constitution. Fund raising is a means to a worthwhile end, not an end in itself.

FOURTEEN
TRENDS AND ISSUES
IN EDUCATION

Educators and noneducators alike are continually developing ideas that they believe will improve the teaching-learning process. Some ideas, such as busing and competency testing, sweep the nation and acquire strong adherents (who claim the idea will solve virtually all the problems facing educators) and equally strong opponents (who believe the idea will plunge the field into irretrievable chaos).

As a teacher you are likely to be asked for your opinion about some of these issues. This chapter is designed to familiarize you with some of the more hotly debated ideas, but the chapter is by no means all inclusive nor does it cover all there is to say about the issues it surveys. To become better versed in the issues discussed and to apprise yourself of other issues of current interest, you will need to read recent educational journals and talk with other educators. This chapter will help point you in the right direction, but staying abreast of the field will be your continuing responsibility.

OBJECTIVES

When you complete this chapter, you will be able to:

1. Given a trend or issue of current interest to educators, explain, in writing, the specific deficiency in education allegedly addressed by the idea and how the idea proposes to remedy the deficiency. (Analysis)

2. Take a position for or against an educational issue of your choice and defend that position, in writing, by developing a three-point rationale that is supported by specific facts and examples. (Evaluation)

COMPETENCY TESTING—STUDENTS

The issue of competency testing is unique, first, because it has no true opposition (no one wants to come out for incompetence) and, second, because of its age. The Hebrews were concerned about reading competence five thousand years ago because they wanted their young men to be able to read the *Torah*. We are still concerned about reading competence today. When the Soviet Union beat us into space by launching Sputnik in 1957, our concern broadened to include competencies in science. These concerns, too, are still with us. In fact, one of the reasons that competency testing is such an important issue today is that it has ceased being a single-subject concern (reading or science or math) and has come to include all the basic skills and knowledge we consider essential for coping with today's world.

The roots of the nationwide concern over minimal competencies are widespread, but a major catalyst, and the thing that has made competency testing a "cause célèbre," was the reports during the late 1970s that *Scholastic Aptitude Test* (SAT) scores had "dropped steadily, after remaining relatively stable during the preceding decade. Verbal scores have dropped 49 points, from 478 in 1963 to 429 in 1977; mathematics scores, 32 points, from 502 to 470."[1] These reports were reinforced by complaints from the business community that the high school graduates being hired were frequently unable to read the instructions for operating simple machines and/or were unable to make change in retail stores. The military joined in by explaining that all its inductees are given a battery of tests to group them according to mental ability with category I being the brightest and Category V being the dullest. In 1980 the pentagon reported that "A study this summer showed that a disturbingly high 46% of the 1979 recruits ranked in Category IV. Those in Category V are automatically rejected as unfit."[2] Further, "on a test that evaluated on-the-job performance, 89% of the motor vehicle drivers and 85% of the Huey helicopter repairmen failed."[3]

Although some people have attempted to rationalize the low test scores and low performance on the basis of the focus of the tests and/or the larger percentage of the population taking the tests, many citizens are demanding

[1]John Ryor, "Declining SAT Scores," *Today's Education*, 66, no. 4 (November–December 1977), 6.

[2]"Battle in the Pentagon," *Time*, 116, no. 13, September 29, 1980, p. 28.

[3]Ibid.

that the schools do something to increase the abilities of graduates. This is true even though the Scholastic Aptitude Test (SAT) scores for students graduating in 1981 were the same as for those students graduating in 1980, thus indicating that the 18-year decline in SAT scores has, at least temporarily, halted.[4] Further, even reports of rises in standardized test scores[5] have failed to quiet the fears of the general public, and pressure continues at the state level for increased standards.

At the beginning of 1980 at least thirty-eight states had taken some kind of action concerning the establishment of minimal competency tests. In some states, as in Florida, the action took the form of a legislative mandate establishing competency tests. In others, as in Illinois, the state board of education recommended the tests. In most, however, the mandate has required individual school districts to establish competency tests in basic skills and has required them to provide instruction to students failing to meet acceptable standards. Most school districts are developing competency tests to be administered throughout the students' school years (as opposed to a screening-type test administered immediately prior to graduation) with the intent of identifying weak students early enough to provide appropriate and timely remediation.

Since no one wants to be "for" incompetence, it might seem that competency testing would enjoy virtually unanimous support, but such is not the case. The reasons are fairly obvious. There are disagreements about just which competencies should be tested, when they should be tested, by whom, and according to what standards. There is also disagreement concerning how many "failures" school districts are able to remedy given their limited budgets. Disagreements not withstanding, however, teachers are having to adjust to the idea of competence testing.

In those cases where competency tests have already been established (as in Peoria and Chicago, Illinois), teachers are finding that their freedom to select material is limited by their need to be certain to cover the skills included on the competency tests. In some cases instructional styles are also being altered as teachers find that they need to assess their students more rigorously and more frequently.

There seems to be some evidence that minimal competency testing can help to increase student performance,[6] but the whole issue of student competence (or the lack of it) has given rise to another issue: teacher competence.

[4]Lawrence Biemiller, "18-Year Decline in Aptitude-Test Scores Halted This Year, College Board Reports," *The Chronicle of Higher Education*. Oct. 7, 1981, Vol. XXIII. No. 6, p. 1.
[5]"What Those Soaring Scores Mean," *Time*, 118, No. 2, July 13, 1981, p. 56.
[6]Ralph D. Turlington, "Good News from Florida: Our Minimum Competency Program Is Working," *Phi Delta Kappan*, 60, no. 9 (May 1979), 649.

COMPETENCY TESTING—TEACHERS

In June 1980, *Time* magazine ran a cover story entitled "Help! Teacher Can't Teach!"[7] The story gave a fairly balanced view of some of the strengths and weaknesses of American education, but its main point was that "quite a few teachers (estimates range up to 20%) simply have not mastered the basic skills in reading, writing, and arithmetic that they are supposed to teach."[8]

Many teacher educators have tried various ways to increase the competencies of prospective teachers and to assure that those who do not meet acceptable standards do not graduate,[9,10,11] but the demonstrated incompetence of some teachers has prompted renewed calls not only for stricter standards for certification but also for the licensing of teachers and the periodic retesting of their general teaching skills and their knowledge in their particular subject areas.[12]

The issue of competencies for teachers shares many of the same points (pro and con) as the issue for student competencies. The problems of which competencies to measure and how to measure them, the restrictions competency testing imposes on academic freedom, and how to best help those who do not attain the minimal competencies are common problems of the two issues and they call to attention another, related issue: individualization.

INDIVIDUALIZATION

Most educators favor individualizing instruction to the extent possible within the framework of public and mass education, but most also agree that, while individualization can be effective,[13] it can also pose significant new problems for teachers. We have seen, in Chapter 11, how self-instructional packages can be used to help individualize instruction for average students. As a teacher, however, what do you do with atypical students?

---

[7]"Help! Teacher Can't Teach!" *Time*, 115, no. 24, June 16, 1980, p. 54.

[8]Ibid., p. 55.

[9]Michael A. Lorber, "From Traditional to Competency-Based Education and Back Again: An Eight-Year Experiment," *Phi Delta Kappan*, 60, no. 7 (March 1979), 523.

[10]Hayden R. Smith and Thomas S. Nagel, "From Traditional to Competency-Based Teacher Education—and Never Back Again," *Phi Delta Kappan*, 61, no. 3 (November 1979), 194.

[11]Michael A. Lorber, "Molding CBTE to the Satisfaction of Students *and* Faculty," *Phi Delta Kappan*, 61, no. 3 (November 1979), 196.

[12]"Licensing Plans," *Time*, 116, no. 13, September 29, 1980, p. 80.

[13]Rita Dunn, "Another Look at Individualized Instruction," *Phi Delta Kappan*, 59, no. 6 (February 1978), 400.

Individualization—Mainstreaming

In 1975, Congress passed the Education of the Handicapped Act (Public Law 94-142), which, among things, defined the term "handicapped students"[14] and provided that they be "educated in the least restrictive environment—in the regular classroom with their nonhandicapped peers, unless their particular educational needs cannot be met in that way."[15]

The reason mainstreaming has become a hotly debated issue is because, while everyone wants to help the handicapped as much as possible, there is the fear on the part of teachers that they lack both the training and time to meet the needs of these handicapped students who were assigned previously to special education teachers. The lack of adequate training is a legitimate concern, and many teacher education institutions are trying to find ways of incorporating this kind of instruction into a curriculum that is already packed tightly with skills and information deemed necessary.

The lack of time teachers need to make mainstreaming effective is yet another issue and is tied to both the issues of declining enrollments and increasing class size.[16] The last factors are full-scale issues in themselves.

Individualization—Multicultural Awareness

At the same time that questions are being raised concerning the adequacy of teachers' preparation for mainstreaming,[17] teachers are also being faced with the necessity of dealing with students from different cultures and subcultures. Although many schools have attempted to deal with many of the special problems faced by blacks, few schools are prepared, with either adequate funding or adequately trained teachers, to deal with the more than 11 million Hispanics living in the United States[18] or with the increasing numbers of Asians, Haitians, and other immigrants seeking a better life in this country.

Attempts by teacher preparation institutions to sensitize prospective teachers to cultural differences are hampered by the same problem ham-

[14]Martha Summers, "Learning Disabilities . . . a Puzzlement," *Today's Education*, 66, no. 4 (November–December 1977), 40.

[15]Edward Brooke, "PL 94-142—Getting the Money to Make It Work," *Today's Education*, 66, no. 4 (November-December 1977), 50.

[16]Dorothy Massie, "Update on Education of the Handicapped," *Today's Education*, 67, no. 3 (September–October 1978), 60.

[17]James R. Flynn, R. C. Gacka, and D. A. Sundean, "Are Classroom Teachers Prepared for Mainstreaming?" *Phi Delta Kappan*, 59, no. 8, (April 1978), 561.

[18]Carlos J. Ovando, "School Implications of the Peaceful Latino Invasion." *Phi Delta Kappan*, 59, no. 4 (December 1977), 230.

pering preparation for mainstreaming—teacher preparation programs are already overloaded with expected competencies and schools are reluctant to add additional courses to those already required for certification. Nonetheless, teachers must deal with both handicapped students and with students from different cultural backgrounds and some of them are doing it well.[19,20] Your task is to prepare yourself with as wide a variety of pedagogical and interpersonal skills as you can so you will be able to deal effectively with the many atypical students you are likely to meet.[21,22]

DECLINING ENROLLMENTS

Compounding the problems inherent in all the issues discussed so far are the interrelated issues of declining enrollments, declining financial resources, and increasing class sizes.

During the decade of the 1970s public school enrollment in the United States declined by about 5 million students (approximately 11 percent).[23] Educators viewed this decline with both hope and fear—hope the decline would mean smaller class sizes and increased opportunities for individualization, and fear the decline would mean fewer dollars for education and thus less of everything. Unfortunately, many of the hopes have been dashed and many of the fears realized.

Many teachers have long contended that they could do a better job if their class size was kept low (less than twenty). Their position became even firmer as handicapped students were mainstreamed into their rooms and as the proportion of culturally different students increased. Now, even though there is evidence demonstrating that student achievement increases as class size is reduced (particularly to fifteen students or less),[24] many administrators are finding it necessary to increase class sizes to cope with the financial hardships accompanying the enrollment decline.

"According to the National Institute of Education, in 43 states it now costs nearly 50% more to operate primary and secondary schools than it did in 1971."[25] Why does it cost so much more today to educate fewer

[19]Thomas E. Robinson, "The Waldtopia School System: A Program for Secondary Education, 1985," *Phi Delta Kappan*, 61, no. 7 (March 1980), 465.

[20]Judith Bernstein, "Kim Is Handicapped, but . . . ," *Today's Education*, 69, no. 1 (February–March 1980), 76.

[21]Jack Frymier, "The Annehurst System: Built on Recognition That People Are Different," *Phi Delta Kappan*, 61, no. 10 (June 1980), 682.

[22]David N. Aspy and F. M. Roebuck, "Teacher Education: A Response to Watt's Response to Combs," *Educational Leadership*, 37, no. 6 (March 1980), 507.

[23]Diane Divoky, "Burden of the Seventies: The Management of Decline," *Phi Delta Kappan*, 61, no. 2 (October 1979), 87.

[24]Leonard S. Cahen and Nikola N. Filby, "The Class Size Achievement Issue: New Evidence and a Research Plan," *Phi Delta Kappan*, 60, no. 7 (March 1979), 492.

[25]Divoky, "Burden of the Seventies," p. 87.

students? "There were many reasons—the way state aid formulas work, the implementation of new federal laws for the handicapped and the bilingual, the cost of desegregation—but mainly it was the rise in teacher salaries and general inflation that made schooling fewer children cost more."[26]

The combination of pressures relating to competency tests, mainstreaming, multicultural students, increasing class size, the financial problems (not to mention chronic absenteeism, drug abuse, and violence) have contributed to a phenomenon known as teacher "burnout"—a sense of hopelessness that overcomes many teachers and causes them to leave the profession. As one "burnt out" teacher put it, "The good teachers have all quit to save their sanity."[27]

Obviously, not all good teachers have left teaching, and one who stayed on gave her opinion about why so many teachers do stay! "Most teachers don't teach for the money. They teach for that recognition they see and feel when a student learns something. I think most teachers do a terrific job."[28]

The authors of this text, along with your instructors, believe that you, too, are capable of doing a "terrific" job. Although many of the issues we have surveyed so far are complex and disheartening, there are some things you can do now to help prepare yourself more adequately. One of those things is to become knowledgeable about new instructional tools that can help you to do your job better. In an effort to help you learn about one of the most powerful new instructional tools, we will conclude this chapter with a look at computers in education.

MICROCOMPUTERS

We have already looked once at computers in education (see Chapter 7), but their impact on education is so great that they warrant a second look. According to one source, "Nearly three-fifths of all secondary schools were using computers in 1975, compared to one-third only five years earlier."[29] Admittedly, much of the computer time has been devoted to administrative tasks, but with the advent of inexpensive microcomputers, more and more time is being devoted to instruction.

Many administrators are recognizing the need for teachers prepared to teach both with, and about, computers, so acquiring such knowledge will not only help you to do a better job in the classroom, but it can help you to get into the classroom in the first place. In a recent survey of 686

[26]Ibid.
[27]"Help! Teacher Can't Teach!" p. 57.
[28]Ibid.
[29]Robert J. Seidel, "It's 1980: Do You Know Where Your Computer Is?" *Phi Delta Kappan*, 61, no. 7 (March 1980), 481.

secondary school principals in Illinois, it was found that (1) 71% saw a need for computer science teachers, (2) 55% saw a need for state certification in computer science, and (3) 82% felt that some computer science is valuable in the background of any teacher."[30]

With such widespread agreement concerning the worth of computers for both administrative tasks and for instruction, you might wonder why computers are included in a chapter devoted to trends and issues. The answer is that, while there is a clear trend toward the rapid expansion of computer utilization in all areas of education, there are some educators and noneducators who are opposing the trend.

One faction believes that every dollar available for education should go for more teachers and/or teachers' salaries. Their position is strong because virtually every educator is in favor of both ideas. Nonetheless, to oppose the use of a tool that cannot only reduce instructional time but can also make possible educational experiences previously impossible[31] does not make good sense in the long run. The question these people must address is whether we can afford *not* to utilize computers in education. Can we afford *not* to prepare our youth for the future?

A second faction is manned by teachers themselves. Few teachers have worked with computers, and thus many are hesitant to learn about a tool they consider terribly complex. The answer here is that, while microcomputers *are* terribly complex, *their use is not.* Teachers in this camp are in much the same position as were horse and wagon owners when the automobile was introduced. Both computers and the automobile are complex products of a technological age. You do not, however, need to be a technocrat to use either.

The fact of the matter is that many secondary school administrators are looking for teachers who can either teach about computers or who can use computers to help provide instruction in specific subject areas. "The demonstrated capabilities of microcomputers selling in the $800 to $1,800 range compares favorably with those of large time-sharing interactive systems. Courseware is emerging that provides drill and practice, simulations, tutorial instruction, graphic displays, and animation."[32] If you want to be part of the future, begin preparing yourself now. Learn about computers.

[30]Stuart D. Milner, "Teaching Teachers About Computers: A Necessity for Education," *Phi Delta Kappan*, 61, no. 8 (April 1980), 545.

[31]Seidel, "It's 1980: . . . ?" p. 482.

[32]Lee Marvin Joiner, S. R. Miller, and B. J. Silverstein, "Potential and Limits of Computers in Schools," *Educational Leadership*, 37, no. 6 (March 1980), 499.

SUMMARY

In this chapter we have surveyed the issues of competency testing as it relates to students and teachers, individualization as it is affected by mainstreaming and students with multicultural backgrounds, declining enrollments and the attendant problems of fiscal stress and increasing class sizes, and microcomputers. Each of these issues, and each of the other issues mentioned or alluded to in this chapter, are more complex than they might appear at the outset.

To find out more about these and other issues of the day, you will have to read professional journals both in your own field and those concerning education in general.[33] Only in this way will you be knowledgeable enough to contribute to the solutions of education's problems rather than being part of the problem yourself. Education needs alert and aware teachers—be one.

---

[33]To determine which professional organizations publish journals that may be of interest to you, write for the *Directory of Education Associations*. It is available for $3.75 from The Superintendent of Documents, U.S. Government Printing Office, Washington, D.C. 20402. The stock number is 017-080-01882-9.

APPENDIX A
SOURCES FOR PRECISE INSTRUCTIONAL OBJECTIVES

The CO-OP Center of Educational Research
University of Massachusetts
Amherst, Mass. 01002

Florida Center for (Competency-Based) Teacher Training Materials
William Spino, Director
College of Education
University of Miami
Miami, Fla. 33100

Institute for Educational Research
1400 W. Maple Ave.
Downers Grove, Ill. 60515

Instructional Objectives Exchange
Box 24095
Los Angeles, Calif. 90024

IPPES
Jackson Public Schools
1400 W. Monroe
Jackson, Mich. 49202

National Evaluation System, Inc.
P.O. Box 266-p
Amherst, Mass. 01002

Oakleaf Elementary School
Mathematics Continuum (and)
Behavioral Objectives for Reading
Baldwin-Whitehall School District
Pittsburgh, Penn. 15200

Pre-Service Secondary Teacher Education
Department of Curriculum and Instruction
Illinois State University
Normal, Ill. 61761

Project Spoke
Mr. John A. Stefani
37 W. Main St.
Norton, Mass. 02766

VAE Pre-Certification Teacher Education Program:
Competencies and Performance Objectives
Department of Vocational and Applied Arts Education
College of Education
Wayne State University
Detroit, Mich. 48202

Also available:

John Flanagan, William Shanner, and Robert Mager, *Behavioral Objectives,*
vols. I, II, III, and IV (Palo Alto, Calif: Westinghouse Learning Press, 1971)

APPENDIX B
SAMPLE UNIT PLAN

Color and Design[1]

I. Introduction
   A. *Course:* Home Economics
   B. *Target Population:* 11th Grade—Average Students
   C. *Title:* Housing and Home Furnishings—Color and Design
   D. *Overview:* "Color and Design" is intended to prepare students with terminology, concepts, and principles involving color and design as used in furnishing a home. This unit will be preceded by "Buying, Building, Renting," a unit concerned with the living, working, and storage space considerations crucial to decisions about buying, building, or renting shelter; and it will be followed by "Furniture Styles and Accessories," a unit that concerns fabrics, textures, color harmonies, wall arrangements, furniture styles, accessories, and floor coverings.
   E. *Length of Time:* About two weeks
II. Unit Objectives
   At the completion of this unit, you will:
   A. Write the definition of, and cite an example of, each of the following terms and phrases: *the four elements of design; hue; value; tint; shade; intensity; warm and cool colors; primary, secondary, and intermediate colors; Prang and Munsell color charts; structural and decorative design; five principles of design; monochromatic; analogous; contrasting; complementary; split-complementary; triad; and accented-neutral harmonies.*

[1]This unit plan was conceived by Linda Kruger.

B. Given three pictures of completely furnished rooms, identify the line direction in each room and state, in writing, the mood that the line direction suggests.

C. Given five colored pictures of furnished rooms, label, in writing, the color scheme as being predominantly warm or cool; identify the hue, value, and intensity of the main color being used; and classify the color as being a primary, secondary, or intermediate color.

D. Given two color charts, label each, in writing, as being either a Prang or a Munsell chart, and cite at least one reason for your choice.

E. Given a colored picture of a furnished room, list, in writing, examples of each of the four elements of design (line, form, color, texture), and cite one factor that helped you decide which element it represented.

F. Given two pictures of the same room with identical furniture but different arrangements, identify the picture with the best arrangement using rhythm, proportion, and balance and guides and write four reasons why the other picture exemplifies a less desirable arrangement.

G. Given a list of colors (black, red, yellow, white, blue, green, gray, brown, and purple), list, in writing, at least two symbolic meanings and/or ideas associated with each color.

H. Given diagrams of seven different types of color harmonies, correctly label each diagram as to type.

III. Content
  A. Introduction: Beauty of design (lecture, transparencies)
    1. Satisfaction in the home
    2. Reactions to surroundings
    3. Causes of good or bad impressions
      a. Elements of design
      b. Room planned as whole
    4. Good taste; harmony of color and design

    (Materials and procedure: Using pictorial examples mounted on construction paper, show examples of the items listed, along with examples of different types of rooms to introduce the topic color and design. Show different room arrangements, color schemes, and moods of rooms.)

  B. Elements of design (lecture transparencies)
    1. The live, basic element of beauty
      a. Psychological effects
        vertical—carries eyes upward; masculine in effect; severe, strong; creates feeling of height (e.g., doorways, draperies)
        horizontal—solidity, (e.g., repose, tranquility; breaks effect of vertical lines (e.g., cornices, bookcases, baseboards, low tables)
        diagonal—action, forward push (e.g., staircases, diagonal line in fabrics or wallpaper)
        curved—feminine in effect; graceful, subtle, gay (e.g., tied back curtains, arches, curves in furniture)
        zig zag—movement, excitement

(Materials and procedure: After correlating pictorial examples with the lecture, show the different psychological effects that line can create. Use a self-prepared transparency. Discuss.)

2. Form (shape)
    a. Created by three dimensions
    b. Line that encloses space
       curved—oval, dome, circular, rounded
       straight—square, rectangle, oblong shapes
3. Texture
    a. Suggests fabric
       roughness versus smoothness
       shininess versus dullness
       softness versus stiffness
    b. Wall finish, rugs, woodwork, wood in furniture
    c. Must go with style and use of object

(Materials and procedure: Show examples of upholstery fabrics to clarify texture. Discuss.)

4. Color and qualities of color
    a. Hue—name of color, family name
    b. Value, or amount of lightness or darkness in a color
       tint—light or high values (good wall colors)
       shade—dark or low values (good rug colors)
    c. Intensity—brightness or dullness of color
    d. Properties of temperature and force
       warm colors—convey feeling of warmth; seem to advance; make room appear smaller (yellow, red, orange)
       cool colors—convey feeling of coolness; seem to recede; create illusion of space (blue, green)
    e. Classifications of color
       primary colors—cannot be broken down into other colors, and no combination of other colors can produce them (red, yellow, blue)
       secondary colors—mix two primary colors (orange, violet, green)
       intermediate colors—mix primary color with adjacent secondary color (yellow-green, blue-green, etc.)
    f. Color charts
       Prang—traditional; three primary colors: red, yellow, blue
       Munsell—five principal colors: red, yellow, blue, green, purple

(Materials and procedure: Devise a flash card game using words and phrases involved with color terminology. This can be used for review as well as for evaluations. The students will seat themselves in a semicircle. Stand in the middle with the flash cards. When the teacher holds the cards up, the first student to raise his or her hand answers the questions involved. The answer appears on the reverse side of the card; it may, therefore, also be used for individual review. The students will bring into class three examples of rooms furnished with cool colors. From these pictures the class will choose the best examples of warm and cool colors used in room decorating and create a bulletin board.

Before proceeding to new material, the students will be involved in a group discussion. The students will form into small groups. Each group will be appointed a specific element of design for which they will find pictorial examples to best describe that element. One member from each group will present the groups' element and explain how and why they chose that picture to represent their element. Discuss.)

C. Classification of design (lecture, transparencies)
   1. Structural—good line, form, texture, and color as a result of the way something is made; functionalism—design concentrating on a function; keynote for modern furniture
   2. Decorative—starts where structural ends. Styles are
       naturalistic—something in nature
       conventional—stenciled design on wallpaper, fabrics, and rugs
       abstract—plaids, dots, stripes, checks, or geometric patterns

(Materials and procedure: Use pictorial examples of the preceding elements to correlate with lecture to clarify further. Students will choose, out of five pictures, the furniture that is structural and the furniture that is decorative. Give the factors that enabled them to classify them structural or decorative. After discussion and clarification, ask the students to bring in an example of each for the next class period. Discuss.)

D. Principles of design (lecture, transparencies)
   1. Proportion—space divisions pleasingly related to each other and the whole
   2. Balance—even: formal or symmetric; equal distance uneven: informal or asymmetric; one closer to center to balance one heavy and one light object
   3. Rhythm—movement of eye as it follows line
       repetition—repeating shapes, sizes, lines, or colors
       gradation—progression in sizes
       opposition—lines come together at right angles
       transition—carries eye gradually from one place to another
   4. Emphasis—eliminating competition creates center of attention
   5. Unity—harmony: elements brought together as connected whole; sizes, shapes, textures, colors, and ideas related

(Materials and procedure: After a lecture correlated with pictorial examples, attention will be focused on the bulletin board. There will be a separate heading for proportion, balance, rhythm, emphasis, and unity on the bulletin board. Working individually, the class will analyze pictures brought into class. Then as one group the class will decide on the three best examples of each principle. The students will then arrange the pictures on the bulletin board in an attractive manner for display under the correct heading. Discussion will follow explaining why the class picked the pictures they did to represent each principle.

Picking one of three pictures, each student will write an evaluation of that picture. The evaluation should consist of a list of the good and poor elements and principles of design found in the picture, and should give reasons why they are considered good or poor.

For review of the elements and principles of design, refer to the bulletin board that has been prepared from the mounted pictorial examples used with the lectures. Have the students discuss the pictures pointing out the elements and principles of design used in each. Then see if the students can pick out the primary, secondary, and intermediate colors used in the color scheme. After thorough discussion of the bulletin board, have the students divide into two teams. Go through the examples of the elements, color terminology, and principles of design one by one. The students will take turns, individually, on each team, and the teams will alternate with each picture. Each correct answer is a point for the team. A wrong answer gives the next member on the opposite team a chance to answer the questions. This procedure will continue until a correct answer is given. After both teams have gone through the stack of examples, the team with the most points wins.)

E.   Color associations (lecture, transparencies)
1.   Emotional appeal
   a.   Black—first color recognized by man; used for mourning in the Western World since sixteenth century; symbolic of evil, old age, silence; strong and sophisticated; used in decoration for small quantities of accent
   b.   Red—second color recognized by man; associated with blood and life, fire and danger; symbol of love, vigor, action, danger; bright reds are forceful and are used in small areas as accent; light values make warm background colors
   c.   Yellow—symbol of power; associated with deceit, cowardice, and jealousy, as well as wisdom, gaiety, and warmth
   d.   White—symbolic of purity, innocence, faith, peace, and surrender; off-white used extensively in home decoration
   e.   Blue—not identified as separate color at first; thought of as a form of black; blue rarest color in nature hence the origin of terms "true blue" and "blueblood"; symbol of happiness, hope, truth, honor, repose, and distance
   f.   Green—symbol of life and vigor; associated with luck: denotes life, spring, hope, and envy; cool enough to be restful, yet warm enough to be friendly
   g.   Purple—symbol of royalty; associated with the spiritual, mystery, humility, penitence, and wisdom; a dignified color used in elegant rooms
   h.   Brown—designated for peasants during Middle Ages, and thus associated with humility; reminiscent of autumn, harvest, and decay; ranges from yellow to red in cast; wood used in most traditional furniture is brown
   i.   Gray—somber color; associated with retirement, sadness, modesty, and indifference; may have warm or cool cast; good background color in decorating
2.   Color preferences
   a.   Tans, greens, browns popular rug colors
   b.   Black, blue, gray, and green popular car colors
   c.   Men prefer blue; women prefer red

(Materials and procedure: After the lecture, discuss and analyze three pictures listing the emotions that are expressed through the use of a particular color or color scheme.)

  F. Principles of design applied to color (lecture)
    1. Balance
      a. Colors must be balanced to give feeling of rest
      b. Light, dark, and dull colors used in largest areas
      c. Intense or bright colors in smallest areas
    2. Rhythm—use of color can make a gradual transition from one room to the other
    3. Emphasis
      a. As people enter a room they should be conscious of one color, with other colors subordinated to it
      b. Blue family adds emphasis to rich, dark woods
  G. Standard color harmonies (lecture, transparencies)
    1. Similar or related harmonies—restful but sometimes monotonous; produced from colors that lie near each other on color wheel
      a. Monochromatic harmony—one-color harmony; several values of one hue; hues must match, but value must contrast; example: light bluish purple should not be used with a dark reddish purple
      b. Analogous harmony—combination of neighboring hues that have one hue in common
      c. Contrasting harmonies—produced by combining colors that are far apart on the color wheel; should differ in value and intensity
      d. Complementary harmony—use two colors opposite each other on the color wheel
      e. Split-complementary harmony—combine one color, such as yellow, and the colors on each side of its complement
      f. Triad harmony—combination of any three colors that form an equilateral triangle on the color wheel
      g. Accented-neutral harmony—harmony in which the largest areas of a room are neutral with small areas of bright color used for accent

(Materials and procedure: Using colored construction paper, create an example of each of the harmonies listed and mount them. Hand in at end of class period.)

  H. Guides in planning color harmonies
    1. Cool background—use picture or other accessories with warm colors
    2. Figured drapery fabric as central idea for color scheme in room, and other colors keyed to those in fabric
    3. Wall and floor covering should be appropriate background colors
  I. Influences on choice of colors (lecture)
    1. Family tastes
      a. Family room should not have colors that are predominantly female or male
      b. Individual rooms offer chance for expressing individual tastes
    2. Physical characteristics of room
      a. Warm colors best on wall for rooms with north or northwest exposure
      b. Cool colors for rooms with south or southeast exposure

    c. Room with high ceiling will seem more cozy and less high if ceiling is painted slightly darker than wall

    d. Room will appear shorter by painting one end wall a warm color

3. Color of furnishings already on hand

4. Effect of lighting—artificial light changes effect of color

5. Texture—colors good in homespun textures often appear too strong in smooth or glossy textures

6. Manner of living

(Materials and procedure: For review of the unit on color and design, bring to class actual samples or pictures of wallpaper, paint, floor covering, furniture, draperies, and accessories. During two class periods use basic information concerning elements and principles of design, including color schemes and textures, to decorate and furnish one room of your choice. Discuss final products.)

**Housing and Home Furnishings
11th Grade
Unit Test: Color and Design**

Name: _____   Date:

Matching: Identify by letter the word in the right-hand column that suggests a mood of the word in the left-hand column.

MOOD   **LINE**

D	1. Gracefulness	A. Vertical
B	2. Repose	B. Horizontal
C	3. Push	C. Diagonal
A	4. Masculinity	D. Curved
D	5. Femininity	E. Zig-zag
C	6. Action	
C	7. Pull	
A	8. Dignity	
E	9. Movement	
E	10. Excitement	

Multiple Choice: Fill in the letter of the correct answer.

    B   1. The basic element of design is

          A. texture.

          B. line.

          C. color.

          D. form.

          E. balance.

D   2. Lines have an effect on an observer. This effect is
- A. architectural.
- B. physiological.
- C. functional.
- D. psychological.
- E. structural.

D   3. Form is
- A. solid.
- B. three dimensional.
- C. shape.
- D. all of these.
- E. none of these.

C   4. The rarest color in nature is
- A. black.
- B. purple.
- C. blue.
- D. gray.
- E. brown.

D   5. Proportion is
- A. spacing of windows in a house.
- B. arranging furniture in a room.
- C. hanging pictures over a fireplace.
- D. all of these.
- E. only A and C.

B   6. Which of the following represents *poor* balance?
- A. Two chairs, one on either side of a fireplace
- B. Five windows on one side of a door and two on the other
- C. Combination of heavy and light furniture throughout a room
- D. None of these
- E. Symmetrical arrangement on either side of a central point

A   7. How does rhythm help produce beauty in design?
- A. Suggests connected movement
- B. Provides several directions of movement
- C. Prevents eye from following smooth line
- D. Enables eye to jerk from one side of room to another
- E. Creates feeling of a musical atmosphere

D   8. Emphasis is the principle of design that creates
- A. three-dimensional effect.
- B. competing centers of interest.
- C. confusion in figured rug and floral draperies.
- D. interest on most important items.
- E. all of these.

<u>B</u>   9. The color light blue is classified as
   A. a hue.
   B. a value.
   C. an intensity.
   D. complementary.
   E. split-complementary.

<u>D</u>   10. Considerations that influence choice of color in the
      home are
   A. amount of light in room.
   B. furniture already in room.
   C. family members who use room.
   D. all of these.
   E. none of these.

Define the following words or phrases and give an example of each.

1. Structural design (good line, form, texture, and color as the result of the way something made—designed to concentrate on function—like a plain, straight-backed chair).
2. Asymmetric balance (informal or uneven balance—an arrangement with heavier object placed nearer center than light one).
3. Character of home (surroundings of home—impression one is left with—relates to family members' personalities).
4. Hue (name of color—family name—blue, red, green, etc.).
5. Tint (light or high values—good wall colors—sky blue, etc.).
6. Shade (dark or low values—good rug colors—forest green, etc.).
7. Primary color (cannot be broken down into other colors—no combination can produce primary color—red, yellow, blue).
8. Intermediate color (mix primary color with adjacent secondary color—yellow-green, blue-green, etc.).
9. Intensity (brightness or dullness of color—bright Kelly green or dull moss green).
10. Warm colors (convey feeling of warmth—seem to advance and make room appear smaller—yellow, red, orange).

Label and define each of the following color harmony diagrams.

1. Monochromatic   2. Analogous

Define: (several values of one hue)   Define: (combination of neighboring hue with one hue in common)

3. Complementary   4. Accented-Neutral

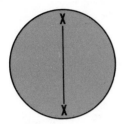   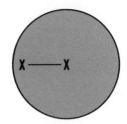

Define: (two colors opposite on color   Define: (harmony in which large areas
wheel)   of room neutral with small areas of
                                           bright color for accent)

What is the name of the color chart on the blackboard? Prang or Munsell

Explain the difference between the two.
(Prang—three primary colors, red, yellow, blue; Munsell—five principal colors, red, yellow, blue, green, purple)

Choose one of the three pictures on the blackboard and evaluate it. List at least five things about the picture that show use of color, elements, and principles of design, and explain the good and/or bad points of each of the five things you listed. (Depends on which three pictures are used.)

TEACHER-STUDENT BIBLIOGRAPHY

Books

CRAIG, HAZEL, and OLA RUSH,   *Homes With Character*. Boston: D. C. Heath, 1962.

GREER, CARLOTTA, and ELLEN GIBBS,   *Your Home and You*. Boston: Allyn & Bacon, 1965.

LEWIS, KORA; JEAN BURNS; and ESTHER SEGNER, *Housing and Home Management* (Macmillan Family Life Series). New York: Macmillan, 1969.

STARR, MARY CATHERINE,   *Management for Better Living*. Boston: D. C. Heath, 1963.

Encyclopedias

The American Woman's New Encyclopedia of Home Decorating. Chicago: Book Production Industries, 1964.

The Practical Encyclopedia of Good Decorating and Home Improvement, vols. I and II. New York: Greystone Press, 1970.

*Teacher bibliography only.

INDEX

A

Absence, extended, 198
Achievement
  evaluation issues, 131
  groups formed by, 102
  standardized tests, 148
Activities. *See* Instructional activities;
  Co-curricular activities
Adjunct programming, 112
Administrative evaluations, 164-65
Adolescents, psychology of, 69-71
Affective domain, 44-50
  characterization level, 49-50
  organization level, 48-49
  practice exercise, 62-63
  receiving level, 45-46
  responding level, 46-47
  and sociodrama, 98
  summary of levels, 50 *tab.*, 65
  valuing level, 47-48
Agility, 54, 58 *tab.*
Air, physiological need, 214
Alcorn, Marvin D., 70
Allergies, 70
American Medical Association, 235

American Telephone & Telegraph
  Company, 113
American Youth Commission, 19
Amidon, Edmund J., 163
Amphetamines, 235
Analysis
  and categorization of questions, 86
  as cognitive skill, 42, 44 *tab.*, 65
  use in organization, 48
Anecdotal records
  of disciplinary problems, 233
  problems with, 73
Apple II computers, 124
Application
  and categorization of questions, 86
  as cognitive skill, 42, 44 *tab.*, 65
  eliciting in objective tests, 135
Appointments to office, 248-49
Aptitude tests, 148-49
Aristotle, 106
Assemblies, 251
Assignments
  out-of-class, 103-5
  punitive, 223-24
Attitudes, and affective domain, 45
Audio aids, 112-14